'A much-needed and delightful book, written with great enthusiasm. It shows how history can be taught with the meaningful experiences of each child at its centre, then making connections between the child, the locality and community, the national and global past and concepts of time. Inclusion and the importance of different perspectives underpin the book. Throughout, the authors empower teachers to adopt their philosophy by showing them how to plan, select resources and strategies, and reflect on ideas and case studies. The book is embedded in references to existing literature on primary history education.'

Hilary Cooper,
Emeritus Professor of History and Pedagogy,
the University of Cumbria, UK

Bringing History Alive through Local People and Places

Bringing History Alive through Local People and Places puts the local environment and community at the heart of history, showing how it can be used as the context for successful history teaching across the primary age range. It considers how to develop children's concepts and skills through local history, how to link local, national and global aspects of history, and helps to develop your own historical knowledge, understanding and confidence in teaching the subject.

Practical topics explored include:

- Investigating children's cultural and geographical roots through fieldwork
- Finding and visiting local museums, archives and heritage sights
- Choosing and using resources
- Using significant people, events and buildings to link with national history
- Environmental education and sustainable development through local history
- Understanding the links between history and everyday life
- Planning and assessing history.

Based on the latest research and practice in the field, *Bringing History Alive through Local People and Places* offers an exciting template of creative ideas and activities to show teachers how they can make history relevant to all children.

Lynne Dixon is Senior Lecturer in Primary Education, Geography and History at the University of Greenwich, UK.

Alison Hales is Senior Lecturer in Primary Education, History and Early Years at the University of Greenwich, UK.

Bringing History Alive through Local People and Places

A guide for primary school teachers

Lynne Dixon and Alison Hales

Routledge
Taylor & Francis Group
LONDON AND NEW YORK

First published 2014
by Routledge
2 Park Square, Milton Park, Abingdon, Oxon OX14 4RN

and by Routledge
711 Third Avenue, New York, NY 10017

Routledge is an imprint of the Taylor & Francis Group, an informa business

British Library Cataloguing in Publication Data
A catalogue record for this book is available from the British Library

Library of Congress Cataloging in Publication Data
A catalog record for this book has been requested

ISBN: 978–0–415–53585–4 (hbk)
ISBN: 978–0–415–53586–1 (pbk)
ISBN: 978–0–203–11196–3 (ebk)

Typeset in Galliard
by Swales & Willis Ltd, Exeter, Devon

MIX
Paper from responsible sources
FSC
www.fsc.org
FSC® C013056

Printed and bound in Great Britain by
TJInternational Ltd, Padstow, Cornwall

Contents

Figures, tables and teachers' toolkits

Figures

Tables

Teachers' toolkits

Acknowledgements

We would like to thank all the learners and educators: in schools in and around London; at the Greenwich Foundation for the Old Royal Naval College; at Hammersmith and Fulham Urban Studies Centre and at the University of Greenwich whose involvement in local history and geography projects has fed into our case studies.

There are also individuals who have given time to discuss aspects of the book with us: Professor Andrew Lambirth – who encouraged and guided us in the early stages of the book and involved us in his 'Writers' Retreats'; colleagues from the School of Education who attended the Writers' Retreats and performed the role of critical friends as we began our first chapters; our colleagues along the 'primary corridor' at the university who listened, advised and supported, and in particular to Phil Jefferies and Iain Kitchener for their help with technical 'stuff'; Sue Ingham, Juliet Desailly and Tony McTurk for inspiration through their own local work with children and for material for case studies and for providing listening, professional ears; Simon McKeon from Bexley Local Studies and Archives and Peter Daniels from Westminster Archives for their contribution and continued passion for local history and other dedicated staff in local history centres who support the work of local history in schools.

Finally, the patience and support of friends and family and their contributions to our local and family history stories must not go without saying.

Introduction

The purpose of this book is to demonstrate how to use 'the local in history' as an approach to teaching history in the primary school. We use the term 'the local in history' deliberately as a means of emphasising particular aspects of our approach which we feel takes it beyond the more traditional local history. One aspect we pay particular attention to is that of personal and family history as part of this; another is the significance we place on the wider links. We also coin the phrase 'the child as the local', again to emphasise the importance of the child as being at the centre of our approach. In doing this, we hope to convince the reader this approach has much to commend it.

We believe the use of 'the local' can be a starting point for all history, and where not possible, it can be embedded within any topic or unit of work. The approach is not only valid in terms of history as a discipline but it is also justifiable on pedagogical grounds. We believe that teaching and learning through the local can help to build a coherent 'bigger' picture which will support children's historical development as they move into secondary education and prepare for lifelong learning. However, we also believe that approaching history in this way is invaluable for helping the non-specialist trainee or practising teacher develop their own historical knowledge, skills and understanding. For this reason, this book encourages the reader to become an 'historian' – starting with the local and going on to build confidence about the subject in a way which will support their teaching. We provide a series of reflections and activities along with essential 'toolkits' which we hope will help in this process.

This book originates from our own deeply held beliefs in the value of personal, family and 'the local' in making history more accessible, relevant and potentially exciting and engaging for young learners. In this, both place and people are of importance. Our journeys to this point are different, however, and as they reflect part of our personal histories and also help to explain the origins of the book, we wanted to outline them briefly.

Lynne's story

Academically I am a geographer, one who did not do school history after the age of fourteen. However, I was lucky enough to discover historical geography at university, and became fascinated by deserted villages and the landscape of medieval ridge and furrow. My dissertation was the study of an historical hinterland, a wonderful amalgam of history and geography. Professionally I arrived at primary education after working for several years as a town planner which inspired an interest in urban environmental education. This led to a career with lots of locally based history and geography work as a teacher, adviser, writer of local resources and

teacher educator. I have enjoyed teaching not only primary children, but also secondary. I have worked with adults on oral and community history projects and on projects which have brought together adults and children. Oral history provided an introduction to black history which was reinforced by discovering the 'Peopling of London' exhibition at the Museum of London in the early 1990s.

Threading its way through these have been the influences of my personal geographies which bring together the north east and London, and family geographies which reach out to Yorkshire, Scotland and the south west. They have given me a love of places and have been explored through my family history researches over the years. Just about all my history, therefore, has been learnt since I left school, piece by piece in patchwork and layers, together with working on that chronological framework, which has managed to form my own 'bigger picture'.

Alison's story

The start of my 'historical' journey was unfortunately not an enjoyable one, however its continuation is one of jubilation. Early secondary education experiences left me with a distinct dislike for a subject I could not see any value in and therefore had no interest in pursuing beyond formal education. This remained until, as a mature student, I had the great fortune of meeting and listening to Hilary Claire during an induction seminar for my teacher training at South Bank University. Her inspiration and passion for social and economic history transformed my view and so my love of history was conceived and my journey began!

My academic studies led me to learning history through ordinary people and places, coming to a realisation that 'their' histories are of the utmost importance and play a major part in our 'story' and 'the bigger picture'. Much of my early historical learning was in my local environment and with local people, both of which I discovered had rich and vibrant pasts. The study of history, under the careful guidance and nurture of my mentors – Hilary Claire and Dr Alan Parkinson – not only gave the skills to uncover these stories but instilled a passion for learning which extended far beyond that of history. My love for children and enthusiasm for learning has enabled me to combine the two and pass on that passion through primary education and later as a teacher educator and senior lecturer in initial teacher education. My interest in inclusive history leads the way for my current research in early years education. Today, I continue to learn with and through the children, teacher trainees and colleagues whom I am fortunate to meet.

Coming together

We came together as teacher trainers at Avery Hill and shared our experiences, embedding parts of our approach to history with our students. In writing the book we have come to realise that we share a mutual respect for the same primary historians and want to acknowledge their importance, in particular, Hilary Claire, Sylvia Collicott, Grant Bage and Hilary Cooper along with Jon Nichol and John Fines, founders of the Nuffield Primary History Project which continues to influence classroom practice.

The current educational context at the point of publication of the book is an interesting and challenging one, but we are heartened by the explicit reference to local history in the new National Curriculum (2014). We are aware that amongst the several excellent books which support trainees and teachers, local history is touched on but not explored in depth.

Furthermore, because of its nature, little in the way of published resources can support a teacher undertaking history locally. Of necessity we have needed to use local examples, and many of these relate to the area with which we are currently most familiar – Eltham and south east London. However, we have also drawn on local history and primary history examples from other areas, reflecting our own travels, connections and interests and we relate these in the first person.

We hope that our approach will empower the learner and the more experienced class teacher by showing how resources can be accessed locally. In undertaking this exploration, we trust that confidence in the teaching of history will also grow. We also hope that, since being a local historian should not be a solitary experience, the teacher, the children and perhaps the whole school will begin to feel more part of the local community.

Moving on throughout the book . . .

In chapter 1 we offer the reader a justification for why we feel history as a subject is vitally important in primary education and as well as a discipline in itself. We will discuss how history through 'the local' can be instrumental in effective teaching and learning and of great benefit to children particularly. It will give a rationale of our concept 'the child as the local'. The next four chapters offer the reader the practical tools in history and how to use them to ensure effective learning through the local takes place. Through place, people and history centres, the chapters guide the reader through the abundance of resources available, and how to select and use them in the classroom with children whilst developing the readers' pedagogical knowledge and subject knowledge in history. Chapters 6, 7 and 8 provide a theoretical understanding of how the local connects to the national and global world and the importance of chronology in this, helping to develop the 'bigger picture'; they also suggest ways in which these aspects can be taught. Chapter 9 looks specifically at the cross-curricular links in history providing the reader with an understanding of how history and 'the local' fits with the other aspects of the curriculum and teaching and learning, and is not a standalone subject in itself. Chapter 10 covers planning and aims to bring all this together. It gives an overview of how to structure both teaching and learning in such a way that the experience is coherent and meaningful for the children in the classroom.

Chapter 1

The 'what?' and the 'why?' of the local in history

What's it all about?

Introduction

This chapter aims to introduce the reader to the notion of the 'local in history' and discuss how we have moved on from the more usual idea of local history to one that can help and inform primary classroom practice. It will offer a fresh insight into the once perceived amateur historian's pastime as being an essential discipline accessible to all. It will emphasise the importance it holds for the teaching of primary history in our schools today and will argue that the 'local' should be at the heart of all primary history teaching. Blyth (1988) commented that for children, 'knowing about themselves, their families and their past, helps [them] to understand why they are as they are' (p.2). This chapter argues the point further; that through 'themselves' and their community, children not only begin to see who and why they are as they are, but where they are and the valuable contribution that they have made to the history of our world today. It will give an initial insight into how the 'local' can equip children to go beyond their locality and have access to a rich, broad and informed history; *their* history, taking *them* from the local in history to the national and global. History gives children what Bage (2000) describes as an 'exciting and lifelong window on the world' (p.79).

Chapter objectives

By the end of this chapter you should:

- understand the importance of primary history as a curriculum area;
- be able to make comparisons between *local* history and *the local* in history;
- have considered the notion of children and the local and children *as* the local;
- have started to question your own values and ideologies surrounding the question 'what and whose history?'

Why history matters

Andretti (1993) raises the question why so many books on the subject of history find it necessary to commence by justifying their discipline. His view is a defining one: 'history is a very powerful force that works on the consciousness of every human being on the planet, and it

is at its most powerful when we do not think too hard about its nature' (p.1). We therefore make no apologies for challenging the reader and presenting questions to consider when thinking about why history matters for us and our children.

Before we embark on our reasoning for including primary history within the curriculum, we feel it is important to take a moment and consider what history means to the individual. It is only by reflecting on our own experiences that we are able to put into context our own standpoint. This reflection will no doubt have consequences for both your understanding of history now and your future teaching and learning.

Reflection

- *What does the term history mean to you?*
- *What was your experience of history at school?*
- *What do you consider the value of history to be, to individuals, children and to different communities?*
- *What history have you engaged in recently?*
- *When does something become 'history'?*

There is an ongoing dialogue between history academics and those from other professional and non-professional backgrounds as to what constitutes history or why history matters. Our starting point is that teachers and educators have the opportunity to ensure that people's histories can be uncovered through the primary history curriculum and more explicitly through the local as an approach. We can provide children with the necessary skills and understanding for them to make an informed decision as to whose history and what history *they* want to uncover and to tell. Therefore history no longer remains exclusive to the elite or academic but becomes more accessible to all.

The role of history: social or political?

When we consider 'why' history, we have to consider the role that it plays in our society and education system. There is, of course, no one or very easy answer and one's standpoint will inevitably influence the perspective of a given explanation. But simply put, history is often defined in terms of its role both socially: how history has shaped us as people and the contributions we have made to society, and politically: how history has shaped us as a nation. This consideration is important as it will no doubt influence the approach to history teaching and learning you may take.

Tosh (2008) turns to two issues surrounding the debate on the role of history in our culture. He refers to the socio-cultural perspective which has resulted in a battleground of cultural politics and political ideology 'variously conceived as national heritage and cultural identity' (p.6). This view, he says, is not concerned with the questions that these particular histories raise but how they serve their social and political role.

The second issue he raises is the following of 'lazy relativism' which sees one perspective on the past as being as good as another, therefore rendering all history as having the same value, regardless of its roots. This derives from the attack on history by the

postmodernists who question the credentials of history and whether it is a valid branch of knowledge at all. Tosh points out, however, that what both cultural politics and the postmodernists have in common is that they miss the opportunity to evaluate the kinds of practical understanding that history has to offer because they firstly 'value outcomes rather than processes' and secondly 'refute the notion of applicability altogether'; both failing to see how history offers insights into the contemporary world (ibid).

Whose history?

An interesting view on history is offered by Jenkins (1991). He defines history as a series of discourses about the world and he makes a distinction between the use of the terms 'the past' and 'history'. He uses a noun/verb analogy when he describes his reasoning: the past as being the *object* of historians' attention and history as the story of *doing* history (historiography). His reasoning being that the 'history' – what has been written about the past – is different from 'the past' itself; history is what historians have made of the past. He considers the difference to be important if we are to understand the nature of history and how the process of history happens.

Reflection

- *What is your understanding of the past?*
- *When does something become the past?*
- *How do you think children would answer this?*
- *What misconceptions do you think children might have about the past?*

The point that Jenkins is making and something that others such as Claire (1996) express quite clearly is: what is seen as 'the past' can be subjective and arguably narrow, as we are often bound by the historian's choice of the past. Historians choose their discourses or stories according to what they feel is important based on their theoretical perspective, culture or societal standpoint and/or political ideology and will retell the history (discourse) from the perspective they see.

Task

- *Pick ten events you consider important in history and place them on a timeline.*
- *Ask a colleague/friend to do the same.*
- *Compare them.*
- *Are there any similarities or differences?*
- *Why?*
- *Does your timeline reflect a political or social viewpoint or both?*
- *What does this tell you about your perspectives on history?*

If we consider what might be left out of the history story, it begins to paint a far more complicated picture. We can use Jenkins' example to illustrate the significance of people's choice and help us understand his distinction between past and history: there have been millions of women in the 'past' but few have made their way into the story of history (Jenkins, 1991). If we concur with the notion that everyone has a past, then why has their history not been told? Their history is *hidden*. For instance, does the absence of women mean that women have not contributed to shaping history, rendering them invalid or worthless? Of course not! Yet we have been, and to a certain extent still are, exposed only to those figures that have been perceived as being significant in shaping our national history. The notion of 'hidden history' and its importance will be considered further in chapter 9.

This has far-reaching consequences, not only for the conceived notions of national heritage and identity (explored in later chapters), but for children's sense of identity, their family and cultural heritage.

Reflection

- *Consider events or groups of people that may have a 'hidden' history.*
- *Why, perhaps, are they not at the forefront of history or included in a primary curriculum?*
- *What is the value of children engaging in and learning about 'hidden history'?*

History not only equips us with a window to the past but provides us with necessary skills and understanding needed to live as informed and rounded citizens. As Claire eloquently wrote in her seminal text *Reclaiming Our Pasts*:

> History tries to make sense of human lives, working with the values and moralities of those who lived them. It also requires interpreting 'what was going on' using hindsight and our own contemporary values . . . history involves accepting uncertainty . . . using imagination and creativity . . . It involves being able to communicate with passion and clarity . . .
>
> The practice of history is truly educative because it develops human powers, concepts, skills, knowledge and reflexivity.
>
> (1996:2)

History's aim is to make sense of the world, something that we all, from the very young to the old, engage in. History is thus an integral part of our being. If we view it in its very simplest terms we cannot live life without our being part of the historical discourse being uncovered. Day to day we live history; we are both part of the history now and history in the making. Claire (1996) suggests that history is never just about the past but always involves reflecting on the present.

If we consider our everyday actions and thoughts we are constantly looking back and reviewing what happened yesterday, last week, last year, reflecting on and contemplating the 'tomorrow'. We consciously and subconsciously compare, contrast and evaluate events and experiences to make sense of what is going on in both our personal lives and the lives of

those around us. We ask questions, look for causes and consider the consequences; we interpret evidence and express opinions on things that have happened, both everyday events and events that may have had a considerable impact on our lives. We would take this one stage further and argue that history is and must be a consideration of the future – future history. If the study of history is learning about and reflecting on the past then we must learn *from* the past; it would be foolish not to use these contemplations when considering the future.

Consider the following reflection.

Reflection

Think back to the 2011 riots and write down all that you remember.

- *Where were you?*
- *What are your memories of the day?*
- *How did the riots impact on you personally or on your local community?*
- *How many accounts can you recall reading or listening to (newspapers, television, oral accounts)?*
- *Did you find one account more plausible or accurate than another? Why was this?*
- *What do you consider to be the cause or instigation of the riots?*
- *What questions do your reflections raise?*
- *What are the implications for the future?*

There is no question that at the time of the 2011 riots, the majority of adults and arguably many children all around the country were engaging in some sort of dialogue along similar lines as those posed in the reflection. This is an example of ordinary people living in and engaging with history – doing history.

Another way in which ordinary people are engaging in and with history is through skills of history inherent in everyday tasks such as the reading and reviewing of written documents.

Task

Consider a personal or professional written document that you have reviewed recently, either as a professional or as an individual. Examples might be: a newspaper story; a set of house deeds; a new job contract; the National Curriculum (2014), or the recently revised Early Years Foundation Stage Curriculum (2012).

With this in mind answer the following:

- *Think about your reading process; did you read through slowly, skim the document or pull out key words?*
- *What existing knowledge did you need to be able to put this document into context or to understand it?*
- *Were there any parts that were not clear? What did you do to help you understand it?*
- *How did this compare to other similar documents that you have had experience of?*
- *How might you use this document for future practice?*

When reviewing any written sources, we engage in and apply a similar process through which to interpret the evidence. Our knowledge and skills become more defined and accurate with practice. Having an understanding of how these life skills might be enhanced through the study of history puts a difference perspective on our engaging in history. This exercise acts as a simple example of how the skills of history permeate everyday aspects of our daily lives – reading and interpreting texts for instance.

The above questions and reflections enable us to begin to consider our perspectives on history. If we are aware of the role history plays at a micro level as well as the macro, we can begin to determine the importance we as teachers place on it and whose history we might cover and how.

Why the *local* in primary history?

Before we think about why 'the local' in history, it is worth noting that local history has been a longstanding feature in the curriculum throughout the United Kingdom; memories of our own history learning before the statutory curriculum certainly include aspects of local history. At the time of writing, the 2014 history curriculum continues to promote it as an area of study.

Local history study is also very evident throughout Europe – Finland for example begin their learning with 'historical knowledge and knowledge of own roots' and state, 'Learning history should also serve to strengthen pupils' own identities and other cultures and their influences' (Eurydice at NFER, 2010). In Austria, children study cross-curricular local history three times a week from the ages of 6 to 10. Within the United Kingdom, Scotland, Ireland and Wales also place a strong emphasis on the value of local history. What is evident in all the above examples of local history curricula is the explicit link between the local area and personal and community identity which will be explored in chapter 4.

Tosh (2008) argues that we are in a time when the study of history has never been so popular. He refers to the explosion of family history, media coverage and historical visits as being the 'new gardening' of British leisure time. His point, however, is not one of celebration but that of concern. He argues that few of these activities bring an historical perspective to issues of real historical importance and that they have little substance in the genuine purpose of history: that so many rightly argue as being fundamentally important to gaining an informed understanding of the present. He states that 'we are confronted by the paradox of a society which is immersed in the past yet detached from its history' (p.6).

The same can be argued for the history being taught in primary schools today. It can be said that during recent times we have seen the expansion of history within our primary schools; an increasing array of topics now emerging to bring relief from the flames of the political fires that surround core subjects, targets and Ofsted inspections. Themes such as 'Florence Nightingale', 'The Great Fire of London', 'Toys', 'The Romans' and indeed 'Local History' studies have been popularised by the familiar QCA schemes of work that have in the past provided teachers with a beginner's '*Gardening Handbook to History*' to go with Tosh's analogy.

As primary school teachers and history leaders for many years we have been privileged to witness many children revelling in the delights of what may be considered a rich and full history curriculum. We have seen activities such as history weeks, Second World War enactments, Roman battles, themed assemblies – some of which will provide case studies throughout this book. We would however argue that whilst we provided many a rich

episode or opportunity in history we perhaps inadvertently did not provide children with the connection or coherent structure in which they themselves could take their history forward. Tosh (2008) suggests that we provided an enjoyable, but amateur 'garden history' approach.

Creative curriculum approaches and the introduction of innovative initiatives such as Black History Month and Refugee Week have perhaps perpetuated this idea. Topics, it would seem, are sometimes being taught in isolation and, whilst exciting and engaging, they appear to have little relevance to the children themselves or to their lives. This has been evident in many primary schools visited in our roles as link tutors and something that has been instrumental in the instigation of this book.

In order to ensure that we do not propagate the 'gardening approach' to history we must consider the type of history curriculum that is taught, with consideration to the 'how' and 'why'. We do not want a curriculum that our children enjoy and enthuse in momentarily but holds little relevance to them as individuals and their place in their community or society; otherwise we are in danger of our children having many narratives of history but no under standing of how these pieces slot together to build the bigger picture (Dawson, 2011).

Of course, we are not suggesting that a creative curriculum or promoting initiatives such as the examples mentioned above are irrelevant; on the contrary, they are fundamental to a child's learning, their sense of identity and understanding of culture. We consider these approaches to be very much at the forefront of historical learning and cannot emphasise their importance enough. Further exploration and justification of these ideas and approaches are covered in depth throughout the book.

However, the point we argue is the need to find a way to make learning more relevant and comprehensible and we propose that a valid approach is through the local. We argue that without putting the child and the local at the centre of as much historical activity as possible the learning may be irrelevant, piecemeal and potentially superficial. It is essential that depth is sought through purposeful activities in and through the local, which we advocate are at the heart of good historical teaching and learning.

Children deserve and can have a history curriculum that provides both enjoyment and meaning; an enabling history curriculum on which further learning is built and taken forward. This requires teacher knowledge, careful planning and a sound pedagogy of how children learn – requisites of all good teachers.

How?

History is certainly a contentious subject – arguably, that is what makes it such an exciting discipline! We are presented with many different viewpoints, debates and questions that are continuously reviewed and responded to by historians, politicians and curriculum policy makers alike. Not so prominent, however, is the question of 'whose?' history and 'why?' We have on the one hand the issue of national identity and the concern with 'British-ness' and how our children might learn about 'our island story'; and on the other, the argument that children need to learn about the wider world. How do we ensure the history we teach does not become a dry narrative of an isolated island story? How do we teach history so that it is not disconnected from the rest of the world, but more a history that is part of a tapestry of the global world we live in today?

The local in history is very much at the forefront of this global connectedness. It is an approach to teaching and learning that moves the child from the local to national and global.

Collicott (1986) stresses this importance of the local stating, 'local history is a piece of a giant jigsaw' (p.1) and uses the idea of story to demonstrate a way of looking from the local, to see connections and relationships on a national and international scale. This is explored in depth in chapters 6 and 8.

As educators, we would wish to show children how they and their history make up that rich and vibrant story; a story that is not and has never been isolated on the proverbial or otherwise island. We believe we should equip children with the knowledge, skills and understanding for them to be able to make informed and sophisticated decisions about the present and influence their future based on a developing understanding of their shared past.

Schorske refers to this understanding as a need to think 'with history' rather than 'about history'. He argues that thinking about history (knowing the story) does not equip people with the tools to orient themselves within society (Schorske cited in Tosh, 2008). If we consider this in relation to our children and their being able to orient themselves in society, making informed decisions about the future, then we have to consider a history taught through *their* history and not just telling them the 'story'. We must give children an historical education that leads them to the realisation that history is an indispensable basis for understanding the bigger picture. Children need to know why they are learning this thing called 'history' and the 'history stories' of the past. As teachers we may possibly fail to make the links for children or more importantly fail to give them the strategies and depth of understanding for them to make the links themselves. It is in this sense that we argue the case for 'the local' in primary history: one that starts with the child and their personal history around them; the context and form may differ from child to child, but essentially it starts with them and their local.

When we are thinking about children in or perhaps *as* the local (explored later in the chapter), we can more clearly see the relevance and the connections to a child's sense of identity and also to citizenship. This is an important aspect if we consider the future to be dependent on the historical narrative of the past. This is looked at in more depth in chapter 9.

Local history and 'the local' in history: a discernible difference

When we were conducting research for this book several academics, higher education students and experienced primary school teachers were asked what they understood by the term local history. As perhaps expected, many respondents suggested it was about finding out about your local area; further exploration of their understanding prompted answers such as: 'it's about where you grew up or lived as a child'; 'where you were born'; 'it's about finding out about the buildings in your area'. There was little clarification as to the time scale of growing up in a local area or indeed when the local area became 'your' local area. The boundaries were blurred as to whether a local area was determined by the place of birth or the longest time spent in a place.

Some answers seem to suggest that it is where family still lived, a place with which there were connections, whether or not it was still the place of residency; others said it was where they (individuals) lived now. This raises many questions for children and their local. Where might a traveller child's local history be – in his/her cultural heritage or where they might have stayed the longest; or perhaps where they are now? What about a refugee child who has now settled here but has his birthplace in another country? Or a child of a military family who moves according to where their parent's job dictates?

Reflection

- *Where do you consider your local to be?*
- *Look at what defines your choice.*
- *What connects you to that place?*

Similarly, when students were asked how far the local was from a given point many answers were vague. The responses focused on how far the local spanned and from what direction. One student said 'it is as far as you can walk in any direction from a starting point'; another, 'it is as far as you can go somewhere and still know where you are '.

Grigg and Hughes (2013) offer the definition of the local as having a radius of less than a kilometre. They refer to this in a geographical context and it may be that our approach to the local in history needs a more fluid understanding of the extent of the local area. Milner et al. (2004) point out that the 'local' should include a wider area as this contributes to the character of the locality. This concept clearly links to Lomas (2002) and others who suggest there is no finite definition of where the local begins and ends; but it offers the idea that when one is thinking of an area, particularly when teaching, one should think of depth rather than breadth. Chapters 2, 3, 4 and 5 will provide excellent starting points to facilitate that depth of learning in the local; the idea that the breadth of the local does not necessarily mean a wide area or 'lots of things' but much historical learning can be achieved by looking at one, sometimes small, aspect.

It is worth noting here that neither the National Curriculum 2000 (DfEE/QCA, 1999) nor the National Curriculum (2014) for history defines local in any specific terms. It relates neither to that of the geographical area nor to the focus of study and therefore the breadth and depth of studying in and through the local is very much up to the professional judgement of the teacher.

Other local history definitions

Local history has for many years been enjoyed and celebrated by people across the world. There is an increasing amount of evidence that local history continues to grow and thrive both here and throughout other countries; local history societies, groups, publications, heritage sites are all indicators of its popularity and illustrates Tosh's analogy of 'garden history'.

However until the seminal works of Hoskins in the 1950s, local history was still very much portrayed and viewed as a separate and subservient discipline to academic history. Whilst there is evidence that this view has been changing, it is slow to do so. Many university courses do not offer bespoke routes into local history and the dearth of academic literature published on local history would suggest a lack of importance given to local history study itself. Sheeran and Sheeran (2009) attribute this slow turnaround to the exclusivity that local historians have unintentionally created for themselves. Dymond (2011) refers to local history as having a 'split personality' with different competitors but having comparable aims. Perhaps there is still a feeling of 'lazy relativism' that Tosh refers to, among the historian 'camps' today?

Dyer et al., writing in 2011, state that 'no branch of history thinks and writes about itself as much as does local history' (p.1). The theorist of local and regional history, Marshall (1992, cited in Jackson, 2008) comes to a particular definition of local history as being a collection of interests rather than a coherent historical discipline. Tosh adds to both these points by stating that 'the greatest interest in a specific locality is felt by those who live there' (2010:81). The suggestion is that local history remains the practice *of* local people *for* local

people, with the significance of such study still not fully being realised by the wider word of academia because of the closed nature of the practice.

Clifford and King describes local history as 'local distinctiveness' and says it is characterised by its elusiveness – 'being instantly recognisable yet difficult to describe' (1993:1). They take Tosh and Dyer's view one step further when they say that whilst many have a strong allegiance to the local, discontinuities in its identity have left few ways of expressing the power that place has. Is this the reason that local history appears not to be as strong a discipline as it might?

With the increased focus on heritage sites and local places with national importance, it is easy to view local history as being about the significant place. However Hunt (1978, cited in Jackson, 2008) considers local history to be much more about the ordinary person, whether relatively rich or poor, pursuing daily labour and enjoying pastimes and humdrum existence, than about the national figure, however prominent his/her part in national affairs.

Riden (1998) and Twells (2008) say that the nature of local history is changing and we are now seeing local history as being more about the community than the physical or the significant individual. Clearly what might be considered significant depends on the context and interpretation. An individual may very well have a great deal of significance in the local but not always on a national level. Likewise, we may fail to see the connection between the national significance and the local. While national significance will remain important within any national curriculum we feel it is important to incorporate the local, whether this is people or place, in a significant way rather than a peripheral one. The idea of 'national' has to be challenged positively if we are to springboard local history from the potting shed to high on our curriculum agenda.

Children and the local

When considering teaching and learning within the primary school we must put the children at the heart of the process. Teaching and learning in and through the local provides an opportunity for children to come to a realisation that history is all around them and in their everyday lives. Through experiencing the past in such a way they come to appreciate 'something of the significance of the commonplace present' (Pluckrose, 1991:67). It provides them with a sense of identity, how they and their family have contributed to societies past and present, thus making the overall study of history more relevant (Bage, 2000). The tangible nature of the local makes the story of history accessible to children; it is no longer remote, but real. They are able to physically see, touch, listen and question to make sense of it. They can begin to comprehend how history happens and how communities, places and events have been transformed and shaped into what they see today. This is explored in further depth in chapter 3. Without this opportunity, learning might otherwise be a series of disconnected episodes which have little meaning.

When thinking in such a way we need to consider the range of children in our class and the diverse backgrounds that they may come from. This poses the problem of where do we start? Should we include all children's starting points and is this practical? Of course not; so it would make practical and curriculum sense to start with the immediate area of the school as the focus of a local history study. This could, for example, be the school building itself. The children in a class would have an obvious connection to it, although 'their story' may be further afield than the immediate area (see case study 1.1 on pp.14–15). If we consider the increasing diversity in schools, it may be this is an acceptable compromise to the dilemma of: 'Whose history?' 'Where?' and 'How far?'

We would suggest that whilst the school might be considered a shared physical starting point when thinking about history in the classroom, it does not necessarily need to be the *only* focus for history in the local or, indeed, end with that. The seminal work of Claire (1996) offers insight into excellent starting points for all children and her book *Reclaiming Our Pasts* is a must for all students and experienced and/or non-specialist teachers.

The child *as* the local

When we are thinking about 'why the local?' in children's learning, a summary might be as follows: for history to be meaningful, children need to make personal connections to it. They need to be able to experience, see, feel and discuss history and this is accessible in and through their immediate local environment. People and places in that environment provide opportunities for real historical engagement – it is not remote but a real story that is tangible. If we are to put the child at the centre of learning in the local by choosing aspects of the local which are pertinent to them, we can think of them as being as important as the local itself; an analogy we therefore introduce is the child *as* the local.

This does not necessarily mean that this is the local environment in which they were born or indeed live now. They may not live in the area at all. They may travel into the area from a different location each day to attend the school. They may, like the traveller child, have only been in the area for a limited time and will only stay in the area for a short period; they may have their roots firmly established in another area. However, through studying in or through specific aspects of the local – school for instance, the child is given the pedagogical tools through which they can assimilate and accommodate information before then individualising and constructing their own history learning (Kolb, 1976, cited in Garner, 2000; Bage, 2000). Using the school itself as a way into using the local as an approach serves both as a teaching tool and as a connection to the learning in history. Children can connect with the local people in and around the school and the immediate community; therefore, all learning is meaningful. In further chapters the local and learning through the local will illustrate how specific skills, knowledge and conceptual understanding can develop children's historical learning.

If we are to consider what it means for a child *as* the local, we offer the following case study as an illustration of how one child's history, including that of his parents, was incorporated into a Key Stage 1 history topic on homes.

Case study 1.1

Jerome had lived in the UK since birth. His parents were of Afro-Caribbean heritage. Both his parents had come over to Britain and settled in London during the 1970s. After his birth in the late 1990s Jerome and his family move to Bexley where Jerome later went to a local school in the area. The school was predominately white with a high socio-economic intake. Jerome was a frequent visitor to Grenada, the birth place of his mother, and despite being raised in Britain he had very strong cultural roots reinforced through his family and long stays in, what he described as, his 'other home'. His history was very much tied up with his parents' history which he inevitably shared; immigration and settlement in England and now Bexley were very much part of his history. For Jerome, history in KS1 bore little relation to his personal or cultural history. The then popular QCA unit Toys and Homes used at the time of

the school history curriculum did not include any reference to his other home or cultural heritage.

In order to bring *his* history into the curriculum and enable him to make the connections with the learning the class teacher decided to link the topic of 'homes' with movement into and out of Bexley. It was decided that the children and their families would be asked to tell us about their experiences of moving. This enabled all children to participate in the project; clearly some had never moved home but had moved classes within the school, so the topic was adapted to suit. Story was used as a starting point and stimulus for the topic and books such as Floella Benjamin's *Coming to England* enabled Jerome to tell 'his' history.

The concept of moving was explored and the reasons why some people moved within the immediate locality or from one locality to another – as Jerome's parents had. Questionnaires were sent home and families asked to share their experiences. Jerome's mother was very willing to come in and share her and her family's history of her '*local*' in Grenada and now her local in Sidcup.

She described her experiences of moving from one country to another and how the family had to adapt to a very different 'local'. Because Jerome had knowledge of both places, he was able to use his experiences to explore the concepts and make links. He was able to begin to ask questions about Sidcup – his 'local' now and compare and contrast those to his '*other home*'.

Other children were also able to draw on his experiences and were able to see how 'homes' and the places were different. The project then took the children themselves outside the immediate vicinity of the classroom and into the local community for the next part of the study.

There are other ways in which we can illustrate our analogy of the child *as* the local; for instance one might consider the arrival of the Vietnamese boat people in the 1980s, many of whom may have children or grandchildren in schools local to their relocation area today. We may want to start with the child in terms of their cultural heritage and look at how the Vietnamese have shaped and contributed to the development and change in the local area. We may look again at the 'local' of their parents/relatives and compare to our local. Clearly, any learning that puts the children in the local or *as* the local needs to be done sensitively and appropriately. We advise you to discuss any aspects of a child's history which might be deemed sensitive with your history coordinator or headteacher.

The local and heritage

Heritage defies precise analysis, although we have come to regard it as the legacy of notable buildings, people and achievements of a particular place. Local histories of the nineteenth and twentieth centuries sought to promote the status of places through the establishment of historical pedigree, even if tenuously based on fragmentary archive evidence, relict landscape and architectural features and hearsay. Whilst there was a lull in the early twentieth century, heritage has, in the last 20 years or so, seen an unprecedented popularisation through organisations such as the Department of National Heritage, established in 1992 and later renamed the Department for Culture, Media and Sport (DCMS), and Heritage Lottery

funding. More recently the Department for Education has committed £2.7 million to English Heritage, the government's statutory adviser on the historic environment, to work with heritage partners to deliver 'the thrilling story of England' to children in schools.

It builds on a principle of localism involving local communities and local school, describing the heritage sites as: 'the physical remains of the rich, controversial and thrilling story of England. All belong to the people locally, and local children who visit them will be inspired to delve further' (Gove, 2012).

Tosh (2008) sees heritage affectionately as a concept that nurtures ordinary people and their historical environment and, as Jackson (2008) says, alongside local history and local history activity we inevitably have heritage. Jackson (2008) goes on to argue that an understanding of what these interests encompass can be best achieved by conceptualising the purpose and practice of local history as both history and heritage.

As shown earlier in this chapter, heritage as history can be viewed in two different contexts. First, we can look at heritage as Tosh does – in the social sense, as a means of nurturing the ordinary person, or second, from a political stance, to conserve our national identity and our 'island's story' which might not necessarily have the ordinary person at the forefront of its intention (Cannadine et al., 2011).

We would suggest that both are arguably valid in preserving our local and therefore our nation's heritage. Heritage is particularly important in times of change; it forms a sense of security and a visual point of reference and even a refuge (Cormack, 1978, cited in Grigg and Hughes, 2013). It is with this view in mind that we put child's heritage at the heart of the local.

The local and identities

Identity is a complex concept which covers language, religion, a shared memory and a sense of identity. It is rich in symbolism: heroes, battles lost and won, national anthems, songs, poetry, paintings, memorials, street names (Ball and Stobart, 1996). Identity is both an interdependent and a mutable concept. We have a person's identity which is shaped by his/her environment, community and cultural heritage, but a community or local environment which is shaped by the individual. The changing nature of one must impact on the other, thus making it difficult to define one's 'identity' in a broad sense.

However Stobart suggests local historical work demonstrates a concern for and a potential to foster contemporary senses of local and regional identity, distinctiveness and consciousness. It can also contribute to local social cohesion and community regeneration (ibid). Chapter 3 refers specifically to this.

Local and regional identities are, of course, neither monolithic nor static. Place identities are socially constructed and reconstructed, contested and debated, and draw selectively and variously on aspects of the past and on contemporary local characteristics (Asari et al., 2008; Jackson, 2008). This is further explored in chapter 2, where we offer valid reasons why place or places in local are important to us and more specifically to children as individuals.

Concepts and skills in the local in history

We cannot begin to think about teaching and learning in and through the local if we do not give immediate regard to the concepts and skills involved. In our experience, many non-specialist teachers of history struggle with the notion of historical concepts and the complexity of understanding and the teaching of these. We have also found there has been a lack of

understanding in differentiating between concepts and skills, so we offer the following, very broad, definition: a concept is an idea that leads to an understanding. It cannot be practised as such, unlike a skill, but has to be repeatedly experienced. We can practise a skill, for example observation, in order to become more accurate and concise, which may in turn help us develop an understanding of a particular concept. A concept will have a defining set of principles and characteristics that lead to that understanding. For instance, the defining principles which might underpin the concept of a house are: a house has rooms, stairs and a roof. It may be a place where someone lives or where someone is intending to live (though not necessarily); whereas a bungalow is not the same concept as a house as it has no stairs leading up to bedrooms. A concept needs revisiting in different contexts, discussed and applied in a socially constructed way in order to develop a level of understanding (Vygotsky, 1962).

The stage of development in our learning will depend on how deeply a concept is understood. For example a young child may have some understanding of time through being able to talk about yesterday and today; however an older child will begin to understand change over time and suggest reasons for it.

Whilst we give only a brief overview here of the key concepts and skills, they will be more contextualised throughout the book. We do in particular explore chronology in more depth in chapter 8 as this is one of the key concepts central to the understanding of history and is notably the most difficult concept to comprehend, for both children and adults alike.

Turner-Bisset (2005) describes concepts in history as first, second and third order concepts. The first includes the overarching concepts central to history and historical enquiry (we place chronology as being central to this also); the second which help us understand historical situations, and the third which help us understand periods of times. Figure 1.1 gives an overview of the concepts adapted from Turner-Bisset and shows the interrelationship of the main ideas. Interwoven within these concepts are the skills of enquiry. Examples of such skills, though not exhaustive, are: questioning; observing; hypothesising; discussing; evaluating; recording; sequencing; deducting and comparing. Some skills and concepts overlap, for example interpreting evidence is both a skill (we do it) and involves a concept (the *idea* of evidence being able to show us something).

To help us relate these concepts and skills to the local, consider the following task.

Task

List the concepts in Figure 1.1.

- *Using a local study and a focus of study (for example, industry, clothing or housing), note down questions/examples that might be applicable to each of the first order concepts, for example: Industry.*
  ***Change:** was there a change to the farming industry in the late nineteenth century in Sidcup?*
  ***Cause:** if so, what might have caused the decline?*
  ***Consequences:** what was the result for the local people?*
- *Consider what second and third order concepts might be applicable to this period of time.*

What skills would you engage in to begin this process of enquiry?

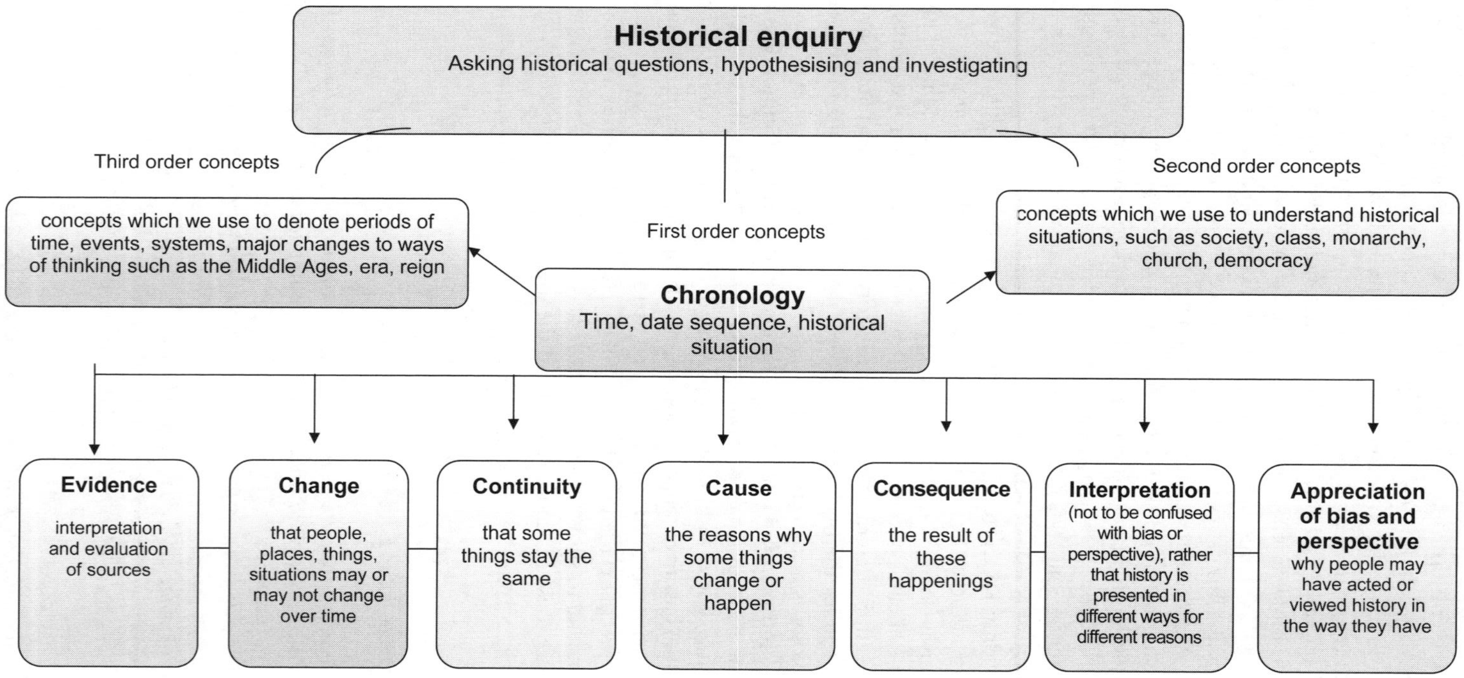

Figure 1.1 Key concepts in historical enquiry.

When considering historical enquiry (what we argue is the overarching concept) we must consider the process of learning history – what Turner-Bisset refers to as the syntactic process. She describes this as being 'the processes by which new truths become established in a discipline . . . in history this being historical enquiry' (Turner-Bisset, 2005:18). By understanding that there is indeed a 'process' which is needed for children to learn effectively and thus adhering to it, teachers will ensure children do not miss vital concepts and skills of historical learning. The steps involved in this process are interdependent and all necessary.

The process can be summarised as follows:

- asking/forming an historical question (if history is taught without questions it is probable that the learning is coming from a fact/information-giving approach derived most likely from a secondary source, which arguably leaves the child in a passive position and not 'doing' history);
- searching for evidence;
- examining evidence;
- recording evidence;
- interpretation and comparison of different sources;
- synthesis of historical argument – what can we conclude from what we have and why?

The importance of this process is that if children miss a step within the structure, they will not develop the important conceptual understanding or skills needed to understand the nature of history and why and how things have happened. Without this full understanding they will be unable to move forward in their learning and there is a danger that negative attitudes to learning history will develop.

Summary

- There is no one way to define local or local history study.
- Putting the child at the local is of paramount importance to developing independent and meaningful learning.
- Our approach to history teaching and learning must be reviewed with a consideration to teaching in and through the local if we are to create a coherent and concise 'bigger picture' for children.
- An understanding of the process, concepts and skills involved in historical teaching and learning is paramount.

Further reading

We include the following books here as well as in the bibliography to highlight their importance further. We feel they are essential reading on the role of teaching and learning in primary history and will prove invaluable resources.

Thinking History 4–14: Teaching, Learning, Curricula and Communities, by G. Bage, London: RoutledgeFalmer (2000)

Reclaiming Our Pasts: Equality and Diversity in the Primary History Curriculum, by H. Claire, Stoke-on-Trent: Trentham Books (1996)

Creative Teaching: History in the Primary Classroom, by R. Turner-Bisset, London: David Fulton (2005)

Useful websites and resources

http://www.history.org.uk/ The Historical Association website and associated publications are an invaluable resource for students, teachers and non-specialists. They provide excellent resources, research and cases studies on teaching and learning and on the theory underpinning history – a 'one-stop shop' for the busy historian.

http://www.english-heritage.org.uk/daysout/eastofengland/

And now to the 'how' . . .

This chapter has explored why we feel history is important and has introduced the reader to the concepts of 'history through the local' and the 'child as the local'; it has offered a rationale for our approach of teaching primary history.

The next chapter introduces the reader to the tools of our approach and looks specifically at places and maps and how to use them.

Chapter 2

Resources and how to use them – place and maps

Putting in place

Introduction

This chapter is about places and their relevance to the local in history and in doing this the link with geography is acknowledged. We consider what places are and why they are important to us. It is also about their representation in the form of maps and what we believe is the central role of these in historical learning about the local area. Underpinning this is the need for children to explore their own local geographical roots in order to give them a sense of identity and community. This is important in its own right but also of relevance as a building block in extending their knowledge and understanding of other cultures and societies, making them more accepting of people and cultures different from them.

Chapter objectives

By the end of this chapter you should:

- understand the significance of places and their importance to us;
- understand some of the links between history and geography;
- know about a range of maps that can be used to support local history;
- be able to use maps with children to help them develop historical knowledge, skills and understanding.

Place

Importance of place to us as individuals

In our everyday experiences as individuals, places are important to us. From the familiar question to someone newly met, 'And where are you from?', to the care we might take in selecting places to live, go for a holiday or go shopping, places have significance for us. In particular the place where we live has a special significance; for better or worse it is our local area, the one we probably spend most time in, and will come to know in a practical and often emotional way. Researchers such as Spencer (2005, cited in Tanner, 2010) argue that the attachments we make which are emotional are an important part of identity while others such as Catling (2003) also argue that it contributes to self-esteem.

Reflection

- *What places were significant to you while you were growing up?*
- *Consider one of them and reflect further on your memories of that place and the associated emotions. Is it a place that you feel is part of your identity? Do you still know that place? Do any changes to it affect you emotionally?*
- *Is it a place you would like to return to more permanently?*

Spencer and Blades (1993) argue that the study of place is important in helping to establish children's identity and they refer to the concept of 'place attachment' as helping amongst other things to provide daily and ongoing security. Relph (1967, cited in Wiegand, 1992) argues that to be human is to 'be in place' and that 'knowledge of place is a simple fact of experience', implying that merely living or working in place is to develop knowledge of it. His reference to experience, however, reminds us that experiences vary. For instance, the locality of the school is very often not the teacher's home locality. This has both advantages and disadvantages. On the positive side it can allow the children to be the experts in terms of the local area that they know 'better' than the teacher. One disadvantage, however, might be that without the insider's view, the teacher may bring value judgements about the area which unduly influence their understanding of it, especially if it is an area with a negative reputation. This does result in a difference in perception and this is acknowledged by Relph in his seminal work *Place and Placelessness*, when he refers to the distinction experienced by 'insiders' and 'outsiders'. (Relph, 1967, cited in Wiegand, 1992). Teachers, however, may be helped in having a fuller understanding of the locality if the school is genuinely part of the local community.

The naming of places enables us to identify them for ourselves, makes them 'visible', enables them to be shared with others, may define and describe their character, and gives them a cultural context. They may or may not have clearly defined boundaries, and places we are familiar with may form part of a hierarchy (as in a street within a town within a county within a country). They may overlap with other areas as in the example of Kent overlapping with London.

Importance of place in geography

For the geographer, place is central to the subject and geographers have in recent decades become more interested not only in studying places, but also in defining and studying the concept of 'place' (Massey, 1995; Holloway and Hubbard, 2001; Cresswell, 2004). A commonly held view is that place is a meaningful location and that the naming of it is significant in this. A place is 'a portion of space with its unique blend of built and the natural, recognised by one person or a huge group of people, as personal to them in some way' (Taylor, L., 2005:14). It has the attributes of location and locale, but also through its relationship with people, a character or personality, a sense of place. Place for geographers is clearly about the physical environment and the human – cultural, economic and social.

Primary geographers in particular see their role as helping children to develop a sense of

place starting with the place they live in and thereby building on children's daily experiences. The term 'a sense of place' may be a difficult one for the non-geographer to define, but it is an understanding which is seen as emerging from both knowledge about a place filtered through an individual's values and attitudes (Fisher, 1998) and mediated by our emotional responses. Geographers would see that development as being aided by an investigative, questioning approach.

Clifford and King (1993) refer to place as being process and story, as being a layered continuation, a description which encompasses the changing nature of places so that they are not static.

Importance of place in learning

Some geographers and others would also claim that place is an important context for learning more generally: learning in a place, as well as learning about a place. Swift (2005) for instance claims that the emotional connection with place is significant in terms of learning. The twin meanings of 'place as a context for learning' may encompass both the use of fieldwork as an approach to learning about a place, an approach we explore in the next chapter; and links to the more complex notion of 'situated learning', a term which also overlaps with the concepts of 'place based learning' and 'area based curricula'. (Royal Society for the Encouragement of Arts, Manufactures and Commerce, 2010; Morgan, 2011; Place Based Learning UK, 2013). These embrace the notion of a curriculum of relevance to children both by drawing on the local area and its resources and by involving the community in its development. These ideas have also been explored by Bage (2000) and more recently Alexander (2010) who identify the importance of a local component in the curriculum, termed the community curriculum, suggesting that about a third of the curriculum time should be used in this way. The arguments behind these ideas and initiatives offer further support for the relevance of place as a basis for learning in both history and geography.

Place, geography and history

Places are also of significance in history, and especially history in the local. It is impossible to think of history without thinking at some point of the geographical setting which is its arena. To use the analogy of story, if history provides the narrative line, people the characters, then geography (place) provides the setting. The analogy should not be taken too far, however, for the geography of a place does not have a passive role. Local historians as well as geographers have tended to see place as separate from people as in the following statement of Rogers (1972:4):

> All history, and local history more obviously than many other branches of that study, is concerned with the interrelationship of people and place. The two have interacted with each other in a manner which is often hard to disentangle but which we will be aware of as individuals.

This interrelationship is important.

Some primary historians such as Harnett (2007) recognise the importance of place in seeing the importance of a history curriculum which encourages a greater understanding, past and present, of the communities and localities where they live. From a slightly

different perspective Hoodless (2008b) claims that the history curriculum is most effective when it is adapted to meet local needs and is relevant to the school and its children. Because children's interests are often local – through friends, play spaces, shopping, leisure activities – working around what they know in the local place is often the best stimulus for learning.

Catling, commenting on the links between the two subjects (2006:14), suggests that the connection between them goes deeper than the physical environment – that they are 'more to do with personal and local identity'. Furthermore, he sees the opportunities of a study linking history and geography as one which addresses identity and a sense of place and involves not only a deeper sense of the local, but also leads to links between individuals and the wider world. This is perhaps the challenge; not to become so immersed in a sense of one's own locality that the perspective becomes introverted, an issue that is one for 'the local in history' therefore, as well as for local geography. Driver and Samuel (1995), drawing on Massey, have pointed out that it is easy to be introverted if we focus only on the uniqueness of localities and that we need to be careful of believing that place has a defined and fixed identity. We need to understand place in 'less bounded' and more open-ended ways, challenging historians and geographers alike. Local histories need to be placed in broader contexts such as the national and global and we need to be aware of:

- commonalities and what they share as much as the difference and distinctiveness between places (that many places will have been influenced by the arrival of the railway or the decline of manufacturing industry);
- the interconnectedness of places (that trade and migration have forged links between places; that ideas travel and influence permeates);
- change and being open to its inevitability (that high streets grow and decline for instance);
- the diversity of places, even those which seem homogeneous.

History and geography have four further components in common. First, they share a range of skills which can be usefully developed for both subjects within the local area. Second, they share the approach of enquiry (Pickford et al., 2013) and within this a number of skills which variously belong to fieldwork and thinking skills – observation, recording, interpreting, analysis, questioning and so on. The key question approach to the study of place has become part of a recognised pedagogy in geography and a number of authors have linked those questions to the study of the local in history as Table 2.1 demonstrates.

Third, significantly, they also share a number of key concepts, a connection which was developed as the foundation for teaching and learning in the 'Place Time and Society' project (Blyth et al., 1976). The significance of the link between the subjects was also more recently recognised by Alexander in linking place and time as one of his eight domains in his curriculum proposals (Alexander, 2010).

Finally, the subjects also use many similar resources for the study of the local area: photos and other visual material; reports; the environment itself; the local community; newspapers and pamphlets. This makes them perfect partners when working in the local area, although in the past geographers have sometimes felt that history can easily dominate a local study partly because of teachers' lack of confidence in the geographical aspects.

Table 2.1 Key questions in geography and history (after Copeland 1993:6)

Questions for local geography (Now)	*Questions for local history (Then)*	*Influence of the past on the present*
Where is this place?	Where was this place?	
What is this place like?	What was this place like?	What elements of the past can we still see?
How is this place linked to other places?	How was this place linked to other places?	In what ways have past connections influenced how this place is now connected with other places?
How is this place similar to and different from other places?	How was this place similar to and different from other places?	What influence have these elements had on this place and how is this influence different from or resembles what has happened at these places?
Why is this place as it is?	Why was this place like this?	How did this place change?
What does it feel like to be in this place?	What would it have been like to live in this place?	How does the past influence what it feels like to be in this place?
How is this place changing?	Why did it change?	

Place and maps

> Geography is about maps and history is about chaps.
>
> (Crosby, 2005:201)

It would be difficult to envisage a focus on place without including the use of maps. They are quintessentially the tool of the geographer but also, in spite of the rather dated adage quoted above, valued by historians, and they now seem to be of significant importance in historical research (Crosby, 2005) both as a subject of study in their own right and as a source to help understand the landscape. Local historians have long recognised their value (Riden, 1998), as have educationalists. Maps represent a place in a two-dimensional form and therefore allow an insight into what a place is or was like. However, because they cannot show everything, what is shown is always a selection of reality and represents the concerns of the map maker whether in the past or the present. Technical issues such as the accuracy of distance measurement may also have influenced them.

There is quite a lot of specialist information about maps which can be overwhelming for the non-specialist, so we are summarising here some key points about their availability and usefulness, and we have provided information about publishers, scales and editions in the resources section at the end of the chapter.

- Both modern and historic maps can help with local history investigations.
- The most useful present day and historic maps to have are Ordnance Survey maps. These are available from about the mid-nineteenth century onwards.

- They are available in hard copy from local history libraries or sometimes as reproductions and electronically.
- The Digimap service for schools is worth investigating to provide access to maps online.
- Other historic maps are available which cover the eighteenth and even seventeenth centuries at smaller scales (i.e. with less detail).

Reflection

- *Are you confident in your own use of maps?*
- *Are large scale maps regularly used in geography or history in school?*
- *In other curriculum areas are maps in evidence?*
- *Is there a collection of maps in the school and does the school subscribe to Digimap?*

Disney and Hammond (2002) suggest three approaches to selecting maps for use in school:

1 all available maps from the earliest map to that of the present day arranged in a catalogue for use by staff;
2 maps to illustrate change over a particular period, e.g. the Victorian era or the second part of the twentieth century, especially relating to significant change such as the coming of the railway;
3 maps that can link with other primary sources, e.g. photos (many will be available from the early years of the twentieth century) or the census from 1841 to 1911.

Teachers' toolkit 2.1 Using maps

1. *On a modern map of the area identify the school and any local features known to you.*
2. *Identify any place names and interesting street names.*
3. *Look at the shape of the streets and clues as to the type of houses. Do these suggest anything about the age of the built-up area? (see p.29)*
4. *When working with toolkit 3.1 (on p.40), use a modern map to help record what you are finding out about the local area as part of your initial walk around the area.*
5. *Use an historic map as part of your own initial research into the area. This will often mirror what can be undertaken with the pupils. In particular:*
    - *identify any familiar features which you recognise from the present day;*
    - *identify features which are no longer there;*
    - *are there any 'antiquarian' features such as ruins, tumuli or earthworks?*

Teaching and learning with maps

Our experience is that maps have an endless fascination for adults and children alike. Early OS maps have a particular appeal, perhaps because of their engaging visual style showing for

instance individual trees. When carrying out any mapping work, it is important to consider both children's knowledge of the local area today and their mapping skills. Disney and Hammond (2002) comment that children will get more from the maps if they have a good knowledge of the local area. They also need to have the experience of using a present day map of their local area as it enables them to make links between the real place and its two-dimensional abstract representation. This means ensuring that when using local maps in history, children's mapping skills and knowledge of their area today are at an appropriate level. However, working with historic maps will help to develop this knowledge and these skills further (Catling, 1998). When working with maps, highlighters and acetate sheets are particularly useful, while projecting images on to the wall is a simple way to create a large scale display map.

Using an historic map: what was this place like?

As a rich primary source for the historian, maps from the past represent many opportunities for the use of enquiry. They can be particularly useful in describing a place at a time in the past (Boulton, 1991).

- Children can begin by finding features they know and can recognise (Disney and Hammond, 2002) before moving on to identifying the unknown features.
- They can ask questions about features they do not recognise or are not familiar with and highlight them on a present day map, and then these old features can be visited.
- An overlay can be used to mark features such as routes and key buildings and then placed on the modern map.
- Roads or fields can be listed and analysed for any clues they give about land use or activities. Are the names still in evidence?
- Questions can be used to extend thinking; for instance, what are the most important changes? Why did change happen?

Local example 2.1 illustrates how an old map can reveal past industries.

Having identified historic features, links can be made with other evidence: for instance, with that from a trade directory listing the shops in a village street or town centre or with a school register to show where the children who attended the school lived. A project by Fines (2010b) introduced maps through a link with oral history. These sources of evidence together can begin to help children answer some of the key enquiry questions in Table 2.1 and the case study on Penge shows how fieldwork and the use of maps can be linked.

Local example 2.1 What was this area like?

The Byker and Heaton sheet (Tyneside Sheet 12, 1898) of the Godfrey Edition shows a wonderful array of clues as to the industrial past of the area. Looking at just a quarter of the sheet, the following were in evidence: potteries; tanneries; glass works; canvas works; flint mill; smithies; electrical works; lead works; clay pit; brick works; corn mills; timber yard, as well as some references through street names – Millers Hill; Foundry Lane; Maling Street (local pottery) and Engine Street. These are all rich clues as to the former industrial nature of the area.

Having become familiar with the key features of an area, children might choose a place or a route on the map for which to describe what they would be able to see and smell. In the role as a builder, they could decide where to build some new houses or shops which could then be compared with the actual locations on a later map (Boulton, 1991). In a similar vein, children could be given an outline map of the area showing physical features and then decide where the Saxons or Vikings might have built a village taking account of water and wood supplies, flat land for building, land for crops and perhaps a means of defence (Turner-Bisset, 2005).

Case study 2.1 Penge

Fieldwork and the use of maps

A class of Y6 children was involved in a local history study of Penge in south east London. The work focused on change and the reasons for change. The work began with a trail of the area which drew on the evidence of the built environment, for instance in dating buildings, identifying change by comparing then and now and by looking for physical evidence, interpreting inscriptions and dates. This was followed up by the use of a sequence of five OS large scale maps from 1864 to the present day. From these the children could see some of the changes that had taken place: change in street names (one had been the site of an infamous local murder); change of building names; the building of the railway; the creation of a local park; the addition of a public toilet and the building of many more houses especially between 1864 and 1894. Building plots could be identified with the help of land auction details and they also revealed why more houses were being built in the area. They noted that Penge was surrounded by many stations and, drawing some of this evidence together, they were able to hypothesise about the role of the railway in facilitating the growth of the area.

Using a smaller scale map, the children also mapped the birth place location of individuals living in the area at the time of the 1881 census and began to understand about migration during the nineteenth century.

For schools in the London area, the Booth poverty maps may provide a useful source. Charles Booth was responsible for the creation of these maps of the area of London in his day. He and his researchers walked the streets with local constables making notes and classifying the houses in terms of social class and character. The descriptions of streets and areas provide a fascinating source (see local example 2.2 and appendix 2.1).

Using a modern day map: what has our area been like in the past?

Using a modern map allows us to look for evidence of the relics of past periods and hence can tell us something about what the area was like in the past. The 1:50,000 and 1:25,000 OS maps show evidence of times past through the use of symbols. Roman and non-Roman

Local example 2.2 Edric Road and the Park Hatcham Estate

Monson Road. 2-st houses like the rest of estate. A few shops near Eckersley Gardens and at corners. Laundry, baker, grocer, etc. PINK as maps

(PINK = Fairly comfortable. Good ordinary earnings.)

Hatcham Park Estate. Wide streets, long gardens, well kept houses and general appearance of comfort and respectability. Railwaymen, clerks and others in regular employment live here. The women are well dressed, the doorsteps are clean and though there are lots of children they do not play about the street. Only two pubs on the estate but there are four grocers' licenses and several pubs on the main road.

(From Steele, J. (ed.) (1997) *The Streets of London: The Booth Notebooks; South East.* London: Deptford Forum Publishing.)

remains where known will be marked, dates may be used, visible earthworks shown, sites of antiquity (meaning before the Middle Ages) and sites of battles named. An overlay of these relict features could be placed over an historic map to see if additional evidence of them was available in times gone by (see local example 2.3).

Local example 2.3 The potential of present day maps to reveal the past

Reviewing a range of 1:50,000 scale OS maps from places across the country as far apart as Port Talbot, Wensleydale, Keswick, King's Lynn and York, revealed an astonishing range of such sites, only some of which are given as examples here:

- Port Talbot – many antiquities, enclosures and dismantled railways
- Wensleydale – rich in disused mines and evidence of earlier settlements
- Keswick – stone circles and disused mines
- King's Lynn – many moats, tumuli, dismantled railways
- York – moats, a mill mound and disused airfield

A modern map can also begin to tell us about the age of an area, although this also needs to be linked to fieldwork and the use of other sources. Take, for instance, the type of houses and the nature of the street layout:

- an area of small winding streets may indicate a medieval area;
- long lines of terraced houses with small gardens on long straight streets are typical of the late nineteenth century in many areas;

- semi-detached houses with gardens of a moderate size on streets that may have a geometric layout are typical of the inter-war period (1919–1939);
- cul-de-sacs with detached and semi-detached houses are more typical of the post-war period

Comparing maps: how has this place changed? How was it similar to and different from the place today?

The use of a modern day map alongside the old map capitalises on children's familiarity with the present day area and allows a direct comparison to be made so that similarities and differences can be identified and recorded. Comparisons will work best if maps of a similar scale can be used. If necessary a photocopier can be used to help change the scale of a map. For older and more able children a sequence of maps can show when the most significant changes occurred. Using a sequence of maps can provide opportunities to look at the chronology of change and it is really important to use a timeline if undertaking this work. Looking at a series of maps can also help children understand that change does not happen in a regular way. Examples of this can be seen in the work of John Fines (2010b) and also of Mackintosh (2004). In the latter example, during work with Year 4 and 5 pupils on change in the centre of Hull, Mackintosh was impressed both with the children's interest in maps and with their mapping skills. Updating a recent but dated map can also help children identify change.

Working on comparison using the historic map and without a present day map can challenge children further and be suitable for older children, i.e. the children are drawing on their recall of the local environment. Fines, working with Year 6 children, used an old map and asked them to record features that they knew from today that were either there then or not there. This simple activity led to some useful speculation including some thinking about cause and effect (Fines, 2010b). Activities such as these will help children develop both their chronological understanding and their understanding of the concepts of similarity and difference.

Building plans

Large scale plans of a building can provide a fascinating insight into changes in use and usage. They may be available from the local history or archives centre, for the school itself, or for other significant public or historic buildings (they may be part of published information for heritage sites including ruins), and occasionally for local houses. Children can explore the significance of the types of rooms there are in a building and that tells them about life in the past – a dressing room in a Victorian house; a bath house linked to a Roman villa; a ballroom in a mansion.

Using place names

Place names are fun! The magical perspective of the writer Bill Bryson reminds us of the delights of the curious and humorous names which are scattered across our urban and rural areas (Bryson, 1996). He states that there are some 30,000 place names in Britain (and we guess these would be place names as in settlements) and lists a number which have particularly appealed to him: Prittlewell; Yonder Bognie; Lickey End; Shellow Bowells; Sockburn and Spitall among them. My father could never help finding Twizel in Northumberland

particularly funny. This gives an added dimension to the use of place names in investigating local history.

There are many clues as to the past settlement of an area through the place names. This was acknowledged in one of the QCA geography units of work, 'Village Settlers', which suggested the use of a map as a starting point for identifying past settlement patterns (DfEE/QCA, 1998). Place names usually reflect a combination of landscape features, local families who owned land or had importance, farming; and the type of settlement (farm, village, hamlet etc). Table 2.2 shows the more commonly seen place names from various periods of settlement. To those could be added French names from the Norman period such as mont (a mound); or bel/beau (beautiful); medieval names such as bury (manor); forum (market); regis (of the king) and grange (monastic sheep farm).

Street names can also provide clues as to the history of an area: events, people and occupations. Local references may be to long-gone occupations – Ropemaker Walk; Clothmakers Street; Weavers Lane; Green Lane (perhaps a drovers' route). Local features no longer in physical evidence may be indicated – Railway Street; Canal Road; Mill Street; Horseferry Place. There may also be other idiosyncratic references such as the group of streets in Ladywell, south east London, reportedly named after the builder's children: Francemary;

Table 2.2 Common place names and their origins and meaning

Celtic		*Anglo-Saxon*		*Viking*	
Aber	mouth of a river	Bourne	stream	Bar	gate
Afon/avon	river	Burh/burg/bury	fort	Barrow	hill
Bal	homestead/ hamlet	Combe	small valley	By	farmhouse/village
		Cot	cottage	Crag	rocky cliff
Bre/don	hill	Croftsmall	enclosure	Dale	valley
Bryn/pen	hill; top	Den	pasture	Fell	mountain
Caer	fortress	Dene	valley	Force	waterfall
Capel	chapel	Dun	hill	Garth	fenced land
Coed	wood	Ey/ea	island	Gate	road/track/path
Cwm/cum	deep valley	Field/feld	field/clearing	Gill	ravine
Dun/dum	hill/fort	Folk	people	Haven	harbour
Lan/llan	church	Ford	river crossing	Holme	island
Pont	bridge	Ham/ton	village	How	hill
Porth	harbour	Holt	wood	Ing	meadow
Tre	homestead/ hamlet	Hurst	clearing in woods	Kirk	church
				Knott	rocky hill
		Ing	people	Lund	grove
Roman		Lea/ley/ ly/leigh	clearing	Ness	headland
Caster/ cester/ chester	camp			Pike	mountain peak
		Mere	pool	Rigg	ridge
		Port	market town	Stoke	place/holy place
Fos(s)	ditch	Stead	large farm	Tarn	pond
Port	harbour/gate	Stock	cattle farm	Thorpe	small village
Street	paved way	Stoke	outlying farm	Thwaite	field/clearing in forest
		Stow	holy place		
		Ton/tun	meeting place	Toft	homestead
		Wey	temple	Wath	ford
		Wic(k)	dairy farm/camp	Wick	market
		Worthy	enclosed land		

Arthurdon; Phoebeth; Amyruth; Gordonbrock; Henryson and Elsiemaud. Other examples of national significance are given in chapter 6.

Maps as a form of recording and communicating

Maps can provide an attractive and relevant form of recording information and communicating understanding. In terms of recording, for instance, the age of buildings could be mapped and historic features not otherwise shown on a map could be added. In terms of communicating understanding, change could be indicated on a map by highlighting, or historical photos could be linked to the location they show on a map as part of recording how an area has changed. An exciting trio of maps by a Year 6 child (Figure 2.1) shows an area of Hammersmith over three successive periods.

Maps can provide a culmination for local history work, and an example of this being done outside of education is the Parish Maps project which is run by the organisation Common Ground. Their website lists maps across the country which have been compiled by local communities. They discuss the content of a parish map as being produced for localities by local people and recording what they value in it, much of which is fragments of history.

Next steps

Having explored the nature of place and its representation on maps, the next chapter encourages the exploration of the local environment as a rich and accessible source for learning about the history of the locality.

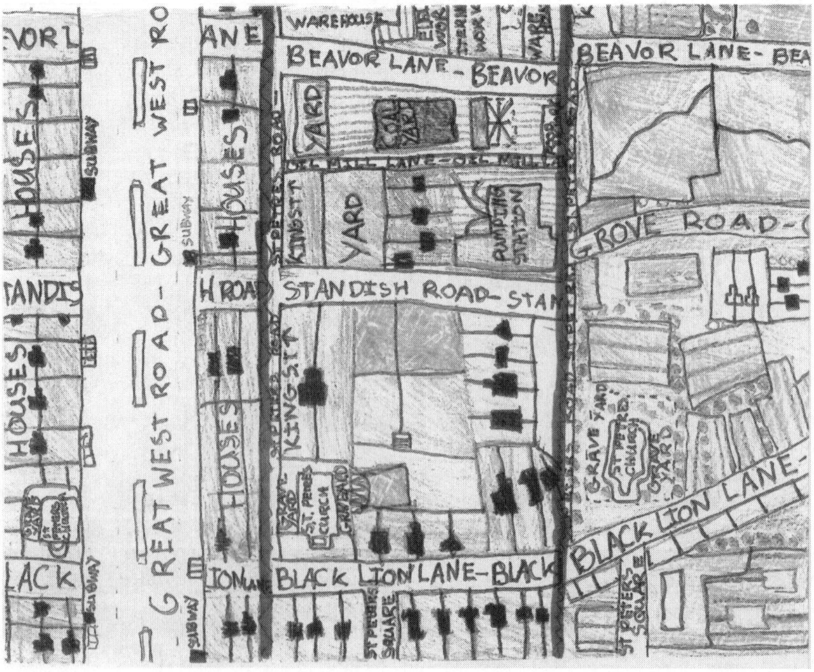

Figure 2.1 Three maps by a Year 6 child showing historical change over one area.

Appendix 2.1 Types of map: an introduction for non-specialists

1. *Everyday maps*

For many people, the easiest maps to access are street maps, either in hard copy or on the web. Street maps are best at showing routes and a selection of key amenities, and less good at showing the detail of areas and individual buildings and for this it is essential to go to Ordnance Survey maps.

2. *Ordnance Survey (OS) maps (old and new)*

OS maps at a range of scales provide a wonderful array of sources across a period of more than one hundred and fifty years. The Ordnance Survey was established in the 1790s for military purposes. The first series of large scale maps (at a scale of one inch to the mile) was completed in the 1870s (Riden, 1998).

Large scale OS maps

(i) **Maps were originally published at a scale of one inch to a mile**
1st edition – 1870s
2nd edition – from 1900s
3rd edition – between the world wars with continuous revisions since then.
Some of these are available as reproductions.
From the second half of the nineteenth century onwards larger scale maps were also produced:

(ii) **The scale of 6 inches to the mile**, which in metric terms has become the 1:10,000, is good for overviews of areas.

(iii) **Maps at the scale of 25 inches to the mile** show much in accurate detail, for instance, field boundaries, railway lines, milestones, footpaths, named public and industrial buildings. In metric terms this became the 1:2500. This was the largest scale generally available. For urban areas two larger scales map be available:

(iv) **Maps at the scale of 50 inches to the mile** may be available for the post-war period and these became the 1:1250 maps.

(v) A scale of **10 foot to the mile or 1:500** was produced in the 1870s. These town plans show not only details of buildings and streets but also the interior of public buildings and street furniture shown to scale and, where they exist, are wonderful documents for showing detail at street and building level.

Digital maps: It is possible to access OS maps old and new and scales ranging from 1:100,000 to 1:1250 on the Digimap service which schools can subscribe to.

3. *Other old maps*

Sixteenth- and seventeenth-century maps by Saxton and Speed: these are essentially small scale and therefore lacking in detail but good at showing the rural nature of areas which are now urban and showing early roads, settlements and names. Also available from the early nineteenth century might be the county maps by Roque.

London maps: London has a wider range of more accurate maps. For instance Ogilvy and Morgan produced the first large scale plan of London in 1676 (required for the rebuilding of the city after the Great Fire). For a later period, the **Booth Poverty Maps** provide a fascinating look at social conditions in the 1890s. Charles Booth was responsible for the creation of these maps of the then area of London. He and his researchers walked the streets with local constables making notes and classifying the houses in terms of social class and character. For south east London these notes have been produced in a book (Steele, 1997), but for other areas there is an online archive.

Tithe maps: Following the 1836 Tithe Commutation Act, large maps were made for most rural areas showing all parcels of land in a parish with an accompanying schedule of owners.

Goad plans: The firm Charles E. Goad has produced large scale plans of towns since the nineteenth century. Initially used for fire insurance purposes, these mainly show commercial uses and are now widely used by commercial organisations. The coverage provided by earlier editions of the plans will vary from area to area but they are a fascinating source for the study of recent change in a high street. There are plans dating back to the 1880s (Riden, 1998). A local history library may well hold copies of some of these.

Large scale building plans: School plans and architects' drawings may be available from when the school was first built, and other plans dating from more recent building alterations may exist either at the school or in the local archives (see chapter 5).

Panoramic views and aerial photos: Neither of these are classed as maps but in different ways they both provide an interesting source of information about the landscape of a place in the past. Panoramic views, especially of London, have been produced as far back as the seventeenth century. They can show what buildings were in existence at the time, and sometimes annotations give additional information.

Likewise aerial views are a useful source of information about the landscape of an area in the past, and as a resource they go back as far as the First World War.

Google Earth 6 has historical imagery.

Sources of maps

Historical maps: The best source of old maps for local history remains the local history library or archive centre (see chapter 5). Maps more than fifty years old are out of copyright. For permission to use all other maps, local authority schools are usually covered by their council's licence from the Ordnance Survey.

Reproductions of historic maps are now available from the following publishers:

- Cassini reproduces historical maps including maps based on the 1 inch OS series from the nineteenth century, enlarged and matched to the present day equivalent. For some urban areas, for instance London, they have these maps in sets of four showing change over time.
- Godfrey produces reprints of old OS maps (1 inch to the mile, www.alangodfreymaps.co.uk).
- Old-maps.co.uk – OS maps from the nineteenth century.

Modern days maps: These may be available to copy for local authority schools at a central reference library. Copies of large scale digital maps can sometimes be obtained directly from

a local authority, often at a very reasonable charge, via the planning department. Alternatively, maps can be obtained from the OS direct or from an approved agent.

Some educational suppliers customise both modern and historic maps for schools in various formats (Wildgoose are suppliers of both modern and old OS maps plus aerial views for educational use, http://www.wildgoose.ac/).

Digimaps for Schools provides access to many present day and historic Ordnance Survey maps. Schools can subscribe to this service: www.digimapsforschools.edina.ac.uk

Good plans can be obtained from Experian: http://www.experian.co.uk/goad/goad-plans.html

Useful websites and sources

Maps

The online Booth archive: http://booth.lse.ac.uk/ The poverty maps can also be bought commercially.

Google maps: http://www.earth.google.com

Ordnance Survey: www.ordnancesurvey.co.uk/oswebsite/getamap

http://www.buildingexploratory.org.uk/resources/

Oblique aerial views dating variously from 1919 to 1953 are available online from the English Heritage Aerofilm: http://www.britainfromabove.org.uk/

An excellent online collection is available from English Heritage's National Monuments Record.

The Geograph Britain and Ireland website has some useful links between symbols and photos of the features (www.geograph.org.uk/article/OS-symbols) and because this is an interactive site, children could add additional ones for their area.

Information on the parish maps project can be found at: http://www.england-in-particular.info/parishmaps/m-index.html

Place names

Many local authorities or history societies have information on local place and street names either published or unpublished (ask at the Local History Library). Some have useful information on a website. A couple of easily accessed examples we found were:

- Tyldesley and District Historical Society have information on local street names on their website: http://www.tyldesleyhistoricalsociety.co.uk/;
- Hampshire County Council provides specific information on names including names connected to the Crimean War: http://www3.hants.gov.uk/localpages/names.htm and http://www3.hants.gov.uk/curtis-museum/alton-history/crimean.htm

For place names generally try: http://kepn.nottingham.ac.uk/ which is the Key to English Place-Names listed by the Institute for Name-Studies – a useful website.

Chapter 3

Resources and how to use them – the physical environment

Walking the area

Introduction

This chapter is essentially about using the physical place as a starting point for learning from and about the locality. We focus on fieldwork, techniques and skills within the local streets and public spaces and are excluding sites (stately homes, castles, cathedrals and reconstructions museums) which are dealt with in chapters 5 and 6. We also provide some background information which will help the reader to develop their own knowledge and understanding of the physical clues in the local streets.

Chapter objectives

By the end of this chapter you should:

- have an understanding of the value of fieldwork;
- have developed children's knowledge of the clues to the past in the local environment;
- know how to find and interpret clues about the past in the physical environment;
- be able to undertake local fieldwork with children to develop historical skills and concepts.

Learning about and from the local landscape

> Nowhere in the UK, I suspect, is there a landscape or a cityscape which is not rich in memory and meaning.
>
> (Wood, 2012b)

In this chapter we are primarily concerned with the physical environment in which children live and in which some of them have grown up. This physical environment is perhaps the most commonly associated with traditional local history. It includes the housing and infrastructure of the locality (road and rail; power and water supplies; schools, libraries, health facilities) plus all the less significant aspects of the physical environment – street furniture, monuments, plaques – that make up the material place. These physical surroundings also

give clues about the social, cultural and economic environments of a locality. This present day environment is of course entirely a product of the past, distant or more recent; it is in varying degrees of transition, and the physical environment is a rich source of evidence for historical enquiry.

This approach in local history has its roots in the mid-twentieth century when, in 1955, the local historian W.G. Hoskins wrote the seminal work on the landscape as a source of evidence for learning about the past – *The Making of the English Landscape*. Looking at both urban and rural landscapes, he demonstrated how to interpret and make sense of the landscape as it has been affected by human activity (Hoskins, 1955). His work has inspired many and he is credited as having pioneered landscape studies and for giving local history, often seen as 'semi-amateur', a more academic profile (Ellis, 2005; Taylor, C., 2005; Lively, 2011). Hoskins stressed the importance of using both fieldwork – 'no historian should be afraid to get their feet wet' (1984:3) – and maps to tell the story of the local while acknowledging the need for archaeology to fill in aspects of the more distant past. He referred to local history and topography in the same phrase, topography being literally the shape of the earth's surface (1984). It is an approach which is taken for granted by many local historians today and one which, in an appropriate form, is ideal for children.

The physical environs are an important starting point for local history because of the visible and easily accessible nature of the evidence. An awareness of the rich layers of our surroundings can also bring pleasure in its own right. We are certainly aware of the pleasure that the ability to date buildings for instance can bring to children.

Out of doors learning and fieldwork

> One lesson outdoors is worth seven inside.
>
> (Brighouse quoted in May et al., 1993)

This oft quoted statement of Tim Brighouse represents the confidence we place in fieldwork. Fieldwork is an approach to a subject which involves collecting information and learning outside the usual place of work – the classroom in education. Joan Blyth (1988) comments that because any local study involves the use of geographical skills and concepts, fieldwork can provide an effective link between history and geography. It involves a range of techniques, some subject specific but many of them common to a range of subjects. It provides an opportunity to learn about the historic environment in situ. The opportunity to undertake local fieldwork is undoubtedly a strength of local history. Claire (1996:182) for instance has commented that 'local history can be the most child-centred and child friendly apprenticeship to the subject' because children can walk around the area they know well, perhaps with the opportunity to be involved in small scale research through the asking of questions, the search for evidence and interpreting the evidence. Indeed, the use of the local as a starting point for history fieldwork generally is also acknowledged, for instance by Walters (2012).

There have been several recent summaries of research into out of classroom learning and more specifically fieldwork which highlights the value of these approaches for enhancing pupils' learning. Dillon et al. (2005) looked at research for the period 1993 to 2003, and Rickinson et al. (2004) for the period 2004 to 2008, and although much of their research was based on secondary aged pupils with little specific reference to history, their findings in support of the value of out of classroom learning are impressive because of the breadth of the studies in other ways. The *Every Experience Matters* research report which endorsed

the value of learning outside the classroom for children's learning built on these findings (Malone, 2008). Additional impetus to this aspect of teaching and learning was given by the *Learning Outside the Classroom Manifesto* (DfES, 2006) which embraced and endorsed all learning in places other than the classroom. The main organisation now promoting learning outside the classroom is the Learning Outside the Classroom Council which formally assumed responsibility and leadership for learning outside the classroom on 1 April 2009. It provides much useful advice.

For the last twenty years, it has been a requirement of the National Curriculum that children learn from a range of sources for history including historic buildings and visits to sites (DES, 1991; DfE, 1995; DfEE/QCA, 1999). It is also a requirement of the Teachers Standards for QTS that provision is made for out of class activities (DfE, 2012b) so that even though the revised curriculum is not explicit about the need to undertake this work, there is hopefully an ongoing commitment to its particular value for primary children.

A number of reasons for working in the environment within the curriculum generally or for a subject like history specifically are widely recognised. These can be summarised as follows:

- Results in motivation, enjoyment and is memorable. (It is easy to find authors who endorse these aspects of the learning, although less easy to provide evidence-based research. The Centre for Architecture and the Built Environment, however, claimed that nine out of ten pupils say they remember more from a school outing than from a classroom lesson (CABE, 2010)).
- Enables learning from real life opportunities to deepen and contextualise learning, including helping to develop locational awareness.
- Provides a sense of scale and of three dimensions.
- Helps the study to be relevant.
- Helps to develop some key skills such as critical thinking and reflection.
- Encourages the use of prior knowledge.
- Social aspects of the experience may help to develop values and attitudes including responsibility towards the local and especially the built environment, and also provide links to current local issues.
- Provides significant opportunities for collaborative learning.
- Appeals to a range of learners because of the range of sensory experiences.
- Encourages a feeling for the environment, a sense of place and a lifelong involvement in the outdoors.
- One other practical aspect of fieldwork in the local area is that it can help to prepare children with the skills that can be transferred to non-local fieldwork helping to make more use of these time consuming visits.

(Kimber and Smith, 1999; Hoodless, 2008b; Corbishley et al., 1999; Dean, 2010; Walters 2012)

Reflection

- *Can you recall any fieldwork experiences from your own primary (or secondary) school?*
- *Can you recall any fieldwork relating specifically to history?*
- *Does this recall include explicit aspects of learning (i.e. not just 'enjoyment')?*

The same authors caution, however, that to be effective these fieldwork experiences need to be well conceived, well planned and well implemented, a qualification which also forms a key finding of the Ofsted report on out of school learning (Ofsted, 2008). They are not, in short, an easy option. Indeed, concern for the safety aspects of school trips is often cited by authors (Vass, 2005; Ofsted, 2008) as a reason that schools avoid undertaking fieldwork. Attempts to address the safety aspects of schools trips have been made recently in order to make them less onerous, and legislation and advice are regularly updated. Although it is not a statutory requirement for schools to have an Education Visit Coordinator (EVC) for every school, as advised in guidance given in 2002, we feel it is useful to have a named person within the school who is fully aware of the detail of relevant school policies as well as other local and national guidance. Current advice should always be checked on the government's website, the website of the Outdoor Education Advisers Panel or with the local authority, and individual teachers may wish to check with their own union.

Planning and organising local fieldwork: a summary of guidance

- Refer to the school policy on out of school learning including that relating to risk assessments, required number of accompanying adults and parental permissions. If you are uncertain or lacking experience in out of school work, talk to the school EVC.
- Undertake a preliminary visit in order to help plan activities, and to assess the practicalities including the safety and size of the space available for groups of children particularly if working on pavements.
- Be clear about the role of the fieldwork in the unit of work.
- Check out children's previous experience of fieldwork and plan any prior learning needed for this visit.
- Set learning objectives related to subject based knowledge, skills and understanding.
- Decide on the approach to fieldwork (see below).
- If possible take photos of the environment which is being explored to refer to during the follow-up work.
- Ensure children are well prepared including pre-visit briefing of learning and behaviour expectations.
- Undertake a second visit as close as possible to the visit date to confirm information for the risk assessment.
- Brief accompanying adults well in advance. (Our own experience is that during fieldwork a teacher without a group herself has more opportunities to overview all the children and is also able to troubleshoot as required.)

Designing fieldwork experiences

There are a range of approaches to fieldwork with varying degrees of teacher control and active involvement of the children. We believe that there needs to be a predominance of the investigative and enquiry approaches, driven by questions many of which can have been set by the children and having much potential for child-led learning. This does not rule out the role of information giving as long as this does not dominate and set a 'passive' learning mode for children. An enquiry approach in fieldwork complements the use of enquiry with evidence in history.

Reflection

- *How much is fieldwork used within the curriculum especially for geography and history?*
- *Is fieldwork undertaken locally in any subject?*
- *Do children experience fieldwork in every year?*
- *Are there particular reasons why fieldwork is not undertaken?*
- *Is any of this fieldwork local?*
- *Are a variety of approaches used?*

The following may be used as an approach to extending your knowledge of the local area and will be especially useful if you are new to the area.

Teachers' toolkit 3.1 Exploring the local area

1. *What do you know, if anything, about the local area already?*
2. *What do other people know? Find and talk to some people who have lived or worked in the area for a long time.*
3. *Study a local modern map and then:*
4. *Walk the area taking the map with you and annotate it to highlight points that interest and intrigue you. A present day, large scale OS map (1:1250 to 1:2500 scale) will show the level of detail that is required for this. The maps will not only show present day human features, it will also show some physical features and historic features and sites. Take a camera and take photos as reminders and potential resources.*
   - *What open space and buildings are there and in what proportions? (is the area predominantly urban or rural?)*
   - *What is the type and density of the housing? Can it be dated? (see Figure 3.2 on p.44 for information).*
   - *Are there many other different types of buildings? Shops, offices, farm buildings?*
   - *Are there open spaces and what are they – fields, woodland, managed parks, playing fields?*
   - *Is there evidence of streams and rivers or ponds?*
5. *If available, read a brief local history. Published local histories are available for many areas either written by keen individuals or produced by local history societies.*
6. *Also look at an historic map of the area, if available.*
7. *Walk the area again looking for links between what you have read and what you can see – do any of the following help to develop your understanding about the area and its history?*
   - *Buildings – the architecture; materials; room design; features etc.*
   - *Sites – derelict buildings, historic sites*

- *Gravestones*
- *Names and initials on buildings*
- *Street names*
- *Dates*
- *Street furniture (objects placed on or near the highway)*
    - *Phone boxes*
    - *Letter boxes*
    - *Lamp posts*
    - *Bollards*
    - *Milestones and signposts*
    - *Shelters*
    - *Signs – direction; indicators e.g. for a fire hydrant, road traffic*
    - *Drain covers*
    - *Sewage stench pipes*
    - *Public toilets*
    - *Litter bins*
    - *Hydrants*
    - *Seats*
    - *Telegraph poles*
    - *Telephone junction boxes*
- *Public buildings and facilities*
- *Transport*

Starting points for teaching and learning in the environment

1. Fieldwork techniques

Although some of the principles are the same, there are particular issues around site visits (whether local or not) as opposed to fieldwork in local streets and parks and so these are dealt with separately. There are a myriad of possible starting points within the immediate public environment, together with a range of techniques which can be used either individually or together in the form of a trail. Figure 3.1 sets out the scope of fieldwork for developing a range of skills and techniques.

Of all these skills, perhaps the most important one is that of observation; helping children to observe carefully, to see as fully as possible the elements of their environment at both a micro and macro level, is fundamental to developing enquiry skills and underpins many of the other skills in the table. Fines (2010a) refers to the need to teach children to look both up as well as down and to develop close observation. Linked to this, talking about and sketching what they can see helps to focus their attention, giving time to recognise and name what they can see. The particular skill of field sketching can be one which teachers avoid for one reason or another, perhaps for lack of familiarity or confidence. It should not be confused with sketching which might be used by an artist although there are links. One advantage over photography is that it slows down the whole process of recording and can provide a focus for discussion between pupil and teacher. However, it can also encourage a

Examples of skills development, techniques and approaches to recording	*Possible use/context*
Observing and describing	Talking about what an old building looks like and how you can tell it is old
Comparing	Comparing two houses, one old and one new, to identify similarities and differences
Enquiry skills – deduction and inference, using prior knowledge	Reasoning from a characteristic or feature to suggest the former use of a building
Naming/classifying categorising	Naming different features on a building Categorising its former use e.g. a shop
Questioning	Identifying what the evidence does not tell you for certain, for instance that a basement door was used by tradesmen
Drawing on two different sources of information	Linking evidence from a map with evidence from the environment e.g. was this building here in Victorian times?
Sound recordings	Recording children's own description of a building Recording a conversation with a resident about life in the past in the area
Make notes	As an aide memoire or to record comments or description in many contexts
Marking information on a map	Age and use of buildings
Highlighting, ringing or ticking words/numbers	Recording the environmental quality of an historical building Selecting descriptive words
Taking a photo	Recording the physical environment, especially useful for a temporary situation such as change happening
Doing a fieldwork sketch	Emphasising features of a static situation such as a building
Annotating a photo/sketch	Showing key features Showing change
Record by listing	Listing type of shops (for comparison with the shops in the past)
Record in a table	Similarities and differences

Figure 3.1 Skills and techniques in fieldwork.

focus on the particular, for instance in emphasising the arrangement of windows, or modern features on an otherwise old building. If only certain features need to be drawn by the child, especially where children have had limited experience of fieldwork sketching, a teacher can provide an outline of the building or of the view. (A useful tip for teachers who are really under-confident in their own drawing is to trace the outline of a building or landscape from a photo.)

Fieldwork can offer a particularly useful way of approaching the development of values and attitudes in history which provides strong links with citizenship education explored in chapter 9: for instance in making judgements about the value of older buildings in the environment, or in empathising with people living in the area in the past. In as much as geography is a context for history, fieldwork also helps children to see the link between the two, supporting the development of cause and effect in history and of explanation in

geography. Examples would be working out why a railway line was built along a certain route such as a valley bottom, or thinking about the importance of a crossing point on a river.

It is also important to be aware of the development of physical and social skills that can be facilitated through working outside: the management of physical equipment such as a clipboard and camera (sometimes all at once), and the collaboration that is provided by working in small groups.

2. *Fieldwork: starting points, focuses and techniques*

Individual starting points such as the ones discussed below can form a focus for, on the one hand, a significant piece of fieldwork and, on the other, a simple introductory visit in which the children observe and discuss a specific feature.

(i) Dating and using buildings

The ability to date buildings is a useful skill and one which in our experience children enjoy especially in relation to local housing. There may be individual buildings, clusters of houses or a street of similar buildings, and whole housing estates which can be investigated.

Children in Years 1 and 2 can use a range of simple indicators such as the presence or absence of chimneys and garages to help them establish whether a house is old. A common misconception of such young children is, however, that the presence of a new feature such as a satellite dish or recently cleaned brickwork means that a building is new rather than old. By Year 6 children should certainly be able to use a much fuller range of clues, including many from the checklist in Figure 3.2.

They will also be able to use a selection of evidence in combination: maps (the absence of a building on an earlier map and its presence on a later map can provide a period during which it was built); people (especially for recent housing, for instance, families moving to newly built housing areas) and sources such as directories and photos.

Buildings themselves provide useful evidence about the past. Analysing aspects of a Victorian building for instance can help children to develop their understanding of what domestic life was like in the nineteenth century. Figure 3.3 shows a list of some of the links that you could help pupils make with careful questioning and prompting.

This approach can also be applied effectively to school buildings. A school building offers rich potential as a starting point for history and is one shared on a daily basis by all the children. A large percentage of children are still taught in schools that are over a hundred years old, a legacy of the boom in the building of school board schools after the 1870 Elementary Education Act. The English Heritage guide on the use of school buildings (Purkis, 1993) offers an extensive guide to the use of schools covering the buildings, the people and documentary evidence. Purkis discusses the changing school styles from the nineteenth century. Her list of clues and what they might tell you about schooling includes the gates marked for 'boys' and 'girls' many of which are still visible; the ventilation lantern on the roof indicating the preoccupation with health and fresh air, a school bell or clock indicating the importance of routine and the lack of personal time pieces; a date or initials perhaps indicative of the significance of the building; doors into classrooms from the outside indicating the importance placed on fresh air.

Housing characteristics that can help with dating

Pre-First World War
Local stone and slate roofs
Sliding sash windows
Angular bays with local stone or stucco surrounds
Smaller houses are usually terraced
More affluent areas will have semi-detached and detached villas
Porches (open or enclosed)
Tiled paths
Chimneys moderately tall
Many decorative features – ridge tiles, brick patterns, barge board
Foot scrapers by the front door
No garages

Inter-war (1919–1939)
Many semi-detached and detached houses
Design often non-symmetrical
Front-facing gables
Brick or pebble dashed walls
Opening casement windows – wooden
Curved bays
Slate or tiled roofs
Leaded or stained glass in doors, transom windows and porches
Some garages
Mock Tudor timber panels
Short chimneys

Post-war (1945–1970s)
Brick walls, tiled roofs
Metal opening casement windows or 'picture' windows
Few or only small bay windows
Garages
Chimneys small or absent in post-1960s houses
Flat or shallow pitched roofs
Tower blocks
Mixed estates of low rise flats and houses

Since the 1980s, styles have changed rapidly. For instance neo Georgian styles were popular in the 1970s and early 1980s while more recently neo Victorian and neo classical styles have become fashionable.

Figure 3.2 Dating housing.

(ii) Open spaces, countryside and parks; trees and plants

In rural areas, the landscape of the countryside contains many clues about the past. Not all of these are easy for children to identify as being the result of past human activity: for instance a railway embankment, a canal or a field boundary might appear to be 'natural' to a child. It is important to correct these misconceptions. It is worth encouraging older children to look at mounds which might be:

- burial mounds;
- uneven terrain which might indicate ruins;

Using the evidence of buildings

- *Chimneys* – indicates the need for fires for heating and can provide evidence for the number of occupied rooms in a house. Can also lead on to thinking about the implications of the dirt and tasks generated by having fires; who laid them, cleaned them etc. Linked to them:
- *Coal hole covers* – coal was delivered to the house in sacks and emptied in the coal cellar, often underneath the pavement. Mess was thereby avoided in the house.
- *Two entrances* – a side or basement door providing access for tradespeople. Enhancement of the grandeur of the front entrance through the use of steps and columns can also lead to discussion about making an impression on others or about the wealth and status of the occupiers.
- *Basement entrance and attic rooms* – might provide evidence of servants.
- *Tiled paths, porches and a boot scraper* – all a practical response to muddy roads: tiles could be more easily cleaned.
- *Dates* – indicate when a building was first built or was renovated.
- *Use of coloured bricks, moulded stucco, patterned tiles, decorative ironwork and barge board* – indicative of the love of decoration especially in the Victorian period. The use of stucco – a specialised type of cement – also allowed the appearance of stone to be replicated without the cost and so heavy ornamentation was possible around doors and windows.
- *Signs of change* – include faded signs painted on bricks; patches of newer brickwork or new extensions; clay tiles rather than slate; double glazing or plastic windows and doors on otherwise old buildings.
- *Building materials* – up until the nineteenth century building materials were very localised and so reflect traditions locally. Once the national railway network was established materials such as bricks of different colours and slates from Wales could be transported easily. Stone slates more recently have been replaced by concrete tiles or artificial slates.
- *Window size* – large windows indicate the most important rooms.
- *Odd ones out* – the presence of a group of post-war buildings in an area of older buildings may indicate bombing during the war. An unusually large building with evidence of residential use may indicate there has been a house with its own grounds which has been 'lost' in the growth of an urban area.
- *Street patterns* – straight streets in the Victorian era and early twentieth century giving way to geometric patterns in the inter-war period. Cul de sacs tend to be a post-war phenomenon.

Figure 3.3 Finding out about the past through the evidence of buildings.

- bumps and isolated bushes which may mark former field boundaries;
- ancient trackways;
- apparently random stones which might indicate stone circles or other ancient monuments;
- smooth hills in a former mining area which may be landscaped slag heaps.

Once such features have been identified as of possible significance, maps, both present day and historic, can be checked to see what additional information is provided.

Most urban areas have a range of open spaces, formal and informal: parks, play areas, playing fields, small areas of woodland, urban squares and allotments. The Nuffield Urban Spaces Project recently developed work with schools on urban spaces in their areas. The

Case study 3.1 Doing fieldwork in south east London

A class of Y4 children undertook fieldwork in a Victorian housing area of south east London as a starting point for a project on the local area. Before the trail they had a lesson developing their understanding of dating Victorian buildings. This session involved the use of photos of local housing and their features; clear use of relevant vocabulary; handing artefacts (wall tiles, finial, roof finial) and discussion of their own houses. Crucially, the adults who were to accompany the children on the trail were present and involved in this. During fieldwork the children used a range of the skills and activities outlined in Figures 3.1, 3.2 and 3.3 which included observation, discussion, labelling and a range of recording techniques in order to help them date the buildings. They also focused on evidence of change; similarities and difference; and used evidence to make inferences about life in the past.

The trail was the starting point for further work on finding out about their area in the nineteenth century.

cross-curricular work, which is published on the Historical Association website, is based around three key questions:

- What are the spaces like now, and how are they used?
- What were they like in the past, and how were they used then?
- What might they be like in the future, and how might we use them?

The project's history activities included fieldwork, for instance, in the form of time walks around the urban spaces finding clues to the past. The children recorded decorative and architectural features of houses, and street furniture. Other activities involved the use of a range of additional primary sources such as photos and the census, and activities such as storytelling and role play.

A particular legacy of the Victorian era is urban parks. Some of these were formed of land previously the grounds of a large house, others might be formed from common land. They are likely to have features dating from the period – bandstands; fountains; shelters; possibly an ice house, lake or avenue of trees; a park keeper's house and iron railings. Later features might include bowling and putting greens, boating lake and flower beds. Older and larger parks might have been deer enclosures.

An idea of the age of trees can be gauged by their size while ornamental planting may be recorded in a published history. Marcus and Barker (1997) give guidance on dating these. Trees and shrubs might provide links with places around the globe (see chapter 8).

(iii) Underground remains: tunnels and caves

Some areas will have underground structures which are evidence of past human activity. Some, such as the caves at Chislehurst in Kent, may be originally natural and then adapted for human use (they were used as bomb shelters during the Second World War). However, many areas have tunnels built for a variety of purposes – smuggling, escape routes, water

culverts – and there may be local myths and stories about these. Not many of them may be open to public access for health and safety reasons, but learning about them adds an edge of excitement to the local area.

(iv) Commemorative plaques, memorials and cemeteries

Memorials may be found in a range of places: at crossroads; on village greens; in churchyards and inside churches; by the roadside; in public buildings. Although the vast majority of memorials date from the last two hundred years, memorials to those who have died have been set up for thousands of years. They are: 'mementoes of individuals, groups or events, made retrospectively by the living' (Purkis, 1995:3). They can involve ordinary people as well as more significant individuals and events and may be to: wars – names, places, victories and defeats; tragedies, disasters and accidents such as floods, fires and plagues; great inventors and inventions. Some of these may have national and international significance and will be referred to in chapters 6 and 8.

CEMETERIES AND GRAVEYARDS

A local church graveyard or municipal cemetery can provide a useful starting point for learning more about an area and its inhabitants. Until two hundred years ago almost everyone would have been buried in a churchyard. As pressure on space in them grew during the Industrial Revolution, private and then municipal cemeteries were provided. Preparation for fieldwork in these areas should take a little more care both in terms of checking with a local vicar, in being aware of any particular health and safety issues especially where the ground is uneven, and in considering the beliefs and views of the children in relation to death and burial. This may be an issue not only for children who have been recently bereaved, but also for children of different faiths, for instance those in which cremation rather than burial is the norm (for instance Hindu, Sikh and Buddhist traditions). In addition pupils should be encouraged to show respect for the dead; graveyards and cemeteries are places of remembrance and visitors to graves may be seeking peace and quiet. Figure 3.4 lists some of the ways in which a typical Victorian (or older) graveyard might provide evidence for a local enquiry.

An exploration of these places can also be a starting point for comparing the burial traditions of another era (Roman) or historic civilisation (Egyptian or Aztec for instance), and also provide links to ancient civilisations through the style of the memorials (Purkis, 1995).

A surprising number of local graveyards may have a nationally known person buried there, providing one of many possible links to the bigger picture of history. Local example 3.1 describes a collective gravestone linked to the nationally significant building and rich in potential for enquiry.

WAR MEMORIALS

Almost every settlement across the country has a war memorial on which the dead of the two world wars are commemorated. (But perhaps you live in one of the doubly blessed villages, of which there are fourteen, where no soldiers were killed in either war!) The website of the UK National Inventory of War Memorials refers to memorials such as sundials, park benches, bus shelters and an island (www.ukniwm.org.uk). According to Quinlan (2005) there are over 37,000 such war memorials in Britain. Heritage Learning, a newsletter by English Heritage published online for teachers and other educators, provides some useful

What can be found out	*Evidence from tombs etc.*	*Possible follow up*
The date the church was built	The earliest date of a burial	Check the date using secondary sources. Try dating from the architecture
The size of families in Victorian times	The size of families buried in a plot	Use census information to confirm specific family sizes and to build up a more general picture. Draw a family tree. Sequence the family events
The popularity of various names in Victorian times	Count of different first names on tombstones	Use census information to identify popularity of names in the nineteenth century
The average age of death in Victorian times	Calculation and recording of age of death	Investigation into causes of death and the prevalence of disease among people
The beliefs people held – sentimental, warning, comic, praising	Examples of epitaphs; sculptures; symbols (e.g. crossed fish)	To establish the meaning of the symbols
The social status of people in the area	The presence of grand tombs or areas where one family has their graves. Is there a mausoleum for a high status local family?	Use census information and street directories to broaden information researching some of the occupations and social status. Use local maps to identify workplaces and likelihood of commuting
The occupations people had	Record any examples	
What the graveyard was like in Victorian times	Age of trees and tomb-stones. Identification of more recent features e.g. notice board	Using possible photos. Discussion of the changes that have taken place including those due to vandalism or neglect

Figure 3.4 Using evidence in a Victorian graveyard or cemetery.

Local example 3.1 A collective gravestone

In the churchyard of St Bartholomew's church, Sydenham, is a gravestone recording the names of ten men who died at the same time in August 1853. The challenge is to think about why they might all have died at the same time and to use that as a starting point for some further investigating at both a local and thematic level. The men in fact were engaged in building the Crystal Palace and were killed in a fall of scaffolding. There is a newspaper report of the accident which can then lead on into learning more of the building and subsequent history of the palace and also into learning about the life of labourers such as these builders and also navvies. In this case there is a large archive of material on the palace as well as publications and a small local museum.

questions generated in relation to a war memorial in Redruth, Cornwall, which could be adapted for a local memorial:

- Why did more people from Redruth die in WWI than die in WW2?
- Was this the same in all localities?
- Look carefully at the names. Did any families perhaps lose members in both wars?
- Find out about individuals by researching then on the Commonwealth War Grave Commission website: www.cwcg.org

(English Heritage, 2010:9)

IN BUILDINGS

Memorials found within buildings can sometimes provide a useful starting point for enquiry (see local examples 6.2 and 8.2).

IN THE ENVIRONMENT

Some events are marked by a stone or a plaque in the wider environment and an example and its use is outlined below.

Local example 3.2 The murder of Mary Bax, 1782

Children have a certain interest in crime and the story of Mary Bax provides an opportunity to delve into the murkier side of life. A stone, which is marked on the OS map of the area near Sandwich in Kent, marks the spot of a local murder. The stone reads:

On this spot
August the 25th, 1782
MARY BAX, Spinster,
aged 23 years
was murdered by
Martin Lash, a foreigner,
who was executed for the same

The story goes that Mary Bax, a young woman – perhaps a local servant – was murdered while she was walking along the coast from Deal to Sandwich. She was apparently carrying a parcel, although the story does not relate what was in it, and was fought for possession of the parcel. That parcel was later found in the possession of a Swedish sailor, Martin Lash, in the graveyard of the parish church at Folkestone and he was apprehended, then tried and executed at Maidstone.

The curious historian will want the answer to many questions:

- What was in that parcel?
- Why was she walking along the coast road?
- Who was the parcel for?
- Why did she hang on to it so fiercely?
- What was the sailor doing in the area?
- Why did the sailor not try to leave the area completely after the crime?
- Did his family ever learn the truth about his disappearance?
- Who buried her?

Part of the interest generated by discovering the memorial stone is about the atmosphere of the locality: a windswept and flat part of the Kent coast used for sheep farming – the incident was apparently witnessed by a young boy, the son of a shepherd – fairly remote but with a pub about half a mile from where she was attacked. The sailor had allegedly jumped ship while it was in 'the Downs'. Other questions might be:

- Had Mary Bax stopped at the pub?
- Had the sailor been drinking at the pub? Was he drunk?
- Did any of his former mates discover what had happened to him?

Lydden Valley Research Group (2006–2013)

Local example 3.2 helps to show how the asking of questions is really important in history and using a story or a resource to generate interest is an excellent way of encouraging children's curiosity. Because it can be difficult for children to accept the lack of certainty in history and to understand the provisional nature of our historical knowledge, it can sometimes be helpful for the teacher not to know the answers: to be able to share with children that sometimes we have to settle for not being certain!

Local examples 3.3 Memorials

Great fires: Although we tend to think mainly of the Great Fire of London, an incident which is taught in many schools at Key Stage 1, many places had a great fire at some point in the past: Edinburgh (1824); Warwick (1694); Southwold (1659); Northampton (1675).

Bethnal Green tube station: Here there is a plaque commemorating a war time disaster which resulted in the loss of 173 lives when a surge of people were crushed while entering the station which was acting as a bomb shelter (http://www.stairwaytoheavenmemorial.org/).

New Cross Woolworth's bomb: At 277–281 New Cross Road in south east London there is a plaque on a post-war building which reads:

Remembering Woolworth's
168 people killed
In Britain's worst V2 attack
25th November 1944

For this particular incident, a small publication allows children to access the testimonials of local people affected by the bomb, but even without this children can find out about V2s, the bombing of urban areas, the Blitz etc., and for the local area, find out what it was like before the bomb destroyed buildings by using street directories from the 1930s or 1940s (see chapter 5). In addition, many local authority history libraries have maps showing where bombs were dropped or use http://www.bombsight.org/ for the London area.

(*Rations and rubble; remembering Woolworths; the New Cross V2 disaster, Saturday 25th November, 1944*. Deptford Forum Publishing)

(v) Street furniture

There are many examples of street furniture – the fixtures and fittings of pavements and pedestrian areas – which can provide evidence and starting points for investigations.

Pillar boxes will give clues about the age of a residential area through the monarch's initials. The small nature of these features seems to have a particular interest for children.

- *Telephone boxes* – their style is a clue to age; their presence an indication of the absence of mobile phones.
- *Street lamps* – main roads were originally lit by gas lamps from the early nineteenth century onwards. Few of these will remain. Electric lighting was being introduced into urban areas from the early twentieth century. Victorian examples, decorative and of cast iron, may survive. Some have initials indicating the local council which provided them.
- *Clocks* – at stations and on churches we may still expect to see clocks. As well as clocks on buildings, there may be clock towers, often with plaques giving dates and indicating some local information, which form a landmark in a local area.
- *Coalhole covers and inspection covers* – these often list the name of the manufacturer who may have been local, or the utility company. There may be some local curiosities such as the drainage cover in Penge, south east London, with T. Crapper's name as the manufacturer.
- *Railings* – in Victorian times both public and private spaces may have had railings, and their removal during the Second World War provides an opportunity to identify change.

(v) Signs

Signs provide information in the environment. They might include painted signs such as those indicating the way to the public shelters which were used during the war; advertisements painted on the sides of buildings which can provide clues to their former use; old road signposts and milestones indicating which places have been important in the area, leading to discussion of which routes were important in the past and how long journeys might have taken. Pub and street names are considered in chapter 6.

Follow-up for fieldwork

The value of fieldwork lies as much in the quality of the follow-up work as in the fieldwork itself. This in turn is of course dependent on good preparation which has in particular equipped children for the learning experience with a thorough briefing about what they will be doing and how it relates to the previous learning. In the longer term, developing children's familiarity with the routines, skills and techniques of local fieldwork will undoubtedly aid its success.

Immediately after the fieldwork, it is useful to have a discussion to draw out initial learning points; provide opportunities for children to compare findings if they have been working in groups; note down any questions which have been raised which could form the basis of research. Following on from this, further investigation and research may be needed to confirm findings from the use of evidence for instance about age, change, use or events. There are numerous possibilities in terms of presenting findings at the end of a piece of work. Regardless of whether the fieldwork leads on to extensive work using documentary material, findings may be presented as reports, displays, web pages, publications. It seems particularly appropriate to find ways of sharing information with the local community through a display at a local library, in an empty shop window or community hall.

3. *Using a history trail*

An educational trail provides an opportunity to introduce children to a range of aspects of the history of the local area. It also provides excellent opportunities to develop the group of skills which form historical enquiry and can help to develop understanding of concepts such as change and continuity and what it was like at a period in the past. An educational trail links a number of places in an area through a particular route with one or more learning activities at each of the stopping points (Fyson and Ward, 1973). There can be a balance between the giving of selective and relevant information and activities which engage the children in thinking and doing and developing enquiry skills.

Trails can have a theme and, depending on the area, possible focuses might be:

- what our area was like in a specific period such as Victorian or Tudor;
- introducing our area's links with time past;
- our area through time;
- change;
- a significant person;
- a theme such as transport or employment.

The learning activities can be supported by illustrative and informational material such as an historic photo or picture, extract from the census, extract from an historical map, an oral history quotation.

Not only does the use of a trail help to develop skills for history, it can also contribute to the development of the key historical concepts. The examples in Figure 3.5 from a number of different trails serve to illustrate this.

A trail can also give children the freedom to choose what they would like to research in more depth. For a more confident teacher they provide a useful more open-ended approach to enquiry.

Case study 3.2 A trail in Crystal Palace Park

A class of Y4 children undertook a trail in Crystal Palace Park in south east London as part of their work on the Victorians. The park contains the remains of the Crystal Palace at Sydenham. (This was the glass structure that was used for the Great Exhibition in Hyde Park in 1851. It was transferred to Sydenham and rebuilt within a landscaped park. The park added another dimension to the attraction with fountains, a maze, a reconstruction of geological structures and dinosaurs, racing track and fairground rides.)

The trail took the children around the different areas of the park covering the original site of the palace and the grounds, both of which contain varied remains from the Victorian period and the early twentieth century. Working in groups, each with an adult, the children used a combination of visual evidence, old maps and old photos to begin to develop their understanding of what the palace had been like.

There was a strong emphasis on observation and the interpretation of evidence with children justifying their answers prompted by the framing of the trail questions and the involvement of the adults – 'Why do you think that?' 'What reason would you give for your answer?' 'Can you explain that further?'

Examples of questions, discussion points and activities from a range of trails	*Concepts being developed*
• Compare the view in the photo below with the view today (early twentieth-century street scene). Note the similarities and differences in the space provided.	Similarity and difference
• As you walk along these roads, look at the way people have changed their houses. Look out for any of the following: Pebble dashing over the bricks New doors A tiled roof instead of a slate one.	Change
• This is a very old area of woodland which has been here for over two hundred years. Look at the map below which dates from the 1930s and find and mark this same long, thin strip of trees.	Continuity
• This small grassed area looks tempting for children to play on, but one local resident remembers, 'You had to keep your children under control at all times. They couldn't go on the greens, or climb trees or anything like that.' Where do you think children might have played?	Historical situation
• Note the initials on the letter box in the wall. What or who do they stand for? Try to find out what that tells you about when the letter box was put here.	Chronology Enquiry
• What do you think this little niche in the wall (around the churchyard) might have been used for? A statue The milk bottles A boot scraper.	Evidence
• Find some evidence that this building was once used as a school (referring to an entrance with 'Boys' above it).	Evidence
• Why do you think this house has two entrances, one up the steps and one down?	Evidence Historical situation
• Look up at the imposing dome here. Sketch it carefully, labelling all the things that add decoration and using the words below. Can you see a date anywhere?	Chronological understanding
• Look for evidence on this building of the links this area used to have to the sea.	Cause and effect
• The census for this house shows that in 1871 ten people lived here – the parents and eight children. Look carefully at the number of windows and chimneys to work out how many rooms there might have been. Discuss where all those people might have slept.	Historical situation
• There is a clock above the building here. Why do you think people needed clocks in public places?	Cause and effect

Figure 3.5 Developing historical concepts through trails.

Versions of trails can easily be used with younger children. Adults can outline the activities and scribe for the children or responses can be recorded. The focus could be more familiar – the school, local park or street of houses – and the route more limited. Activities would focus on description, identification, similarities and differences.

4. *Other teaching and learning walks*

The use of a simple walk around an area can be made more engaging for children through the use of a form of role play. This technique has been adopted by some museums, for instance for the Titanic exhibition at the National Maritime Museum, and on guided walks for instance at Saltaire Village in Yorkshire. Here, the guided walk includes the use of small role play cards, one per participant, describing a former inhabitant of the village and based on census information. This is used to engage the participants as the walk progresses (where that person would have lived; what their work would have been like, for instance). This could be adapted for use with learners as we have done on the Avery Hill campus, which was the former mansion of the Victorian nitrate magnate 'Colonel' North (see Figure 3.6).

A further example of a learning walk – 'If Buildings Could Talk' – is available on the website of the Building Exploratory Trust in which the buildings are given a voice through accounts of the people and personalities who have used a local street along a stretch of the Regents Canal over the last 150 years. As well as being a resource for the area, it provides an

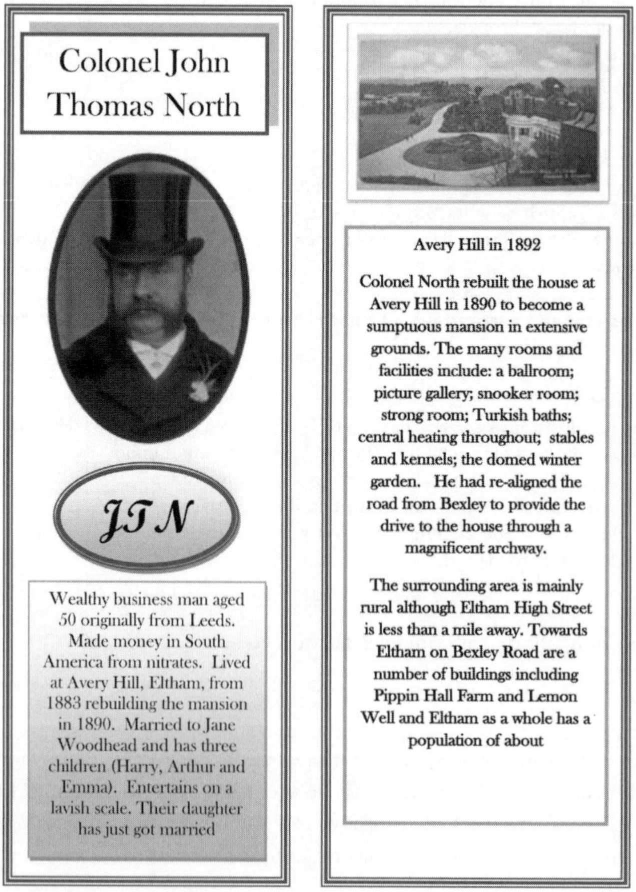

Figure 3.6 Colonel North and his house at Avery Hill.

interesting idea to develop as an introduction to an area, or as a means of children presenting their findings.

Archaeology

Archaeology, the study of our past through the physical remains of human presence and activity, has become of greater public interest over the last couple of decades, although it is perhaps an area that few primary teachers see as being relevant to young children. Nevertheless, the success of Channel 4's *Time Team* programme, and the excitement generated over the find of the Staffordshire Hoard or of the skeleton of King Richard III, and the continued interest in re-enactments which have been based on experimental archaeology indicate its appeal to non-specialists. This apparently dry academic subject can be brought to life for children by the use of practical activities, or by the involvement of articulate practitioners, helping children to understand a time not only before written records but also as recent as the Second World War. It is likely to be even more important with a Key Stage 2 curriculum which includes the Stone, Bronze and Iron Ages.

Some possible practical approaches would be to:

- take advantage of any current archaeological digs in the local area – can they be visited? Looking in the local newspapers can reveal what is happening in the local area. The exciting finds such as the Staffordshire Hoard, a collection of Anglo-Saxon gold objects found in 2009, of course make the national papers (http://www.staffordshirehoard.org.uk/about) but even that is local to someone;
- find out if there is an archaeological organisation locally that might support children in undertaking an aspect of archaeology in the local area, for instance field walking (the process of literally walking in a systematic way across ploughed land and picking up any items of interest for later analysis) or metal detecting;
- find out about and visit any recent digs documented in a local museum. Even local museums may have finds from locations abroad, however, and this is worth investigating as a possibility for widening the scope of 'local' history. If you are lucky enough to have a specialist or national museum in your area, this may offer outreach support. These and other ideas are explored by Lomas (2009);
- undertake a real or mock dig in the school grounds or use metal detectors to locate metal items of interest;
- devise a small scale simulated dig in the classroom (an excavation in a sand tray for buried objects; drawing items in different strata in an old fish tank; or visit a local museum offering this service);
- recreate some of the processes involved in the making of things in the past, e.g. basic dyeing and weaving; making food; making jewellery or writing on clay tablets.

Recording what is found is an important part of the process; it helps to interpret findings and leaves a record for the future. Children should therefore have the opportunity to note down some of the following information about found items:

1. The material
2. Where found (ideally located on a gridded plan of the area)
3. Whether complete or broken

4. A drawing
5. Why it might have survived
6. Initial ideas about what it might be
7. Questions to ask

Other activities might be to analyse a selection of clean rubbish to find out about the people who threw it away or to conduct some experiments to find out how quickly things decay once buried in the ground; to see how long an item takes to be buried once placed on the surface of the soil (Corbishley et al., 1999)

Time capsules

The idea of children contributing to the archaeology of the future is a useful one and a way in might be provided by the picture book, *The Sandal*, by Tony Bradman. This book visits the past, the present and the future using the idea of a sandal which is lost in one time period and reappears in a museum in the next time period. This use of thinking about the future is one which we believe can also help to develop children's chronological understanding.

Case study 3.3 A time capsule

A project linking together past, present and future was undertaken by a class in west London with the support of their local urban studies centre. The work began with some historical investigation, stimulated by a local history trail, moving on to looking at the quality of the present day environment and leading on to children developing their ideas about the area in the future. These wishes were written down and placed in a time capsule which would be opened in twenty years' time. Perhaps some of the children will still be around in the local area to see what did happen!

Next steps

Having established how the physical environment can inform us about the past, the next chapter looks at another significant resource for the local in history: people.

Useful websites and resources

Ideas for built environment

Useful Teachers' Guides from English Heritage:

Geography and the Historic Environment, by T. Copeland (1993)
Using Houses and Homes, by S. Allen, L. Hollinshead and S. Wilkinson (1998)
Using Memorials, by S. Purkis (1995)
Primary History: Using the Evidence of the Historic Environment, by M. Corbishley (1999)
Using Historic Parks and Gardens, by S. Marcus and R. Barker (1997)
Using School Buildings, by S. Purkis (1993)

In addition:

English Heritage's *Heritage Learning Magazine* – resources and ideas: http://www.english-heritage.org.uk/education/heritage-learning/

For inspiration on a small starting point using a range of approaches: http://www.thecornershopproject.co.uk/

Images of England is a 'point in time' photographic library of England's listed buildings, recorded at the turn of the twenty-first century. There are 300,000 images of England's built heritage from lamp posts to lavatories: http://www.imagesofengland.org.uk/

Heritage Explorer: http://www.heritage-explorer.co.uk/web/he/imagebytheme.aspx where you can search for memorials and war memorials.

English Heritage site – Heritage Gateway: http://www.heritagegateway.org.uk/gateway/localeducationandoutreach/default.aspx

Local Education and Outreach: This area contains case studies of different types of educational and outreach activities undertaken by Historic Environment Records, written by heritage professionals to share their experiences and lessons learned.

Material from CABE providing teaching resources for the built environment is archived: http://webarchive.nationalarchives.gov.uk/20110118095356/http://www.cabe.org.uk/education and our street: learning to see http://webarchive.nationalarchives.gov.uk/20110118095356/http:/www.cabe.org.uk/files/our-street.pdf

Online archive of printed adverts: http://www.ghostsigns.co.uk/

Building Exploratory Trust website, 'If buildings could talk' . . . : http://www.buildingexploratory.org.uk/resources/

For Historical Association members the Nuffield Open Spaces material can be accessed at: http://www.history.org.uk/resources/primary_resource_2965.html

Advice and guidance on all aspects of working outside from the Council for Learning Outside the Classroom (LOTC): www.lotc.org.uk

Ideas for archaeology

Chapter 6 'Ancient history: things to do and questions to ask with young children', by Moore in Cooper (ed.) *Exploring Teaching and Learning Through Play: Foundation Stage to Key Stage 1*, David Fulton Publishing (2004)

Primary History Issue 51, Spring 2009, on doing archaeology with children

www.channel4.com/programmes/time-team

www.bbc.co.uk/history/handsonhistory/

The PASt Explorers website is hosted by the British Museum and contains material for both children and teachers: http://www.pastexplorers.org.uk/teachers

There are particularly proactive archaeological organisations in west Yorkshire and Canterbury.

Chapter 4

Resources and how to use them – family and community

Talking to someone

Introduction

History is essentially about people – 'the story of the human past' (Brand et al., 1980). What happened in the past before the evolution of humans is the province of other disciplines: palaeontology; geology; even cosmology. We think it relevant therefore to have a significant focus on people – the individual, the family and the immediate community.

This chapter is about the history children can access through the people around them. It is both the history of those people and the history that is accessed through the experiences of those people. The involvement of people, especially those known to children, in the process of exploring and communicating history helps to bring history to life for children and to link it fundamentally to their own experiences, allowing them to take some ownership of their learning.

Chapter objectives

By the end of this chapter you should:

- understand something of the nature of community, family and personal history;
- have an awareness of how one's own personal and family histories can be used to support children's learning;
- have confidence in the use of oral history as a teaching and learning activity.

A clarification

Because there are many definitions and interpretations of both the terms 'family' and 'community' we give below the simplified working definitions we prefer.

Family: the immediate adults and children with whom children live or to whom they are related:

> The immediate group of people with whom a child shares a home
> The extended 'family of blood' and
> The extended family including close friends who may well have a history in common
> (Based on Claire, 1996 and Hume and Sevier, 1991)

Local community: the people living in a particular place who have interests in common, but not identical, because of their shared location.

Task

- *Draw a poster which includes an image of yourself at the centre. Around it place all the things and people that are important to you and help to define yourself.*
- *How much of your identity do you see as being linked to aspects of your personal history?*
- *If someone asked you to give a brief account of your personal history, what would you tell them?*
- *How comfortable would you feel sharing your personal history with others?*

For us, family and community history is about the history of and through and to a certain extent by local people.

Family

It is widely acknowledged that family structure does not now conform to a standard pattern. It is important to unpick some of this variety, if only briefly, and to consider implications for our teaching. Consider Figure 4.1 on the following page.

How does this relate to your own family?

Task

- *Draw your own family tree, deciding on a format with which you are most comfortable. How many generations can you go back?*
- *How much information can you fill in, e.g. birth, marriage and death dates, occupations?*
- *Do you know where your various family members live now? Where they were born?*
- *Do you have photos of any of them?*
- *Do you know what your relationships to these people are; who are first or second cousins? (second cousins are the children of first cousins)*
- *How many of the people on your tree have you actually met?*
- *Can you identify a 'core' family and an extended family?*
- *Are there any aspects of your family that you feel are hidden from you, or that you would not want to share with anyone else?*
- *Refer to the points made in Figure 4.1 about the diversity of family structures. To what extent do you feel your family conforms to a 'norm'?*

The variations in families suggest that we must be careful not to make assumptions about the family composition of the children when planning activities in the classroom. Authors such as Claire (1996) and Harnett (2007) are at pains to point out that an awareness of children's family and home situation is important so that issues can be dealt with sensitively.

Single parent families: across the country approximately one quarter of families are single parent families and this proportion may be higher in some areas. The reasons for this are several, the commonest being divorce or separation. Others such as the death of a spouse or a prolonged absence because of a prison sentence or working away from home are also possible. Alongside that there are situations where an individual has become a single parent as a conscious choice (Syson, 2009).

Same sex partnerships: these are increasingly common with the advent of civil registration.

Step families: re-marriage or living with a second or third partner can bring some complicated relationships between adults as parents and step parents and children and step children.

Adoption and fostering: the degree to which children who are fostered or adopted have contact with their birth parents will vary.

Looked after children: there is a particular issue for these children around identity and self-esteem which may affect their achievement in formal school.

The span of generations: the age of parents, grandparents and siblings should not be taken for granted. In my family the gap from birth of grandparents to birth of their third grandchild has been 90 years. Situations like this may result in children in a class having parents separated in age by up to thirty years, with some grandparents and parents being the same age. In this situation, what life was like when children's parents were growing up may vary considerably!

It is worth noting that not only is the average age of first time mothers increasing (now standing at about 27), but there is an increasing number of children born to mothers over the age of forty, especially in the London area (*Guardian*, 6 December 2012).

Family composition and size: increasing numbers of children are only children and about a quarter of children may be living without siblings. Family composition can vary considerably. There may be step parents and step siblings; uncles and aunts; grandparents. Census analysis suggests a decrease in the number of extended families.

Figure 4.1 Some variations in family structure.

With this in mind we need to consider what are the general implications of this awareness for our history teaching?

- Parental permission should be sought.
- Review the language that you use so that it does not make assumptions. For instance, that there are two parents; that there are siblings; that there is a 'father' present in the household; that parents are of a certain age. Use more general phrases such as the adults in your home rather than your parents and words such as kin, relations, family circle, household, close friend, family friend. (My own sibling-less child has sister-friends who represent family when we celebrate significant events.)
- Ensure children do not feel pressured into revealing things which they feel are private, being aware that it is ultimately a child's choice as to whom they might include on their family tree and provide an alternative family (see p.63).

Community

Within a specific, small scale area, we tend to think of the inhabitants as the local community regardless of the characteristics they might demonstrate of a 'community' in a sociological

sense. All children and their immediate family are a part of this local population and are thus part of this community. The significance of a school's contribution to the community of their catchment area was recognised in the 2007 Ofsted inspection framework in the use of the term, 'community cohesion'. Although the duty to report on the school's contribution to this has now been removed, schools still have a duty to promote such cohesion under the Education and Inspections Act, 2006 (DfE, 2011). Advice given at the time indicated that schools should view their community as the community within which the school is located together with the wider communities of the UK as a whole and the global community (DCSF, 2007), a perspective we are also adopting.

The relevance of local history to community cohesion is through the contributions it makes in terms of teaching and learning, which is one of the three areas where the school can make contributions to this dimension. The guidance specifically mentions activities which develop pupils' understanding of community and diversity and includes fieldwork visits and ways of involving members of the local community. Local history offers rich opportunities to do this and its role in contributing to community cohesion adds another rationale for its importance.

Within all versions of the National Curriculum up to 2013, there has been reference to children needing to learn about the changes in the lives of adults in their family and around them within the Key Stage 1 Breadth of Study ((1) DES, 1991; (2) DfE, 1995; (3) DfEE/QCA, 1999). At Key Stage 2, where the local is the context for history, as in the local study or in exemplifying national history, then local people have also been an essential ingredient.

Teaching and learning

1. Personal history

Separated out from the partner term 'family history', the term personal history can have an institutional and possibly intrusive feel to it. However, we would not want this to be the case in the context of teaching and learning. We need to be aware that as adults how we see and describe ourselves does vary according to context, and that as children develop their self-awareness, this will also be true for them.

The following activities can be used to help children explore and communicate their personal histories:

- Memorable moments – a record of events the child will never forget, perhaps in a simple scrap book.
- Places in my world – photos of the places the child spend time in – home, school, friend's house, park, shops – with a brief comment.
- A map of my world – the places shown above could be included on a child drawn map of the local area.
- People in my world – a diagram with illustrations or photos of the people who are important to the child. They may be family, friends or neighbours.
- Talking about a specific event such as the first day at school; when a sibling was born.

(Adapted from Hume and Sevier, 1991 and Hewitt and Harris, 1992)

2. *Personal and family history*

It seems, given the development of internet access to a wide range of records and the popularity of television programmes with a focus on genealogy, that family history has become a favourite national pastime (Vass, 2006). Yet in our experience, paradoxically, less is heard about its use in the primary classroom now than it was twenty or thirty years ago. One factor may be that personal and family history has had a relatively low key presence within the QCA units of work which many schools have used as a basis for their planning. It is worth noting that it is recommended that the prior learning for the first unit should include, 'listening to and telling stories about what has happened to them and/or their families in the past' (DfEE/QCA, 1998), showing there was an expectation that these aspects would be being covered with three and four year olds. The Early Years Foundation Stage curriculum specifies that as part of developing understanding of the world, children need to explore, observe and find out about people and places (DfE, 2012a) and the early learning goal refers to children talking about past events in their own lives and the lives of family members.

Another factor might perhaps be that our commitment to inclusion and our awareness of and sensitivity to the diversity of family structures and cultures has made it more challenging for teachers to develop family history in the classroom. And yet, all our understanding of the importance of making learning relevant to children indicates that this should be important in helping to make history relevant to them; we see personal and family history as being a particularly important strand in children's history education. Family history is an important means of helping to develop a child's sense of identity and to strengthen self-esteem. This can provide a starting point for learning about other families and people, exploring similarities and differences and for helping to build respect and awareness for other people's lives. Part of this will be about giving children the chance to tell others about themselves (Claire, 1996). There is an opportunity here to ensure that local history does not remain parochial and introverted, an aspect explored further in chapters 6 and 8.

The following examples can be used to develop aspects of family history:

- special family occasions can be shared and discussed;
- memories of individual family members can be listened to;
- an album of pictures and mementos of family members can be collected;
- making a patchwork quilt with scraps of material;
- map family members' places of birth or current residences.

3. *Developing concepts through personal and family history: understanding of time, change and historical situations*

Family history can provide an accessible context in which to develop knowledge and understanding of life in the past through oral histories, pictures, artefacts and documents and an introduction into the idea of independent research. Using it within the curriculum should also allow the development of concepts such as change, similarity and difference, time and historical situations.

The use of evidence and the enquiry process to find out about the past are fundamental aspects of children's development as historians. Families can provide rich evidence – accounts of life in the past, photos of domestic and family life and documents and artefacts of family significance. There are, however, a number of issues that may arise and these mean that

involving children in bringing this material into the classroom is not straightforward. First, the extent to which families have kept photos, artefacts and documents from the past is likely to vary for a number of reasons. These might include a tradition of not keeping (not hoarding some might say!); general lack of material possessions; lack of space; family break-up; and moving home which might in some cases include the enforced moves of refugees. Second, the nature of people's memories might mean that they do not want to talk about aspects of their past, or might only be able to do so without the rekindling of difficult emotions. Third, the extent of a family in time and space will vary; family members may be absent or out of contact (in another country; in prison); there may be no grandparents; all of which may affect the amount of memorabilia or old possessions. Fourth, some cultures are less inclined to share experiences or may associate requests for information with uninvited prying. Finally, some people may feel diffident about the nature of the life experiences – that they lack excitement, relevance or interest for others.

There is, therefore, a need for sensitivity and flexibility in drawing on these approaches in the classroom. As well as the general points made earlier, we offer below some comments and ideas which help to take the above into account.

- Children should always be provided with a choice – whether to talk about/draw on their personal and family history. Alternatives include involving someone else: the teacher, another familiar adult, a fictional character, a member of the royal family or other well known family.
- Children could choose to work in pairs to share material.
- Have a range of photos and other material for children to choose from as substitutes for photos of their own family members.
- The use of story books about families can help to reinforce messages about diversity.
- Use any of the following to broaden children's experiences:
    - oral history from adults in the wider community;
    - stories (such as 'My Grandma has Black Hair' by Hoffman and Burroughes; the family books by the Ahlbergs);
    - artefacts and family photos provided by you or other adults in the school community.

As primary teachers it is worth remembering how much children value hearing about our own experiences, and our personal and family histories can be part of that. Ian Dawson acknowledges this as an experienced teacher of history at secondary school (Dawson, 2010). Finding relevant family stories is at the heart of his ideas to enliven history and, made appropriate for the primary school classroom, this might involve:

- a story about migration;
- the experiences of a relative during the war;
- family memories of everyday life in the past;
- the experiences of growing up at a particular time;
- illustrating changes in everyday life.

Byrom and Riley (2011) have also promoted the use of the personal as a teaching approach and they also link this with the use of place. In my own teaching with students I have used the example of my great great grandfather and his migration to London.

Local example 4.1 Family migration and urbanisation

John Wise, born in about 1836, was an agricultural labourer living in rural Oxfordshire with his parents. By 1861 he had married and moved to Southwark in south London where he was a police constable. He was probably recruited into the service during the 1850s perhaps while he was still living in Buckinghamshire. At the time the newly formed Metropolitan police service was recruiting agricultural workers who were attracted by the prospect of a secure job with a pension. John and his family continued to live in south London and on retirement he was able to secure a job as a door keeper at one of the London theatres. Within one generation the family moved from rural to urban, from agriculture to service industry, part of the influx of people into the capital city.

For other family stories, see also Corrigan's article on family history describing the story of her great great uncle who was trampled to death in a music hall in Victorian times (Corrigan, 1995) and the examples of Byrom and Riley (2011) and Dawson (2010).

The use of our own histories in our teaching is supported by Hilary Claire: 'All of us have a story, and as teachers we perhaps need to find ways for children to bring their own stories into the world' (Claire, 2006:12). We can use our own personal history or aspects of our family history if we feel able to share them. Try out the following task.

Task

- *Reflect back on a significant day in your own childhood such as your first day at school, getting a bicycle, going on a particular holiday.*
- *How much of it can you recall? Try sharing it with a friend or writing down your memories. Can you place it accurately in time? How long ago was it or can you date it?*
- *Can you make any generalisations from it by placing it into its wider historical context, e.g. all children had milk at school then; it was becoming popular to go on package holidays abroad; computers had just been introduced into schools. In other words, how typical might your experience have been?*
- *Are there questions that flow from these generalisations, e.g. when was free milk for all stopped? What enabled package holidays to become popular? When was the desktop computer invented? What other significant things were going on at these times?*
- *Contextualise this in a basic timeline.*

The use of a photo, document or artefact from yourself, another adult or a child, can provide a useful starting point for discussion and questions helping to form a basic understanding of what life was like in the past, how it was similar to and different from today and how things have changed. Additionally, for us, these stories, personal and family, also have potential as a springboard for strengthening our own historical knowledge. Reflections on the family mementos in local example 4.2 helped to develop personal understanding of the First World War.

Local example 4.2 Two family photos (Figure 4.2)

I have photos from both sides of my family showing each parent as a child with their own parents and siblings. In neither family is the father present. The photos were actually taken during the First World War, and one has the date 1916 pencilled on the back. They are in postcard format. As in many families across the country I imagine, they were taken to accompany the father to war. In each photo the mother is accompanied by four children – a coincidence of course, whereas the absence of the father is certainly not a coincidence. Children could talk and ask questions about these photos which were taken about one hundred years ago on the edge of time 'within living memory': the clothes of the girls and boys, the poses, the settings and of course the absence of a father. There are differences between the photos, one being the difference in quality of the clothes, in spite of them being the 'best' for each of the families. In some cases children could refer to family photos of their own and why they were taken. There might be resonances about absence and deprivation.

The photos are given a context by a memoir written by my mother's eldest sister:

> When I was seven the First World War started. My father who was then 33 was 'called up', but as he had flat feet was not sent to France but to Colombo, Ceylon [now Sri Lanka]. He was away for three years and was a stranger to us when he returned. Looking back I realise we were deprived during those war years and were sometimes hungry. There was strict food rationing with ration books of food coupons as well as clothing coupons. As the eldest it was often my job to stand in queues for meat, fat, sugar etc. and we never seemed to get sufficient sleep with air raids night after night. The Germans were trying to bomb the Woolwich Arsenal where munitions were made, and in the early days zeppelins and later planes passed over and dropped bombs, disturbing our nights. One night a bomb was dropped in the playground of our school at one end of the road and another in the laundry of the hospital at the other end. We tried various ways of taking shelter. At first under the grand piano. Then in the cellar of our house. Later with many neighbours in the basement of the fever hospital, where it was warm due to the hot water pipes heating the wards above.

We further demonstrate the potential of such personal experiences in chapter 6, exploring connections with the national context.

Young children and their understanding of time

For chronological understanding, in terms of very young children, the use of daily routines and the development of clock and calendar time underpins the development of historical time (Simchowitz, 1995). Personal and family history also allows an opportunity to explore the use of timelines with children as they begin to become aware of the past in their own lives, and there seems to be common agreement that children's emerging sense of historical time is helped by the use of these contexts. These early timelines can be produced in a number of different ways and can be structured around:

Figure 4.2 Photos of mother and children taken during the First World War.

- age in years – when I was one, when I was two etc.;
- key events – when I went to school, when my sister was born;
- the number of years ago – one year ago I started reception class, two years ago I . . .;
- using the year date – 2013, 2014 . . . for children confident in the use of dates.

As well as a simple sequence or line format, zig zag books can be made.

In Megan's timeline (Figure 4.3) made in response to a request to draw the timeline of her life, she has projected the line forward to show her future, the next generation and her own death, a reminder not only that future thinking is an important part of the development of chronological understanding, but that in dealing with time we are dealing with issues of mortality and sometimes with existential questions such as, 'Where was I before I was born?'

Personal timelines are about developing a child's memory, the first part of an initial first broad structure for the understanding of time – 'During my life' and 'Before I was born'. As children become older, this second division of time can be further structured into 'within living memory' and 'beyond living memory' creating a threefold division:

- Within my memory
- Before I was born: within the memory of people I know/within living memory (approximately 100 years ago)
- Before I was born: beyond living memory

These areas can be linked in a number of ways through memory and experience (Figure 4.4).

Figure 4.3 Megan's timeline.

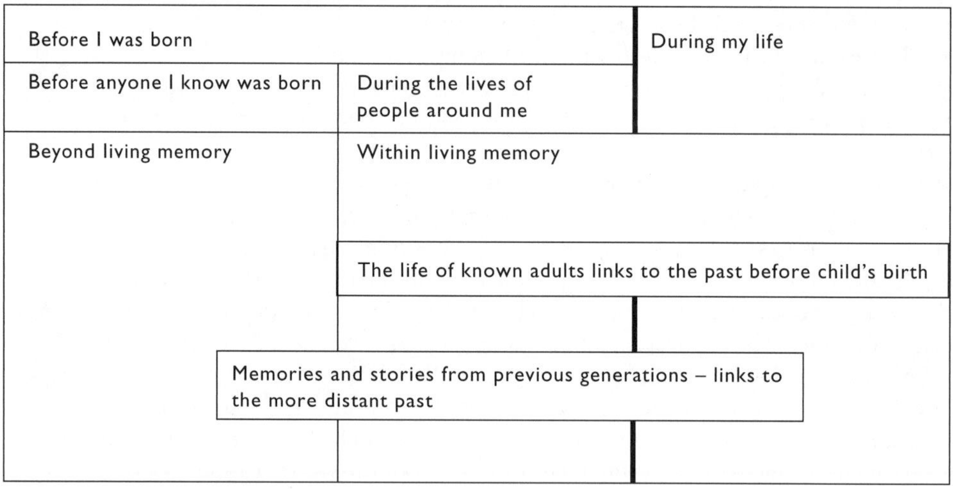

Figure 4.4 Developing an understanding of time for young children.

This latter expression ('beyond living memory') has references to the notion of a shared community memory of the past through the recall of all people still living – recall that can take us back approximately one hundred years. The cultural significance of this way of thinking about time is evident in the recent focus given to the death of the last individuals remembering the First World War, and in our growing awareness of the fading memories of the Second. The significance of this one hundred year period is also recognised within the concept of the 'two hundred year present' which has been developed within education for sustainable development and used amongst others by Hicks (2001). It is essentially a family chain linking to both the past and the future through the generations for one hundred years in either direction from now. Hicks and others suggest this is a useful period for immediate comprehension and we have found it a useful concept for exploring the idea of time in a meaningful way.

More detailed timelines can be shared collectively for the school year. They can be developed and added to as the year progresses (a photo of the class at the start of the year; an item from an outing; a reference to a class assembly; a piece of memorable work; a photo of the Christmas play), and referred to on a regular basis. For younger children a timeline of the day can be 'grown' during the day and then reflected on at the end of the day. All use of timelines should allow the opportunity to use time-related vocabulary: *when* we started in this class; *before* Christmas; *after* our outing.

In local history children can begin by noting down what they recall about changes in their area – a building which has been demolished; a change of a shop's use; a road closure; a new playground; some planting in their school playground. This might also include ongoing change linking effectively with geography in which current and recent change is important (see chapter 7).

An additional structure for developing the understanding of time is provided by the family tree which can allow the identification of different generations. This would appear to be a useful device both in terms of personal identity – 'how do I relate to other

people in the family?' – and in terms of the emerging sense of chronology using generations to go back in time in a structured manner. A broad definition of a 'family tree' is provided by Manning and Granström: 'a kind of map or plan that shows all our relatives and how they are related to us' (2001:32). The traditional family tree used by family historians with its focus on marriages, couples and their children poses a number of issues if we take into account diverse family structure. Alternatives can be modelled with children, and many are provided in a useful book on family trees by Karen Halvorsen Schreck (2006; see resources list at the end of the chapter). For instance she uses a standard genealogists' wheel pedigree as a basis for a child showing both birth family and adoptive family. A simple basic alternative is also provided by a generation chart which can show the generations in a family without showing the relationships. Chronological understanding is considered further in chapter 7.

In my family	*Names*	*Possible ages*
Older people		
Grown ups		
Children		

Figure 4.5 Generations chart.

Task

- *Make a time chart representing the generations in your family. How many generations take you back to the Victorian era? Use this as a timeline with dates of birth rather than events (children doing this could then form a human timeline).*
- *Consider the oldest person you know. How far back will their memories take you? This is the bit of history they could help you to connect with. Beyond that is the unknown territory.*

4. Community history

Community history is generally referred to as being researched and written within a local community with its roots in people's history and with an awareness of history about non-elite groups. Tosh (2008) reminds us that history is a community possession, and there are opportunities for children to be involved in this community history through their work, especially as we are aware that there are many rich areas of a community's history that will never have been researched or recorded. The involvement of children in community history can be a two-way process. First of all is the possibility of including people from the community in the work they are doing. This is not only through the oral history process we describe in some detail below, but also through the involvement of local historians, for instance through a local history society or a branch of the Historical Association whose members may be able to offer help and advice. They are less likely to be familiar with working alongside children in the classroom, however, and so if this is required they will need careful briefing. The local history library will also have expertise which can be drawn on in different ways and this is explored in chapter 5, while a local reminiscence or oral history organisation may be happy to advise on interviewing.

In return, the sharing of children's findings within the community can be considered, with possibilities ranging from a publication available locally to children sharing their findings informally with family and neighbours.

5. Oral history

Oral history has developed since the 1960s as a valid aspect of academic history and can be seen as an authentic technique in the tool bag of the historian. In a formal sense oral history is a process of collecting and using memories of the past (Redfern, 1996). We can, however, also see it as history which people, including children, can help to compile and narrate for themselves. It is in particular a powerful tool for linking children with the recent past, the past within living memory. It can sometimes take us beyond that to the time before living memory through the memories passed down from generation to generation. Peter Vass has commented on the long tradition of using witnesses in the primary classroom (Vass, 1993) and Hewitt and Harris (1992:1) have made particularly strong arguments for oral history as a means of including 'the lives of children and the many different communities in a typical inner city school'; it has the potential to be an inclusive classroom approach. They also

highlight the importance of oral history in building bridges between the school and its local community in a mutually supportive way and this is an aspect of community cohesion.

Redfern (1996) in his seminal work on oral history in schools lists twenty-one points in support of oral history. These range from its cost effectiveness to the sense of ownership. Use the teacher reflection below to consider these.

Reflection

- *Look at the nine reasons given below and arrange as a diamond (see diagram below). This 'diamond 9' activity allows you to rank the advantages in what you feel is their order of significance. This activity will work best if you do it with a colleague and discuss the reasons for your decisions.*

1

2 3

4 5 6

7 8

9

Why oral history?

- *Encourages children's active involvement in the learning*
- *Can promote a collaborative approach to learning*
- *Encourages purposeful use of technology*
- *Places an emphasis on the development of communication and social skills – listening, speaking and in particular questioning*
- *Is relevant and interesting*
- *Gives a voice to those whose history might not otherwise be heard*
- *Helps to forge purposeful links with the community*
- *Provides opportunities to explore different viewpoints*
- *Can become an ongoing resource*

Oral history can fill in the gaps left by historians thereby helping to build a fuller picture of a time, place or events by giving a voice to people who are less often heard (including children) and by shedding light on aspects absent in other sources (Hewitt and Harris, 1992). It has been particularly associated with recording working class lives and working circumstances.

Oral evidence can be accessed by interviewing individuals about their own lived experiences; by listening to recorded interviews and by reading transcripts. It is only in the case of the first of these, however, that the historian is in a unique position; that of producing and

influencing the evidence directly through the questions they ask (Claire, 2004). In other situations, evidence is provided for the researcher. For children, being in the role of interviewer is a powerful way of being actively engaged in the historical process.

Writers agree, however, that care needs to be taken with the use of oral history both by the historian and by the educator (Parsons, 1996; Claire, 2004). First, children may believe anything they hear from an adult and what they are told may become the definitive version of events. Yet memory can be faulty, can be influenced by subsequent experiences and we need to remember that an individual's memory is also in effect an interpretation of history. We should not be blind to the fact that, just like other sources used in history, we should be aware of both bias and reliability and it is therefore helpful to consider whether what the children have been told can be substantiated – can we investigate this information from another source? Second, in practice there may be a limited number of people who can be invited to participate. It may depend on who happens to be available, who is willing or who has been asked before. It may be possible to seek help in identifying people, for instance from a parent-teachers association or community organisation. Finally, there is of course limited control for the teacher as to what the interviewee will say, and the feelings of the individual being interviewed may also be an unexpected factor, for instance if discussing the past upsets them. Some of this, such as references to the Second World War, may be more predictable than others. There is also the issue of language – both 'pitch' and suitability for children. We feel that by thoughtful choice of person and discussion with them beforehand, these problems are minimised. However, if for generational reasons for instance, inappropriate terminology is used (such as 'coloured' rather than 'black'), this should be balanced with the inclusion of more suitable language and discussed with the children after the interview.

There is an importance distinction to be made between children being told about a period (even by a lively and engaging adult) and interviewing an adult who is recalling their own experiences of it. Both the skills involved and the nature of the history being told will be different. Less confident adults may feel they are being expected to give a history lesson if they are not carefully briefed, and this would lose all the advantages of oral history we are promoting here.

The history that comes from people's memories may well be the sort of history that takes children beyond the local area. Local history for us is about local people's experiences, wherever – geographically speaking – those might have been, as well as being about the immediate physical locality. This is an aspect of putting history in a wider context which will be explored in chapter 8. It is also important to remember that people do not have to be 'old' in order to have memories which are relevant to the study of recent history.

Task

- *Is there someone in the community or your family you can interview about a time in the past? At a personal level, the capturing of a loved one's voice can be something to cherish.*
- *Set up the interview in a semi-formal way; prepare your questions in advance thinking carefully about how you will record it.*
- *Make the setting comfortable and in some way set aside from the usual routine. Check for any background noise that can be easily eliminated.*

- *After the interview reflect on the following:*
  - *What did you learn that you did not previously know?*
  - *How effective were your questions in accessing information?*
  - *Was any of the content surprising or upsetting to you?*
  - *Was any of the interview difficult for your interviewee?*
  - *Do you think your interviewee enjoyed the interview?*
  - *What have you learnt about the interview process and how can this be transferred to the classroom situation?*

Developing the skills of children as oral historians

In describing how to develop the skills of children as oral historians, we start from the premise that the person providing the evidence of the past will be interviewed rather than talking to the children on a particular theme with questions only being allowed at the end. The case study illustrates a number of aspects of good practice contributing to a successful oral history project.

Case study 4.1 An oral history project

Two classes of Y6 children in a school in south east London were involved in an oral history projected initiated by a local charitable organisation – the Greenwich Foundation for the Old Royal Naval College. They were also supported in their work by a local oral historian who worked alongside the education officer and the two class teachers. The outcomes of the work were interview recordings and a memories book to be used in an exhibition. The learning objectives were around the development of the interviewing skills and for children to understand that history is about the lives and experiences of real people.

The work began with several activities which were intended to develop the children's understanding of evidence. An initial activity focused on toys which they had brought in from home and these were used to help them understand that objects can trigger stories and that these personal stories and memories are helping us to learn about the past. In a subsequent session the focus moved to the context for the work – the Naval College – and photos of the bomb damage at the college were used to encourage children's questioning. The photos were accompanied by audio recordings of naval officers describing the bombs they had witnessed. In the third session, children's own family photos were also used as a basis for discussion and questioning.

At this point the work moved more explicitly into developing the children's interviewing skills and the Yes/No game was used to help children to understand the nature of questions that encourage people to talk more fully about past experiences. There were then opportunities to take part in a staged interview and to observe and comment on a mock unsuccessful interview. This led to a discussion on how to interview and in particular how to take account of the interviewee.

At this point the children were ready for their own interview session. The interviews took place in the classroom and children had prepared questions which were put to the interviewee in a session managed by the oral history worker. A feedback session with the children encouraged them to discuss the experience and their learning. The children were invited to the Old Royal Naval College to see where the exhibition would be displayed. Their work was developed into a memories book using extracts from the interviews, drawings of the college related to the interviews and photos of the children and interviewees. Recordings of the interviews are now a part of the Old Royal Naval College Archive and are also used by the school.

An evaluation of this funded project was helpful in appraising the approaches and techniques that had been used for the teaching and learning, from the practical aspects of background noise during the recordings and the awareness that the arrangement of the room for interviewing matters, to the social aspects of the respectful and considerate behaviour of the children and to their learning demonstrated, for instance, in the thoughtful and interesting questions that they asked.

(i) Questioning, listening and interviewing/social skills

The development of these skills is fundamental to this form of history and an interview needs to be clearly set in the context of what the children are trying to find out. Vass (1993) provides an excellent example of how focusing children on what they wanted to find out helps to develop the focus of their questions, in this case when they were given a second chance at the interview. Children will need opportunities to practise questioning: how, for instance, to ask open questions, to elicit more than factual answers, and to ask follow up-questions. It is really important that the development of children's ability to ask questions begins in the foundation stage. This is discussed in depth in chapter 10.

Teaching and learning activities

Open and closed questions – the yes/no game. *Children in pairs question each other about a chosen topic (their favourite sport; holidays). They need to go on as long as possible without the interviewee giving a 'yes' or 'no' answer. This will help them develop skills as questioners.*

The listening game. *Children in pairs tell each other about a chosen personal topic, e.g. what I did at the weekend, while the other person listens and asks questions. At the end the 'listener' retells what they have been told either to their partner or to the rest of the group/class so that the accuracy of their listening and remembering can be considered.*

The potato game. *Each child describes in detail one potato from a group of potatoes. The other children have to identify which potato each child has described.*

Telling a story. *In groups, children tell each other a story of an everyday event such as a journey or going to the shops.*

Learning from an interviewer. *Watch a televised interview or classroom based interview and discuss which questions are most successful in gaining a full response.*

Learning from an interview. *Children can also be asked to listen for particular bits of information during a recorded interview, or to listen to an interview and share what they have learnt with other pupils.*

Learning from interviewing. *Practice interviews can be set up so that children interview each other and then the teacher on a topic such as 'my first day at school'.*

(ii) Recording and organisation skills

You will need to consider how the replies will be recorded especially if you wish children to develop particular skills. Audio, visual or written approaches to recording can be used and it is possible for children to record in different ways according to their abilities. For instance, individual children could record through drawing or note taking or using a simple recording sheet. Information collected could be divided into what the children believe to be fact, for later verification, and opinion. Tablets and smart phones can be used for video and audio recording or an Easy Speak microphone which can be downloaded as an mp3 file on to a computer. Digital cameras can be used to record the occasion. The free software Audacity can be used to edit an audio recording and can be downloaded free. Children can think about the physical organisation of the interview and also how a group of them can be involved in interviewing one person, e.g. taking turns to ask questions; to have different roles.

(iii) Critically evaluating

After the interview, children should have time to reflect on and, for older children, evaluate the information provided and also to evaluate the success of the interview. Figure 4.6 shows ideas for an interview record and evaluation sheet.

Oral testimony is a form of evidence for the historian, and finding ways to look at it for reliability or bias would for older children be an important part of the process. Parsons (1996) goes so far as to suggest that children gain very little from an historical point of view unless the statements of the interviewee can be verified. Claire (2004:22) poses the question, 'How, then, can we help children to work as good oral historians, in the same way that we hope they will learn to select, evaluate and interpret other sources in methodical, rational ways?' For younger children, she suggests that the interview should be seen as a way of supporting or contradicting *what they already know*.

This is particularly challenging, especially where children know the visitor. One useful strategy recommended by Claire is to deliberately invite two interviewees with contrasting experiences. If the aspect of evaluating the evidence is the most important aim of the process, then it might be more effectively achieved by children listening to recorded interviews which they will have less personal engagement with. It is also important that children are reminded how long ago the event/period in question was. They could also be asked how they could check whether some of the factual information is correct or whether another person (a woman for instance as opposed to a man) might have had a different experience. To understand more fully from their own perspective, children could be reminded that memory is selective. A discussion of their own memories such as their first day at school for instance;

1. Record

- Name of interviewers
- Name and address of person interviewed
- Date and place of interview
- What did they talk about?
- How long was the interview?
- Were there any problems?
- How did you record the interview?
- Have you written and thanked them?
- What will you do with the information you have gathered?
- The Interview Evaluation

2. Evaluation

- Did you find out the things you wanted to know?
- Which were the most interesting parts?
- Which parts would you like to share with the class?
- Were there any problems?
- Were there too many yes/no answers?
- Choose one example and suggest how you might have got the person to say more
- Was there any information that surprised you?
- Was there anything that contradicted what you know already?

(Adapted from Hewitt and Harris, 1992)

Figure 4.6 Interview record and evaluation.

they may remember that, but do they remember the day after? They could also listen to a group of children from the school describe their experiences of a shared event, and realise how different accounts vary, or even witness a contrived event which has been set up by the teacher and then to compare their descriptions (Parsons, 1996).

(iv) Communicating and researching further

What children have learnt from the interview can be communicated in a number of ways:

- reporting back orally to those who were not present;
- transcribing a small part of the recording (transcribing at length is unnecessary and tedious);
- making transcriptions into a book;
- using a selection of quotations and some accompanying photos to make a display;
- making a presentation using Prezi, Powerpoint or Google Docs;
- enacting scenes from the memories through role play;
- making a timeline of key events that the speaker has referred to;
- making a diary of events described and illustrate them.

It is also considered to be good practice in oral history to provide the interviewee with a copy of a recording or transcript which can be treasured by them and their family.

Some practicalities

The choice of person makes a difference to the success of the interview and the quality and nature of the information obtained. The different aspects of this will need to be balanced. For instance, the choice of someone within the school community with whom the children are already familiar and who is comfortable talking to children, or the choice of someone who represents a particular range of experiences. If you are focusing on a particular period such as the 1960s, the age of your interviewee will make a difference to the perspective given (whether they were at primary school or university for instance).

Figure 4.7 provides some guidance on preparation before and after the interview.

As well as inviting interviewees into the school, much can be gained from taking children into a community facility such as a residential home or community centre. Relationships developed in this way are demanding on time but can be very rewarding for the children, the school and the wider community.

Now revisit the earlier case study in relation to the reflection on the following page.

Some considerations before the interview

It is helpful if the person to be interviewed:

- is able to know the questions beforehand so they have a chance to retrieve relevant memories and think about what they would like to say. (It is important however, that they do not write down their answers as this then changes the nature of an interview into a questionnaire and will undermine the interview experience);
- has been briefed for instance about any sensitive issues from the children's perspective; about responding to the children's questions; what the pitch of language might be;
- knows how many children there will be and of what age;
- is comfortable with being recorded;
- will be physically comfortable – think about where the interview will take place; where will be a comfortable place to sit; can a glass of water be offered; are there any mobility issues?;
- has been asked if there are subjects they wish to avoid;
- has had a chance to think about whether having some props available such as clothes, photos, artefacts would be useful;
- knows the time limit on the interview.

Some considerations after the interview:

- thanking the person – personally and in writing;
- making a transcript or recording as an ongoing resource – for the school; for the local history library; for the interviewee;
- inviting the interviewee and family members back to the school to view the children's work;
- producing a product – a display within the school or a community venue; a book; a drama;
- maintaining links with the interviewee.

Figure 4.7 Teachers' checklists before and after the interview.

Reflection

- *Itemise the aspects of the project that may have helped to contribute to its success such as the nature of the final product and the careful preparation.*
- *How might an oral history project be different without the involvement of outside agencies?*

The teachers' toolkit will help reveal the potential contribution of oral history within the school and wider community.

Teachers' toolkit 4.1 Using oral history to add to your own knowledge and understanding of the local history of the locality

- *On the basis of your previous knowledge of the locality, consider some specific things you would like further information on around the themes of:*
  - *the school itself*
  - *the local area or*
  - *moving to the area*
- *Approach someone in the school or wider school community whom you know or can be introduced to and see if they are prepared to spend some time talking to you or being interviewed.*
- *Record your findings digitally or by note taking (having asked permission to do this).*
- *Consider how what you have learnt links to your previous findings about the area and whether this is information that would interest children.*

Recordings and transcripts

In many areas, oral history projects over the last few decades have recorded the memories of local people on a general or thematic basis and these may be available in written form, but sometimes as sound recordings, at local history libraries. There are also, as Hewitt and Harris (1992) have identified, even older interviews which can be used in the classroom such as extracts from the interviews of Henry Mayhew, published in *London Labour and the London Poor* in 1861.

The oral tradition

Material which does not derive from the direct/lived experience of the individual but is something which they themselves have heard, usually from a member of a previous generation and which has been passed on to them in turn by a senior of theirs, is considered to be part of an oral tradition. This gives access to more distant memories of the past, although these may not always be accurately placed in time. Some cultures are particularly rich in the oral tradition which may include songs as well as stories.

Next steps

In the next chapter, the final link in the chain of evidence for the local in history takes us into local history and archive centres to access the photos and documents which will help to complete the picture of what is available to help understand the people and place which comprise 'the local'.

Useful websites and resources

Oral history

Useful reading in Sally Purkis's chapter in *Teaching and Learning in the Early Years*, edited by D. Whitebread (2003)

An excellent practical guide although now twenty years old is: *Talking Time! A Guide to Oral History for Schools*, by Maggie Hewitt and Annie Harris (1992)

The website of the Oral History Association has links to local projects and oral history organisations: http://www.ohs.org.uk/resources.php

Many areas have oral history projects which have resulted in published printed material or an archive of recorded interviews

A reminiscence organisation with a national reputation is: Age Exchange http://www.age-exchange.org.uk. They have many publications and can work with school locally. http://www.age-exchange.org.uk/eastend/secondworldwar/index.html

Another significant organisation working in east London is: Eastside Community Heritage: Hidden Histories: http://www.hidden-histories.org.uk

Family history

The English Heritage Guide, *History at Home: A Guide for Parents and Teachers* by Rob David (1996), provides useful ideas

What's My Family Tree? by Mick Manning and Brita Granström (p.32), London: Franklin Watts (2004)

On family diversity:

Lucy's Family Tree, by Karen Halvorsen Schreck, Maine: Tilbury House (2006)

All Families Are Special, by Norma Simon, Illinois: Albert Whitman and Company (2003)

The 1881 census is available free online via several organisations: Findmypast: findmypast.co.uk; LDS FamilySearch: familysearch.org/; Ancestry: ancestry.co.uk

Chapter 5

Resources and how to use them – local history resource centres

Having a rummage

Introduction

This chapter will build on chapters 2, 3 and 4 and explore further resources available in the local beyond those found in the immediate environment and community. It will look specifically at:

- archives
- local studies
- libraries
- museums
- specialist societies
- voluntary community organisations.

With these places in mind we will explore the resources which can be accessed by teachers and how they might be used with children both on site and for further study back in the classroom. It will illustrate how history centres will both support the teacher in specific subject knowledge and extend children's learning.

Chapter objectives

By the end of this chapter you should:

- know where and how to locate primary and secondary sources;
- have a clear understanding of the nature of research and historical enquiry;
- be able to use primary and secondary sources with children confidently, applying appropriate pedagogy to develop children's knowledge, skills and understanding.

Why investigate local history resource centres?

There has been much discussion recently that children's historical knowledge and conceptual understanding is perhaps not as strong as it might be, particularly their sense of chronology. This is typified by Ofsted (2011), which states that: 'Although pupils in primary schools generally had good knowledge of particular topics and episodes in history, their chronological

understanding and their ability to make links across the knowledge they had gained were weaker' (p.5). This, we argue is not due the lack of history teaching within primary schools; on the contrary, as explored in chapter 1, there would seem to have been an explosion of interest with history often taking centre stage in many of the creative curriculum topics and approaches. The dichotomy here is: on the one hand history is more popular than ever but conversely historical learning, as suggested by Ofsted (2011), is not as strong as it might be.

Ofsted (2011) also reports:

> there is a pressing need for primary teachers to be better supported in their professional development in history, and for the curriculum to ensure that pupils study overview, as well as in-depth topics so that they can develop a coherent chronological framework for the separate periods and events that they study.
>
> (p.4)

Phillips (2008) draws on Pollard's need for teachers to be reflective practitioners and makes the point that teaching history is:

> far more than knowing facts . . . to be a good reflective history teacher you need to develop an appreciation of how history works. . . . This involves developing a more self-conscious understanding of historical methods and procedures.
>
> (p.7)

How?

An approach we advocate throughout the book is that teachers themselves become historians in the field. We reiterate the need to have a good understanding of history and how history in the local can be used to develop children's historical learning.

For busy teachers a further way of achieving this is to experience research, access practical resources and use the knowledge and expertise of professionals available to them. Clearly archivists, librarians and local historical associations are invaluable resources and should be utilised when planning teaching and learning.

Many teachers will be familiar with using artefacts and secondary evidence within the classroom but fewer teachers will be familiar with or would have used documents and other resources offered in either the local studies or the archives centre. As tutors we have been surprised at how many initial teacher trainee students have never been to such local resource centres or considered the wealth of information they have to offer. Consider your knowledge of such historical centres.

Reflection

- *Have you ever visited a local studies and/or archive centre? Consider the reason why you may have not.*
- *Can you explain the difference between the two or what would be found there?*
- *Do you know where your local studies and/or archives centre is and who your archivist is?*

Local studies and archive centres

Most local authorities will have both a local studies centre and local archives, many attached to a main library. There is a discernible difference of function between the two, though within smaller areas the two may be housed in the same building, often with one archivist overseeing the centre as a whole. Some will have an educational officer who will be more adept at presenting sources to children and will often support and work alongside the archivist. Do check out the range of experience within the centre to ensure that any advice given is child relevant.

Archives

The job of the archives is to preserve, catalogue and store documents and evidence in order that we have a documentary record of our history and heritage. Many of these records will be original (primary) sources and often unique in their nature, one-off rather than published material. The delicate nature of many sources available will mean that varying restrictions will be in place when accessing and reviewing the documents. For instance you may only use pencils when making notes or may only access a limited number of documents to handle or look at at any one time (Halewood, 2000).

Archive centres will vary in size and will hold thousands of sources which will have already been sorted and boxed according to place, theme or period of history, some specifically aimed at popular educational projects such as the Victorians or the Second World War. Some may hold unique collections as illustrated in the following local example.

Local example 5.1 Collections

The London Metropolitan Archives holds a large collection of documentary sources relating to the Black Caribbean community in London during the 1960s. This includes personal accounts and letters and documents which were donated to the archives by the Huntley family; Eric and Jessica Huntley came to London from Guyana (formerly British Guiana) between 1956 and 1958, where they had been active politically in the People's Progress Party of Guyana. The collection holds a fascinating insight into the educational treatment of black Caribbean children who came to join their families during the 1960s and 1970s. Many of these children were erroneously sent to schools for the educationally subnormal, not because they were 'subnormal' (a term not used today), but largely due to the language barriers that these children inevitably brought with them. As Coard (2004) points out, this had devastating consequences for the overall performance of black children throughout Britain. This important and personal history of many local people may have otherwise been lost or hidden away if it were not for the work of the local archives.

As avid historians ourselves, we have spent many an hour sifting through a mass of evidence but as practising educationalists we also appreciate the time constraints of the busy teacher! An archivist will most certainly help you to navigate around the search catalogues, which are increasingly available electronically, to locate a particular local place or theme and will, on request, call up or direct you to particular collections.

Many archive collections have now been placed online and this is clearly a way for busy teachers to access materials remotely. Bexley for example have 3,500 images available electronically (see further resources for further examples). However we need to be aware, as Temple (2013) suggests, that much of what we find online is of national importance rather than the documents of the local people in our areas, and therefore we may need to be selective in its use. We would also suggest that for children and teachers to experience the work of and become an historian, there is nothing quite like being able to see, handle and investigate physical documents, letters and sources. As a young history graduate, the thrill of being able to read Victorian crime and punishment gaol records, marvelling at the elegant pages of the court books and reading wonderful phrases to do with local crimes, for example the running of a gaming house and 'encouraging idleness and dissipation', are still very vivid memories: an experience that all children should be given the opportunity to engage in if we are to keep history alive in our classrooms. We would therefore advocate that online research materials *supplement* the resources and services that local studies and archive centres offer rather than being used as a first or only source of information.

Local studies centres and libraries

Local studies centres and/or libraries generally contain published materials such as newspapers, pamphlets, books and other secondary resources. They will have a selection of maps including Ordnance Survey maps – reproductions can sometimes be purchased or they can be reproduced at a cost (see chapter 2). There are likely to be fewer restrictions when accessing and working with these resources. Whilst some material will only be available as reference, there will be others that can be loaned. It is worth making a note of loan material as part of your preliminary planning. The study centre may also have an education officer who will be able to assist you in the planning and delivery of historical learning.

Children and history centres

When children are introduced to using the local as a basis for historical enquiry, the starting point is often within the environment itself, through a walk, a visit or talking to people, as this is often what springs to mind first when planning a study. The direction of the enquiry will very much depend on whether you want to focus on place (the built environment) or people (the local community) as explored in chapters 2, 3 and 4. However, documentary evidence itself gathered by the teacher during the initial planning and research, perhaps from a history centre (or by the children themselves) can equally act as a starting point for investigation into the local. It is important to stress that, whether the learning originates from the local itself or from evidence gathered from a teacher's preliminary investigations, teachers will need to ensure that the learning is not lost or superficially covered once the walk/talk/visiting/reviewing evidence has taken place, bringing the role of local history centres to the forefront.

It may well be that there has been a variety of evidence gathered but these will merely be pieces of a much larger picture. For children to understand how this picture is pieced together they will need to experience how to evaluate, use and follow up the evidence. This will entail looking for similarities and differences between sources, making connections, disregarding some findings and asking lots of questions. Too often teachers set children off

on a task of 'go and research. . . .' without giving due thought to what this actually means or whether children have the skills required to *research*. It is therefore important that teachers know what prior learning children have and it is essential that they have a good understanding of the process themselves in order that learning is not lost.

As explored in previous chapters, we very much advocated '*doing* history' as opposed to learning *about* or *studying*. As Temple (2013) says, 'children need to understand how real historians work' (p.51). Children need to be active, looking at evidence such as documents, pictures and artefacts, looking for clues whilst piecing together information; they need to become historians. Pluckrose states:

> Human beings do not learn only from books and the spoken word. They learn best by being immersed in experience which calls for a response from their whole being, which fires the imagination and triggers off a desire to discover more.
>
> (Pluckrose: 1989:2)

Children become very excited when we give them the opportunity of being history detectives or an archaeologist. They become even more excited when they are looking at something that has relevance to them such as a map, a building they are familiar with, a name on a census linked to their name or an old picture of the street that they are now living in.

We are suggesting that local history centres offer a valuable way to extend the learning for children either before, within or as a continuation of history being studied. But, we reiterate that for teachers to be confident, skilled practitioners and ensure that children have a clear understanding of historical enquiry and processes, they themselves must be proficient in finding, researching and evaluating sources and seeing how these sources piece together to make a coherent and comprehensible story.

In order to begin this the following activity can be used as a preliminary introduction to using local resource centres. For this purpose we will refer to the local studies and archives centre, although the same activity can equally be adapted for any history centre found in the local, for example a museum, historical society headquarters or a specialist society, such as an archaeological group – many of which will have an office/building or place of contact.

Teachers' toolkit 5.1 Using history centres

- *Locate your local studies and archives centre and block out a time for a visit.*
- *Consider the range of evidence that can be found there by using the suggestions in this chapter and select an area that you might focus on.*
- *If possible try to match this to a question/area that may have arisen from your preliminary walk around the local area.*
- *Ring the centre and talk to the archivist – he/she can then prepare some material for you. This is part of their service and in our experience one they will revel in!*
- *Make the visit . . .*
- *When there, allow some time to get familiar with the process of: retrieving evidence; using the reading/study room and handling documents. This is invaluable.*

- *Using a piece of evidence and one of the suggested activities later in the chapter, become familiar with the syntactic process of historical research (as discussed in chapter 1).*
- *Establish a list of services that your archivist can offer either within the centre or as an outreach visit and note these down as a possible, later resource when planning.*

The above teacher activity may seem time-consuming and one that some may not wish to engage in or see the relevance of; however, this is a way of experiencing the process of enquiry for yourself and also ensure that any possible starting points for history in the local are relevant to the children. This is where you local archivist will help. Teachers need to be ready, informed and confident that the context of historical learning is appropriate.

In order to highlight the value of becoming familiar with and using local history centres we use a case study of initial trainee teachers at the University of Greenwich to illustrate the benefits of teachers experiencing research in the local.

Case study 5.1 Trainee teachers' awareness of archives

Initial teacher training students at the University of Greenwich are offered a two-week enrichment programme in alternative settings as part of their Y2 school experience. This takes them into various settings which include libraries and archives where they have the opportunity to experience education in the wider context. The programme was designed to develop trainee teachers' personal and professional knowledge, skills and understanding using the theory underpinning learning outside the classroom (DfES, 2006).

When the project was developed, the initial pilot was evaluated and the results were revealing. Students were questioned before and after the experience and selected students were interviewed as part of a case study to assess the impact of the project. The initial questionnaire indicated that a number of students placed in archives had not been in or knew what archives were used for (despite many of these students being on the humanities strand of the programme). Few could see the value of having an experience in archives or made any connection between teaching and learning. They rated themselves as not being confident in historical skills or knowledge.

However, after the experience the research showed that students had developed and refined the skills of finding, evaluating and using a range of sources and evidence. The presentations, interviews, and teaching and learning resources that were made for use in the classroom indicated that the students' use of historical language and understanding of concepts had developed more fully and that they had found creative and engaging ways to involve children in their local (Hales, 2011).

Students experienced the process of generating questions, searching for and then through various documents and other sources (some of which are discussed in this chapter), rejecting some, analysing others and making links. They began to understand the value of various documents, what they offered as evidence and the skills they had to use to make inferences in order to build a picture of the past. Many students reported raised confidence, became excited in their levels of learning and actively voiced how they would be able to engage children in their local, using archive centres and libraries as a point of enquiry.

This case study is intended to highlight several key points. It illustrates the importance of teachers experiencing the process of historical enquiry using local archives, and how this can potentially lead to effective teaching and learning in and out of the classroom with children. Bakhtin's (1981, 1986 in Carruthers and Worthington, 2006) theory of socio-culturalism suggests that learning is not only dependent on social construction (Vygotsky, 1962), but it suggests that culture and community also impact on the way that children learn. Learning in this way promotes culture and community cohesion through developing partnerships between different settings, i.e. university, primary schools and local centres; moreover it develops identity in the local by putting the teaching and learning of children at the heart of it.

Using the historical sources found within historical centres

What are historical sources?

Historical sources are any traces of the past that remain. They may be written, such as documents, newspapers, books or place names; they may be visual, such as paintings, photographs, drawings; oral sources or music; or artefacts, sites and building (Cooper, 2006). What has been covered in chapters 2 to 5 is about sources. Anything can be a source of information; however, it can only be an historical source when it is used by an historian to make a point, and what it provides evidence of, depends on what the historian is trying to say. For example, a train ticket might be evidence of an individual's movements or of the price of rail journeys at a particular date or even of deeper social phenomena: for many years, for example, it was the practice to print a 'W' on a woman's ticket (this was when stations had women-only waiting rooms and trains had women-only carriages) (University of Cambridge Faculty of History, 2013).

The difference between sources

Primary sources

Primary sources are created at the time of an event, or very soon after something has happened. These sources are often rare or unique in their nature. However, some primary sources can also exist in many copies such as the *Diary of Anne Frank*. The following are examples of primary sources: diaries, letters, photographs, interviews, first-hand accounts or stories, eye-witness accounts, newspaper articles, film and directories.

Secondary sources

Secondary sources are sources which have been created or have been published after an event or period of history. They will often refer to primary sources. Examples of these might be historical text books, replicas, re-enactments, historical fiction film, newspapers and cartoons. Secondary sources can give additional opinions (sometimes called bias) on a past event or on a primary source. Secondary sources often have multiple copies.

Primary or secondary?

There is sometimes confusion between primary and secondary sources and children need to be clear about the difference. It is important that children begin to evaluate evidence for themselves and not automatically assume something is correct because it is written down, and here we include written materials found online. There is a misconception that primary evidence can be more reliable than secondary evidence; however, this is not always the case; there are some very good secondary source materials available, which can no doubt supplement primary sources. Teachers will need to guide children in accessing material that is both relevant and reliable. It is important to note that some sources such as newspapers and film can be both primary and secondary; it is the content of the sources that is important. For example a newspaper may have an eye-witness account of an event, therefore making it a primary source; however the same newspaper may have an account written by a reporter some time after the event has happened; thus it is a secondary source. There can be a fine line between primary and secondary sources which may be dependent on how long after the event it was produced. Without critically reviewing the evidence with a sound understanding of enquiry, it may be difficult to make that distinction. Non-specialists and/or early career teachers may find it overwhelming when searching for relevant and useful primary or secondary documents to use with children, either at the archive centre or to take back to the classroom. Again, a local archivist will be able to help you interpret the evidence that you use.

Using resources

Children themselves will need to be taught specific research skills of enquiry in order to locate and evaluate evidence. These skills should be taught from the early years if we are going to make children independent and 'learning' historians.

Very young children can begin to experience looking through and looking at a range of evidence when given the opportunity and sufficient time. A teacher can, for instance, when looking at a collection of photographs, ask a young child to find a picture which tells us something about old shops or a picture which shows us a different way of washing clothes; what can they see in this picture which you have not seen before? Such questions will begin to focus young children on the photograph and give them a purpose for looking and thinking about what they see. Giving children a magnifying glass often adds to the excitement!

When children are more adept at sourcing information for themselves and selecting evidence, they will need to understand that sometimes their searches may not always lead to fruition. We have found this to be the cause of frustration with adult teacher trainees and therefore make the point that teachers need to model to children 'that sometimes, we don't know so we have to make a good guess' based on what we have or can see. There are of course times when we may not even be able to do that! However their questions, hypothesis and curiosity may lead them in another direction and to other sources. It is vital that teachers do not stifle this process of learning but at the same time make sure that children are not left to flounder without the necessary scaffolding.

When trying to find out a specific piece of information or develop a specific historical enquiry skill, it is often better to start with a limited number of sources that have been

selected specifically for a purpose in mind according to the learning needs and age of the children. For example it may be that very young children may start with just one photograph and describe what they can see. As children become more skilled in research, looking at and evaluating evidence, initially for what is presented to them, they will begin to select their own sources in order to find out about the past. As with all evidence children must be encouraged to ask questions about the source they are looking at. This will need to be modelled and extended as children develop, but it is a vital component to historical enquiry (see chapter 10 on planning).

Table 5.1 lists some of the more well-known documentary evidence to be found at the local studies and archives centres. Those in italics will be discussed further in the chapter. All of these documents can be used within the archives and many can be copied or reproduced to be brought back into the classroom for further or more in-depth study.

Other resources can be found in places such as libraries, museums and historical organisations and these will be discussed separately.

When looking at and using documentary evidence, Temple (2013) offers a model to use in assessing its usefulness in which she coins the term: 'The 3 R's of archive material'.

Is it . . .

- *Rich* – is the document rich in detail or information? Will it help children to understand a particular aspect in more depth or give an overview?
- *Reliable* – how accurate is it likely to be? As we have mentioned before, we cannot ever be completely sure, but we can make an informed judgement based on asking some pertinent questions. Who wrote it? Why? Is it biased? Is it a primary source (written at the actual time) or was it written after (secondary evidence)? The answers to these questions can help you to scaffold and extend children's inference and deduction skills as well as your own!
- *Relevant* – does the document give you information about the local area, person, event that you are studying? Is it something that will capture the children's enthusiasm? Often the style of handwriting and use of language will excite children and generate a hearty discussion.

Alongside this, we would also suggest teachers use the model offered by Turner-Bisset (2005) and referred to in chapter 6 as a teaching and learning activity:

- What do we know for certain . . . (dates, places, names, factual information)?
- What reasonable guesses can we make?
- What questions can we ask?

Children and misconceptions when using sources

The study of history is undoubtedly full of misconceptions, some of which will be specifically referred to throughout the book. Children's misconceptions often occur through lack of experience with a particular focus, concept, activity or source. Teachers' lack of subject knowledge is also a factor, again emphasising the need for teachers to have sound understanding of the content and concepts being taught. Lomas (2011) says that one of the most important roles of good primary history is to address and correct pupils' misconceptions about the past. If children are not challenged through specific questioning and discussion and given the time to explore the concept, misconceptions will not be corrected.

Table 5.1 Documentary sources available in local centres

Sources of information to be found in local studies/archives centres	*How these sources might be used in the local*	*Specific concepts or skills*
Advertisements found in newspapers, directories or as individual posters	Can give clues as to the services, shops and goods that were available at that time; can tell us about the audience at which the product/shop/service might be aimed.	Change and continuity Similarities and differences Historical situations
Census returns	Can tell us about the types of families living in the local area, either a street, house or building.	Historical enquiry
Diaries/letters/personal accounts	Can give an insight into the thoughts and feelings of people living in the area, what the area may have been like and how certain events affected them.	Empathy Bias
Directories (trade and street directories)	Provide a comprehensive overview of a town or community. Directories will contain details of trades, services and local people; a useful way to compare the change/continuity of a town within a short amount of time.	Change and continuity
Newspapers/magazines	Can give detailed information as to the specific events and actions of people in the local area. There may be views and opinions expressed in response to what was going on at that time.	Historical enquiry Cause and consequence Historical situations Bias Interpretation
Maps	Give an overview of what the local area looked like at the time; can place a specific street in relation to the rest of the area – see chapter 2 for an in-depth look at maps.	Historical situations Compare and contrast
Visual imagery such as photographs, pictures, posters, cartoon, drawings, portraits	Can give immediate information on how the local streets, buildings and people have changed. They can give clues as to the historical situation of that time, e.g. a group of women washing clothes by hand outside in the street may present a very different picture to washing today.	Interpretation Similarities and differences Chronology
School records such as log books, punishment records, registers	Can tell us about a particular school in the local area – its ethos, why children were absent, punishments administered and lessons taught. Children will be able to compare and contrast with their own school now.	Similarities and differences Historical situations Cause and consequence Change and continuity
War documents: bomb records, letter, diaries, ration books,	Can give insight into the extent local people were affected by war; how much war damage was experienced and what evacuation was like for families and children.	Historical enquiry Cause and consequence
House details such as inventories, deeds, house sale details, family and estate records	Specific houses/buildings can be focused on to find out about the styles, rooms and facilities a house may have had, who may have designed and built the house and why. Inventories give an insight into people's belongings and possessions.	Historical enquiry Change and continuity
Crime records/gaol records	Can tell us what crime existed in a particular area and why. Children can investigate age, gender and punishments given during that time.	Historical situations Cause and consequence

When looking at sources of evidence the following gives a broad overview of the possible misconceptions both children and adults might have. As an adult consider your own views on the following general misconceptions and how you might challenge children in the classroom:

- Black and white photographs are old.
- Photographs must be a true picture of that snapshot in time.
- Newspaper reports must be true.
- Secondary evidence such as historical non-fiction books must be accurate/true.
- Eye-witness accounts must be reliable because the people were there.
- Documents which look dirty or faded are old.
- Illiteracy must mean people were unintelligent or poor.
- Artefacts which may be dirty or rusty must be old.
- All evidence is either primary or secondary.
- Primary evidence must be more reliable than secondary.

Types of sources

The following gives a summary of some of the types of sources you may wish to use with children when exploring your local. It offers some suggestions, though they are not exhaustive, on how you might use them and some questions which may be relevant.

Advertisements/posters

Children can look at and identify the product/s being advertised or message being relayed in the poster. The pictures/dress/style or wording of the document may give clues to the date or era. Older children may question why certain gender or gender-specific vocabulary might have been used. Does this give us clues to the historical perspective of that time? Who is the audience aimed at? Would this be something that people from the local community or family might use/do/visit/promote now?

Groups of children may look at different styles and forms of advertisement, i.e. posters, within newspapers, directories, shop windows. The complexity of a poster used should depend on the age and learning of the children. (Cross-curricular opportunities are discussed in chapter 9.)

As with the example below, it is sometime possible to use an artefact alongside the advertisement which will further bring the resource to life.

Task

- *Look at the advertisement in Figure 5.2.*
- *Look at it alongside the artefact in Figure 5.1.*
- *Use both Temple's 3 R's of archive material and Turner-Bisset's model.*
- *What does this advertisement tell you?*
- *Would you consider this to be a useful source of historical information for children?*

Figure 5.1 Tilley Iron.

Figure 5.2 Advertisement for the Tilley Iron.

Census returns

Census returns have been completed in the UK every ten years since 1801, except during the Second World War. However, census returns before 1841 were not considered reliable due to the way the data was collected; they were essentially notes and did not contain as much information. From 1841 onwards details of all individuals in a house or property were recorded rather than just the main resident (Wall et al., 2004). The 1881 census is the first available online and can be accessed free of charge via http://www.familysearch.org. The census provides a snapshot of the population at that point in time detailing names, ages, gender, places of birth, occupations, family status and residency.

Its intended use was not for the historian, but primarily by the government for long-term planning, studying trends in population growth or decline and analysing data about ages, occupations and places of birth (Wilkinson, 2011). Census material can only be accessed after a hundred years have passed. Unfortunately, we may have seen the last census collection in 2011 as officials evaluate the reliability of data collected and whether more accurate means of collection would be more cost effective, viable and reliable.

This could be a centre point of discussion within a classroom. Children themselves could consider more reliable or innovative ways to collect such data. We could pose the question of: can we collect and use the data in a better way so it will become a more valuable documentary evidence for family and community history?

Census returns can tell fascinating stories and provide a real sense of investigation for children. They can be chosen for a specific street, area or building and children can look at the entries and begin to interpret and hypothesise about the people and the stories behind them. The handwriting may be problematic for children to read and decipher and therefore it may be necessary for the teacher to transcribe parts themselves. However, if children do this it will encourage them to look more closely at the document and discussion can be had over the style of handwriting and how this may have changed. (See Figure 5.3, an example of an original census return and Figure 5.4, the transcription.)

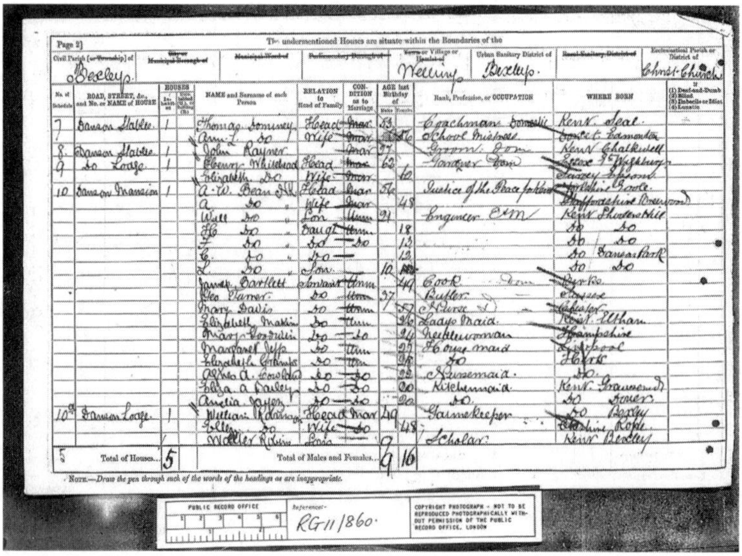

Figure 5.3 A census return.

Name	Relationship to Head of Family	Condition as to Marriage	Age Last Birthday		Rank Profession or Occupation	Where Born
			Males	Females		
A.W Bean	Head	Mar	56		Justice of the Peace	Hampshire Poole
Bean	Wife	Mar		48		Herfordshire Brewood
Will Bean	Son	Unm	21		Engineer	Kent Shootershill
H Bean	Daughter	"		18		"
F Bean	Daughter	"		13		"
C Bean	Daugher	"		12		Danson Park
L Bean	Son	"	10			"
James Bartlett	Servant	"		49	Cook	Berks
Leo Turner	Servant	"	37		Butler	
Mary Davis	Servant	"		57	Nurse	
Elizabeth Makin	Servant	"		26	Lady's Maid	Eltham Kent
Mary Goodwin	Servant	"		24	Needle Woman	Liverpool

Figure 5.4 The local census data transcript of the Bean Family living in Sidcup, Danson House in 1891.

Some generic questions/activities to use with census material:

- Highlight the adults and make a list of their occupations and the places they were born.
- What do the occupations of people in the street tell us about the local community at that time?
- Identify the place of birth on a map of the immediate region, of the British Isles and of the world.
- What does this tell us about the migration and movement of the time?
- Look at the language being used; how has this changed? Would it be allowed today? (Children will be fascinated at the inclusion of words such as 'lunatic, imbecile, beggar' used from 1841 onwards.)
- How have family structures and size changed?
- Create a family tree using the information.
- Investigate the residents of a local non-residential building – many areas had asylums, workhouses and prisons.

- Compare the data between streets/areas/buildings.
- Look at the popularity of first names.
- Become one of the characters . . . Write, draw, role play their story.

Newspapers and magazines

Most archives will hold newspapers and magazines on microfiche and as original copies, with many now being available digitally online (see further resources for websites). Local newspapers provide children with a rich source of activity of the time within a local area and from it they are able to build quite a picture. Teachers will need to be selective in the material that they direct children to within the newspaper so that they do not lose focus and the learning is not superficial. Information may include:

- advertisements;
- local stories/events;
- jobs vacancies/services offered;
- houses for sale;
- particular people within the community;
- particular events within the local community.

Children can compare and contrast different events/stories/pictures of the time and during different periods of time, e.g. at ten-year intervals. Activities might include: retelling a local story either verbally, through drama or writing in role as a reporter; creating an advertisement for another house/object or job vacancy or taking on roles as the characters and hot-seating each other through role play. The following examples are general questions that may act as a starting point when looking at newspapers and magazines:

- What was the main story/event happening at the time? Why was this being publicised?
- Are there any stories/events that we can compare with today? Look for similarities and differences.
- What were the local people concerned with at the time?
- What does the range of advertisements tell us about the employment in the local area of the time?

Directories

From the middle of the eighteenth century until the 1930s, local directories were published to provide information on the trades, residents and local services such as libraries, schools and churches. They outlined the names, occupations and addresses of the most important people within the local community and how the town was governed. Towards the end of the nineteenth century names, addresses and at least one of the occupations of a town's residents was included for the benefit of the post-office, so post could be delivered more reliably. Often a brief history of the locality was supplied within the directory.

Local example 5.2 Penge Directory

The Penge, Sydenham Directory, 1867–68
(Edited Extract)

Within the living memory of many of the present inhabitants, Penge was a thickly wooded common several hours' journey from London by coach or on foot.

When the railways made travelling easier, the natural beauty of the village and surrounding countryside attracted business men. They found that a railway journey of 20 minutes transported them from the smoky City to the pure air of the country where their families could enjoy all the delights of the country.

Another great attraction is the proximity of our beautiful Crystal Palace with its beautiful gardens, park-like grounds, matchless art treasures, music and so on.

Another great attraction is that Penge is surrounded by a circle of twelve railway stations.

Directories were originally published for commercial purposes, a bit like our *Yellow Pages* or *Thompson Local* today, but they also gave a fairly comprehensive view of local communities. They were published more often than the census, so provide an invaluable way to fill any missing gaps. A street or town can be compared within a relatively short period of time – for example over a two-year period or every two years for a given time. This will help children understand the rapid change that some towns went through. Other activities that children can engage in are: mapping the transport activity and destinations within a town; looking at and comparing businesses, particularly looking at more unusual businesses that we may not see today; looking at the different uses of a particular building, or annotating or creating a picture from the description provided of the town.

Diaries/letters/personal accounts

Diaries, letters and personal accounts allow children to develop real empathy with the local people in the community. Many children will be familiar with famous diaries such as those of Samuel Pepys or Anne Frank. However some may not have had experience of written evidence from ordinary people in the local. The National Curriculum (2014) states that children should study significant events and people; the meaning of significant, however, is subjective and open to debate. Who is to say that a local person, who may have fought in a world war and therefore contributed to the national heritage of our country, is not to be regarded as significant?

Often diaries and personal accounts offer insights into very significant events for that community or local area and can demonstrate the achievements and efforts of individual people. For instance the archives of the south east London Borough of Lewisham holds a collection of letters from a local boy who tells his story of evacuation to Devon during the Second World War. (See further resources for reference.) Many such examples can be found across the country and give primary children the opportunity to relate to ordinary children like themselves in their own town or community. The impact of such individuals on a local community can be profound and offer a very different interpretation of the history of a local community.

School log books

School log books offer children an immediate connection with *their* history, as they are able to engage instantly with historical enquiry. Using these books and the 'now' in their school, they are able situate themselves in the historical situation and make comparisons, look for similarities and difference and suggest reasons for why things might have happened.

Local example 5.3, written by a local archivist, Simon McKeon of Bexley Local Studies and Archives Centre, outlines the possible uses of school log books with children in schools.

Local example 5.3 Using school log books in schools

From 1862 to the mid 1990s head-teachers were required by law to keep a daily log of events and issues that arose at their school. Common entries that can be found in most school log books include records of pupil attendance and the reasons for non-attendance; descriptions of the subjects taught, with timetables, and even notes on disciplining the children. Displaying passages from school log books enables children to compare their experience at school with that of their Victorian counterparts. As well as providing a fascinating insight into local history the entries often include references to how national events and celebrations were experienced in the school, such as Empire Day, the ending of the world wars, and coronations etc.

One very fruitful area to investigate in school log books is the entries of school attendance. In an age when many parents did not regard their children's attendance at school as importantly as parents do today, the log books are replete with reasons for why children did not attend school. For example children may have skipped school in order to work with their parents in local farms or even to watch the local circus that had just arrived in town. Easy to use numerical data can also be isolated from the entries to illustrate how simple mathematical enquiries can be used to discover what life was like at Victorian schools.

Gaol records

Gaol records are no doubt a sure way to engage most children, especially boys. Using local gaol records would mean that children will recognise the place names and start to imagine people in these places (Turner-Bisset, 2005). Such records are rich in vocabulary and this in itself generates lots of questions. The use of vocabulary and ensuring children understand what particular words mean in context is extremely important when dealing with all documentary evidence. In our experience letting children look, read and ask questions will lead on to several lines of enquiry and hearty debates! (See chapter 9, 'Cross-curricular history' and the section on asking questions in chapter 10.)

House details/information

House details, particularly when used alongside other sources such as pictures and census details, can help children visualise what houses were like both inside and out; a field trip

before or after looking at documentary evidence can further enrich the learning (see chapter 3). Reading information about larger houses that may now be split into flats or are no longer residential but used for other purposes can again develop children's sense of change, cause and consequence, helping children understand the changing nature of their local.

Local example 5.4 House details

The Avery Hill Campus, part of Greenwich University, is situated in Eltham, a suburb in south east London. Avery Hill was once the home of Colonel North, 'The Nitrate King', a significant Victorian individual, and his mansion was particularly grand, with many unique features of its time, such as a Turkish bath and its own water tower. See Figure 5.5 for further details of its grandeur.

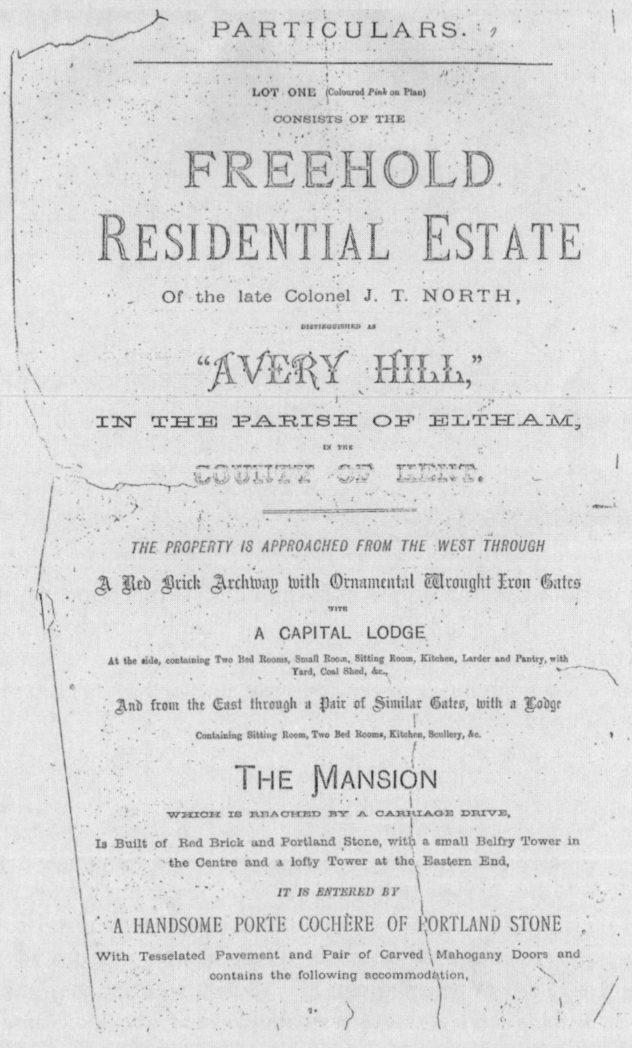

PARTICULARS.

LOT ONE (Coloured *Pink* on Plan)

CONSISTS OF THE

FREEHOLD

RESIDENTIAL ESTATE

Of the late Colonel J. T. NORTH,

DISTINGUISHED AS

"AVERY HILL,"

IN THE PARISH OF ELTHAM,

IN THE

COUNTY OF KENT.

THE PROPERTY IS APPROACHED FROM THE WEST THROUGH

A Red Brick Archway with Ornamental Wrought Iron Gates

WITH

A CAPITAL LODGE

At the side, containing Two Bed Rooms, Small Room, Sitting Room, Kitchen, Larder and Pantry, with Yard, Coal Shed, &c.,

And from the East through a Pair of Similar Gates, with a Lodge

Containing Sitting Room, Two Bed Rooms, Kitchen, Scullery, &c.

THE MANSION

WHICH IS REACHED BY A CARRIAGE DRIVE,

Is Built of Red Brick and Portland Stone, with a small Belfry Tower in the Centre and a lofty Tower at the Eastern End,

IT IS ENTERED BY

A HANDSOME PORTE COCHÈRE OF PORTLAND STONE

With Tesselated Pavement and Pair of Carved Mahogany Doors and contains the following accommodation,

Figure 5.5 Particulars of Avery Hill house sale.

KENT.

By Order of the Trustees under the Will of the late Colonel J. T. NORTH.

Particulars and Conditions of Sale

OF THE

IMPORTANT AND VALUABLE

FREEHOLD RESIDENTIAL ESTATE

DISTINGUISHED AS

"AVERY HILL,"

SITUATE IN THE PARISH OF ELTHAM,

IN THE COUNTY OF KENT,

About a mile-and-a-half from Eltham, and a mile from New Eltham Stations on the South Eastern Railway, from which either the City or the West End of London is reached in about half-an-hour. It comprises an

EXCELLENT FAMILY MANSION

Built in a most substantial manner of Red Brick and Portland Stone, in the most Expensive and Artistic Style and fitted throughout with all Modern Improvements, with a

Noble Picture Gallery or Ball Room,

WINTER GARDEN, LARGE CONSERVATORY AND FERNERY,

Extensive Vineries and other Glass Houses, Engine and Machine House, Two Lodges,

CAPITAL STABLING FOR 24 HORSES, STUD FARM, PARK AND PASTURE LAND,

The whole containing about

143 Acres and 2 Roods;

ALSO TWO LEASEHOLD PROPERTIES ADJOINING,

KNOWN AS

"PIPPINHALL FARM," of 430a. 1r. 6p.,

AND

"AVONDALE," a RESIDENCE, and about 24a. 3r. 2p.

POSSESSION WILL BE GIVEN ON COMPLETION OF THE PURCHASE.

Which will be Sold by Auction, by

MESSRS. G. A. WILKINSON & SON,

AT THE MART, TOKENHOUSE YARD

(OPPOSITE THE BANK OF ENGLAND),

On MONDAY, JULY 27th, 1896,

At TWO o'clock precisely, IN THREE LOTS, (unless previously disposed of by Private Contract).

Particulars and Conditions of Sale, with Plans, may be had of Messrs. BUDD, JOHNSONS & JECKS, Solicitors, 24 Austin Friars; and with Cards to View of Messrs. G. A. WILKINSON & SON, Surveyors and Auctioneers,

7 POULTRY, LONDON.

Figure 5.6 Auction details of the Avery Hill Estate.

Many less grand houses within a local area can be of as much interest to children and should not be overlooked. Children can compare the details with modern homes, suggest reasons for the change of use and consider the impact on a local community. The designs of houses may have multicultural connections, reflecting or having features of significant buildings or places abroad.

Local example 5.5 Multicultural connections in the local

Eight houses in a local road in Bexley, a suburb in Kent, were designed by the Indian architect, D.C. Whadwa, during the 1930s to reflect seafaring vessels and our connections with India. At this period of time it was extremely unusual to have Indian architects design houses; however, for children who may have emigrated from India to England today it would provide a sense of identity for the place they now live in. For other examples or local connections to the national and global see chapters 6 and 8.

Visual images, such as photographs, pictures, postcards, cartoons and posters

Archives will hold thousands of pictures and photographs of both people and place. Pictures are an invaluable source of information and their very nature allows children of all ability to access the learning. Many pictures are multi-modal combining text and image which teachers can use to extend those children who are moving on to the higher order historical concepts and skills (Nichol, 2010). For example multi-modal cartoons are a fascinating and engaging way to look at social situations. Again we would advise a call to your local archivist before to ensure that pictures chosen are relevant for your learning objective. When working with any imagery remember to address the common misconception that black and white must means old!

Card (2010) offers the following guidelines when working with cartoons; however, these can be used as a starting point for any pictorial work:

- Give pupils time to scrutinise the cartoon/picture. We would suggest picture framing sections so children focus on detail.
- Ask children what they can see for certain – this allows you to pick up any early misconceptions.
- Plan leading questions to help children get to the point of the cartoon.
- Be ready to discuss ideas and answers which are mistaken but are rational inferences given the pupils' stage of knowledge and understanding. The key question is 'what in the picture made you think that?' This encourages pupils to articulate, explore and revise inferences.

Other ideas and questions might be useful starting points for using photographs and pictures; the level of questioning will depend on the age and stage of development of children:

- Is the picture staged? If so why might it be?
- Who do you think is taking the picture?
- What does the picture tell us about that period of time, place or people?
- What do you think is happening outside of the picture? Children can discuss, draw, enact or write about the scene they cannot see.
- What do you think the person is thinking/feeling in the photograph? Why?

Using libraries

Libraries will be more familiar to the reader than perhaps other history centres mentioned in this chapter. Generally, secondary sources (though not exclusively, as libraries also hold primary sources) will be held at libraries, i.e. sources such as local history books, information text books, historical stories, biographies, autobiographies, leaflets, pamphlets and newspapers. Historical stories are a valid and accessible starting point to introducing history to children (see chapter 6). There may certainly be locally based stories of real people and events such as Chalky White – the unknown warrior from the First World War: this particular local story from Bexley can be viewed via the link in the resource section at the end of the chapter. Many libraries will offer online access to the internet as well as their online collections.

Using museums

Museums can be defined as 'institutions that collect, safeguard and make accessible artefacts and specimens, which they hold in trust for society'; this also includes galleries that hold works of art. Their job is not just to conserve collections but also their presentation and interpretation (Museum Association, in Grigg and Hughes, 2013).

Whilst many famous national museums such as the British Museum or the Victoria and Albert Museum are located in the major cities of the UK, some excellent museums of national and global importance can be found locally. For instance the Brunel Museum is located in middle of a local housing estate in Rotherhithe, south east London. Its collection is very small, but tells a story of global significance (see chapter 8).

Other local and independent museums may tell stories of equal importance but at a local level, particularly local industrial heritage (see further reading and resources, particularly Culture 24 who provide an online comprehensive guide to museums across the UK).

Museums offer children the opportunity to interact with the artefacts and other resources they may hold such as art and film. Walters (2012) talks about the 'awe and wonder . . . the visceral, affective impact' that the real thing can have on pupils and adults when they are given the opportunity to visit and use museums as part of their learning. However, there is perhaps a risk that some museums, particularly big museums, can leave children having seen a lot but learnt little. He suggests that whilst larger museums may have resources, local museums often excel in other areas; for example, role play experiences, education officers and loan materials. It is therefore worth considering the smaller, locally based museums which will have targeted resources and may offer extra experiences.

When planning a visit, refer to the guidelines given in chapter 3. However, do bear in mind that many museums often offer outreach sessions to schools or loan materials which can be used in the classroom, so a 'visit' might take place in the classroom. It is advisable to investigate your local museum to review the services and resources they have to offer.

Artefacts

Artefacts are easily accessible by the teacher and can be used in or outside of the classroom. They can be used singly or as part of a collection. The type of artefact used will depend on your learning objective and the age and stage of development of the children. For example simply comparing a telephone with a dial alongside a mobile phone could develop children's observational skills (particularly younger children's); a single, unusual artefact from a Victorian kitchen might pose several higher order questions for older children. However, a collection of telephones, irons or even washing pegs can be used to develop a range of chronological skills.

Throughout we have stressed the importance of children becoming 'historians' or 'history detectives' themselves, and using artefacts, as with documentary evidence, really facilitates this. When using artefacts, children need to be able to explore them using all their senses. It is simply not enough to place them in the middle of a table or behind a glass case without letting children touch them. Much can be discovered by looking inside, feeling the weight, smelling or role playing with the object to develop concepts such as understanding what it was like to live with or use a particular object. In our experience as

teachers and working with the most challenging of children, given trust and responsibility, they have never misused or purposely damaged an object or document in their possession. It is important that they are informed about the nature and importance of caring for artefacts and how to handle and look at them carefully and considerately. Requests by schools to parents, family and local community to loan local artefacts will provide an abundance of relevant and interesting resources and with them will often come opportunities for engaging in oral history, as to their use and history by their owners.

There are many good reference books on the use of artefacts and a selection are offered in the resource sections at the end of the chapter. However, some generic questions and activities are offered below:

- Describe the similarities and difference between . . .
- Who might have used this artefact and why?
- How might it have been used?
- What does it tell us about the way of life?

The British Museum's *A History of the World in 100 Objects* provides an excellent example of how objects can be used to represent history and tell the story. This can be easily adapted to work in the classroom and more specifically for work in the local. Children can collect artefacts from local people, family and local history resources centres and tell the story of 'the local' in objects. During a 'History Week' in one of our primary schools, a school museum was set up which displayed objects and possessions from the local community. It provided a fascinating insight into the local activity across approximately a hundred years, including leisure, occupations and ways of life.

Specialist societies and organisations

Specialist societies and organisations are becoming increasing more popular in local areas and communities. Their roots, as explored in chapter 1, largely originate from local history societies very much focused on the immediate area. However, many offer specialised information in a specific context. For example, Age Exchange, based in Blackheath, London, is recognised as the leading UK charity working in the field of reminiscence, and provides (amongst others) many local case studies of people living in and around Blackheath.

Other organisations such as archaeological groups will often visit schools and offer projects and outreach programmes in various areas. It is worth contacting your local borough to find out what groups are available to you locally. Some points of contact are offered below.

Next steps

This chapter has looked specifically at the resources found in local historical centres and brings to an end the section of the book that deals with sources in the local. The following chapters look at how the local links to the national and into the wider world. It looks at how the sources found in people and place can be used to support these aspects of history. The development of a chronological framework is looked at as part of this.

Further reading

The Sandal, by T. Bradman and P. Dupasquier (1999) – a three-part picture story which is a subtle introduction to museums for young children

Using Documents, by I. Davis and C. Webb, Hythe: English Heritage (1996)

A Teacher's Guide to Learning from Objects, by G. Durbin, S. Morris and S. Wilkinson, Hythe: English Heritage (1990)

'Visual literacy: learning through pictures and images', *Primary History*, Issue 49, London: Historical Association (2008)

'Doing history with artefacts and objects', *Primary History*, Issue 54, London: Historical Association (2010)

'Doing local history', *Primary History*, Issue 55, London: Historical Association (2010)

'Doing history with written and printed sources', *Primary History*, Issue 56, London: Historical Association (2010)

Useful websites and resources

http://www.age-exchange.org.uk/

http://www.bexley.gov.uk/ This is an example of a local borough authority website, one used in this chapter. However the search engine will provide the reader with a comprehensive list of local online archives

http://bombsight.org/explore/greater-london/lewisham/

www.culture24.org.uk/home

http://www.crayfordhistory.co.uk/index/

http://www.historicaldirectories.org/hd/ud/usingdir2.asp

http://www.lotc.org.uk/about/manifesto/

http://www.cityoflondon.gov.uk/things-to-do/visiting-the-city/archives-and-city-history/london-metropolitan-archives/Pages/default.aspx – London Metropolitan Archives

http://www.nationalarchives.gov.uk/ The government's national archive for England, Wales and the United Kingdom, which holds over 1,000 years of the nation's records for everyone to discover and use

Chapter 6

The bigger picture

Establishing a national context

In this chapter and chapter 8 we go beyond thinking about local history bounded by its physical territory, and consider the links of a local area with first the national and then the global aspects of history. We start here by looking at the relationship between the national and the local. We look at the potential of local history to provide history content and encourage the use of the reader's own personal and family history as a resource for history. The use of story in the teaching and learning of primary history is discussed and ideas for classroom practice given. Starting points are suggested for linking into wider geographical perspectives.

Chapter objectives

By the end of this chapter you should:

- have an understanding of the relationship between local and national history;
- know how to make links between local and national in teaching and learning;
- have developed understanding of how to use story in teaching the local in history.

The relationship between local and national

> Penge is an unpretentious, ordinary, resolutely unfashionable railway suburb, adrift in the low-rise sprawl of south east London. It is an ordinary little place. But its ordinariness is precisely the point of this book, because the histories of places like Penge are packed with interest, drama and insights into the world in which we live.
>
> (Spence, 2007:viii)

> But to be ordinary is not to be uninteresting, or unimportant.
>
> (Ibid:122)

There is a two-way relationship between the local and the national. In one sense, local history cannot be anything but 'British' (Purkis, 1989) and as Blyth has also pointed out, 'in some sense, all history is local history' since it has to happen in a place (Blyth, 1994:61).

The story of Penge's transition from a rural to a suburban area, described in Spence's book on its development, is one which typifies the urbanisation which followed the coming of the railway to different parts of England. The point he makes helps to illustrate in part the idea which underpins this chapter: that the local in history can help to exemplify the national and reinforces our point that it can be exciting and interesting. Alongside this is the recognition that, albeit in an uneven way, different parts of the national story can be found in every local area: uneven in the sense that aspects of national history may be more evident in some areas than in others, both because they have been part of the national to differing degrees at different times, and also because the evidence of these aspects may be present to different extents.

The local can readily be used as an example of an approach to history that is beginning with the national story. As an illustration, if the Victorians are being studied, examples can be drawn upon from the local area such as the growth of the area as a result of the coming of the railway: this reflects a national to local approach as illustrated by the example of Penge above.

However, we want also to emphasise the advantages of a local to national approach; the study of the development of the area leading into a consideration of what was happening nationally. The principle underpinning this latter approach, and these chapters, is that national (and as we shall see later, global) aspects of history are helpfully accessible to children through the local. For children, we also believe that an approach to the national through local (which includes for us the personal) can be helpful to primary teachers in developing their own historical knowledge and understanding. However, there is no doubt that something of the national framework can help in developing this understanding, so that the two-way relationship is essential. For children we believe that this approach serves both the purpose of history and the purpose of the teaching and learning of history to young children. This perspective, which is explored in more detail below, is supported by both educationalists and historians.

The historian and journalist Michael Wood is committed to this approach and continues to demonstrate this through his writing and television programmes. One of his guiding principles in his 'A People's History' project has been that, 'at the grass roots you can also find the national story' (Wood, 2012a) and his in-depth study of Kibworth in Leicestershire demonstrates in detail the local and national links (Wood, 2010). His approach also acknowledges local and regional differences in the national story, so that for instance he discusses the way in which the decline in the Roman presence in Britain varies across the country. This reflects what Levstik and Barton (2011) refer to when talking about challenging children's assumption of uni-linear historical development; learning that change happens at a different rate and starts at different moments in different parts of a country.

This making of links and finding a wider context within which local, and indeed personal, history is to be placed reflects a particular perspective on history. It is an approach to history which has also found favour with educationalists. Collicott (1986) refers to local history as a piece of a jigsaw, the jigsaw being the national story. She goes on to refer to that picture fitting into the larger picture of world history. This does indeed require us to look outwards from the locality to see the wider relationships. It is an important way in to helping children understand wider, different and complex relationships (Collicott, 1990a). She also argues that the known locality not only provides readily accessible evidence, a principle which underpins our first chapters, but that it is an important building block. She sees this use of the real world as an important way of engaging the children as they embark on beginning to understand these links (Collicott, 1993).

Bage has also argued specifically in relation to children that it is possible to encounter national history largely through the local. He goes on to argue that our curiosity about past and present is driven by the difference between ourselves and others and that therefore this requires history that starts with the local (Bage, 2000). This local history can then be used as the basis for developing further knowledge in regional, national and international contexts. At a practical level, Bage highlights the approaches of Collicott (1986) as a means of localising the National Curriculum.

This approach to history, linking from the local to the wider context, is essentially about making conceptual links in a spatial context as well as the more usual temporal one – the longer-term chronological framework. Both are about seeing the bigger picture rather than stopping with a detail in isolation. The notion that it is helpful for children to begin with the specific rather than the bigger picture is not a new one: in the early twentieth century it had a strong advocate in the work of Mason, to whose work Cooper (2012) draws attention.

> The fatal mistake is in the notion that he [the pupil] must learn 'outlines,' or a baby edition of the whole history of England . . . Let him, on the contrary, linger pleasantly over the history of a single man, a short period, until he thinks the thoughts of that man, is at home in the ways of that period. Though he is reading and thinking of the lifetime of a single man, he is really getting intimately acquainted with the history of a whole nation for a whole age.
>
> (Mason, transcribed by Ambleside online, 1993)

This hints at the two approaches to history – the detailed and the overview – between which there is a tension. This tension is around the views that there is a need on the one hand for the development of a long-term chronological framework – the big picture – and on the other, for the exploration of aspects of history in depth. How can young children usefully work towards the big picture of history, a chronological frame of reference, that will support them in secondary school and beyond? We suggest that this can be done by teaching that includes both a developing chronological framework and the exploration of aspects of history in depth, and moves between the two. The latter provides the context for detailed historical enquiry which will excite and engage children, a context provided by the dynamic and creative history which primary teachers can work well with. The former requires some significant attention to chronology – hence the focus of the following chapter. We believe that both approaches are possible, that they complement each other and that they are important to children's development of knowledge, skills and understanding.

This approach is supported by Riley (1997) who maintains that study in depth is essential to develop an understanding of history while the wider context is essential for making links. He refers to this wider context as overviews. Our secondary colleagues have to engage more significantly with the development of a meaningful framework for a usable big picture of the past (Howson, 2007) but perhaps we can help prepare children for this as primary teachers. Riley (1997) has suggested a number of different ways of approaching history planning, combining overviews with opportunities for children to engage in detailed study, and these are appropriate for older primary children. The overview might for instance be the broad chronological framework, or might provide information on the characteristics of a period. An overview of a period might also be provided by a story. The important feature is that the overview provides a context within which more detailed work can take place. It can allow connections to be made; develop understanding of cause and

effect; reinforce the understanding of key concepts and allow a meaningful framework for the use of evidence.

At some point, therefore, it is helpful to move from the local to the national understanding and to build on this to form a framework within which local understanding can then be constructed. Indeed, national history will always be an important frame of reference for local history and when telling the local story it may be used to develop ideas and to complete the chronological story so as to provide a more complete picture, especially at Key Stage 2. For a teacher whose understanding of history nationally may be insecure, how can the local area truly help to exemplify and link to the national in the teaching and learning of history? A useful starting point may be their own personal/family history.

Developing your own understanding of the national context for the local

In keeping with our philosophy of supporting the non-specialist in developing their historical knowledge and understanding, we begin with the starting point of putting one's own personal/family history into context. Local example 6.1 is based on extensive research, but even one or two examples from a teacher's personal/family history can help to develop this framework of reference. Alongside the personal example has been given the national context with which it links. How these links can be identified is explained in Figure 6.1 later in this chapter. Using the personal/family context not only helps develop historical understanding, it also highlights examples that the teacher may be able to use in the classroom along the lines discussed in chapter 4. These links can be used imaginatively as in the example of Dawson (2010) who uses the experiences of an uncle who emigrated as a comparison point with a Roman soldier arriving in this country, pointing out that both have experiences as emigrants and immigrants.

Local example 6.1 Some aspects of personal and family history in a national context

Some aspects of personal and family history	*The national context*
A great great grandfather was a soap boiler	The urban poor in Victorian times
A great great aunt was a teacher before education was compulsory for all	Education in Victorian times (dame schools)
A great great grandfather was a navvy then a railway subcontractor. He worked in both England, on the continent and then in Australia.	Building of the railways. The notion of betterment. Mobility in Victorian times
A great grandfather, an agricultural labourer in Buckinghamshire, was recruited to the Metropolitan police force	Nineteenth-century agriculture, migration and urbanisation. Development of the police force
Several members of preceding generations in the nineteenth and twentieth centuries migrated to Canada, the United States, New Zealand and Australia	Pattern of migration in nineteenth and twentieth centuries

Both grandparents fought in the Great War, one on the western front and one in Sri Lanka	First World War
A parent's family moved from inner to outer London in the interwar period	Growth of suburbs
Father was in a reserved occupation but was an ARP officer. Grandparents' house suffered bomb damage. Uncle in the RAF	Second World War
Aunt was a missionary in Africa from 1930 to the 1960s	Legacy of Empire
Growing up in the 1950s experiencing the end of rationing, with own identity card	Impact of Second World War. Education 60 years ago
A teenager in the 1960s	Major cultural changes in post war period

A further stage might be to review the potential of the local school area in the national context. How this works for the area where we are based, Eltham, is shown in local example 6.2.

Local example 6.2 Some aspects of the history of Eltham in a national context

Eltham's local history	*Evidence*	*The national context*
Shooters Hill follows line of Roman Road	Line of current road shown on	The Roman era map
Early settlers clear land. Possible settlement	Secondary sources	Saxon era
Farming community	Domesday Book	Early Norman era
Creation of deer park and Eltham Palace. Great Hall built. Henry VIII frequents the palace	Eltham Palace Great Hall and grounds	Tudor period – Henry VIII court life and leisure pursuits
Eltham resident Ingram Friser involved in the murder of Marlowe in Deptford	Plaque in Deptford	Importance of Elizabethan playwrights
Eltham develops as a pleasant town with some wealthy inhabitants	A few buildings on high street date from this period. Daniel Defoe's writing	Links to London in seventeenth and eighteenth centuries

First Eltham station built 1866	The station	The spread of the railway and its impact
Population growth	Areas of Victorian housing	The spread of the railway and its impact
Avery Hill mansion built by 'Colonel' North	Mansion house and parkland	Victorian entrepreneurs
Well Hall (Progress) Estate built to house Arsenal workers (1920s)	The estate	First World War and its impact (Public housing)
High Street widened	Change to street line shown on maps	Extensive suburbanisation between the wars especially around London
Eltham Heights Estate built (1930s). Courtaulds build their house at Eltham Palace	The estates and the house	Extensive suburbanisation between the wars especially around London
Avery Hill Mansion damaged by bombs	Changes to the original mansion	Second World War
A2 bypass and then motorway built	The roads and their impact on street patterns	Impact of the motor car and building of motorways
Death of Stephen Lawrence	Pavement plaque	Catalyst for change in policies in public institutions

Based on Simmons (1990) and Spurgeon (1992) and on local knowledge.

Sometimes a link with other parts of the country will help to develop a wider geographical context for local history. Many are through transport. These may be roads of the Roman era; early drovers' roads; eighteenth-century turnpikes; then canals and railways. Where these routes led and how they were used can help to develop an understanding of trade and commerce. Other ways in which links may be apparent is through place names and family names. We might wonder for instance why names from County Durham are being used in Kent (Stanhope – a family name; Weardale – a place name) or why the Earl of Devonshire has property in Derbyshire.

The toolkits in chapters 2, 3, 4 and 5 will have helped to build up knowledge about the local area, but there are some specific local sources which can help in developing historical understanding in relation to aspects of local–national links. These are considered below under the headings of people, events and characteristics.

Significant people locally

Most local places produce information on their 'famous' residents, individuals of national fame whom they like to claim links with, as well as individuals of lesser significance or whose

significance has perhaps been forgotten. Local history libraries and local history societies are likely to have published and unpublished information on this. The following list (local example 6.3) is based on some of the famous people that the London Borough of Lewisham has identified. It is by no means exhaustive but hopefully throws some light on the range of individuals that even limited research may reveal in any locality.

Local example 6.3 Some significant people in Lewisham

- Edith Nesbitt, children's author who lived in Lee and Well Hall
- Joseph Paxton, gardener and architect of the Great Exhibition building and the Crystal Palace. Lived in Sydenham
- Samuel Pepys, diarist. Visited the naval dockyard at Deptford
- Sir Ernest Shackleton, Antarctic explorer who grew up in Sydenham
- Tsar Peter the Great visited Deptford to study ship building
- Marie Lloyd, music hall artiste. Lived in Lewisham
- Margaret and Rachel McMillan, pioneers in nursery education who worked in Deptford
- John Logie Baird, who developed television and worked latterly at the Crystal Palace
- Sir Francis Baring, a merchant banker who built his wealth on international trade
- Tommy Steele, the 1950/1960s rock and roll singer
- Ignatius Sancho, who was born on a slave ship in about 1729 but grew up in Blackheath and became a man of letters
- Octavia Hill, Victorian campaigner and co-founder of the National Trust who worked in Deptford

Another approach is to consider the potential local connection of significant people who form part of the existing curriculum, those with whom you are familiar or those for whom there is a richness of resources. Teaching in the local does not mean discarding these people; all of them have links with local areas in one place or another. For instance:

- the several residences and work places of Florence Nightingale provide links with Hampshire, Derbyshire and London (a less well-known link perhaps being with Hackney (Claire, 1996);
- Mary Seacole lived in London during the 1870s;
- the places visited by Queen Elizabeth I on her progresses, as well as her palaces, in and around London were in the Midlands, Sussex, Kent, East Anglia and the West Country and
- those visited by Queen Victoria included the Isle of Wight, Balmoral and Sandringham;
- the engineering projects of Brunel feature across the south and west of England and into Wales as well as various railway projects abroad;
- Brunel's nineteenth-century contemporaries, George and Robert Stephenson, also worked on railway engineering projects across the country including in the north east, around Manchester, in the Midlands, in Scotland and Wales.

Local events

Local events may be those only of immediate local concern such as the great fires outlined in local example 3.3. There are experiences such as the Second World War or the arrival of the railway, which are shared nationally. Some of these starting points will allow the study of an aspect of history in breadth and depth. For instance, the Second World War is a very rich period for local evidence and this may well allow much of what we would expect children to learn to be covered in that topic: the key chronology; evacuation; rationing; the Blitz and other aspects of life on the home front. There are many remnants that may be visible in a local area:

- street names;
- air raid shelters left as garden sheds;
- evidence of iron railings which have been removed;
- a break in a line of terraced houses with later infill housing where there was a bomb;
- painted signs to public shelters;
- memorial plaques.

In addition of course, not only will some local people have memories of wartime both locally and elsewhere, local records and archives such as photos, newspaper articles, maps of bombs dropped, the letters of evacuated children, official documents and more will be available at the local history library (see chapter 5). If this study were to be extended to cover aspects of the conflict, there might well be other starting points locally – an airfield; a seaport; coastal defences; training camps; a war memorial; links with a particular regiment; prisoner of war camps.

Another approach would be to consider a single national event such as the sinking of the *Titanic* – national in the sense that it affected the whole of the country at the time, had an ongoing impact, and has subsequently formed part of a collective 'memory bank' which resonates in a number of local areas. Local example 6.4 identifies some of these links.

Local example 6.4

Liverpool – original home of the White Star Line. The *Titanic* had originally been going to pay a courtesy call to Liverpool before her maiden voyage, but in the event did not. There is a plaque marking the offices of the White Star Line in James Street.

Belfast – the Harland and Wolff Shipyards were here. This is of course where the *Titanic* was built with some 3,000 men being employed. There is now a visitors' centre telling the *Titanic* story as it relates to Belfast.

Southampton – the *Titanic* sailed from here on her maiden voyage on 10 April 1912. There are several memorials in the city.

Cobh (Queenstown) – the *Titanic* made her last port of call in southern Ireland. Many Irish emigrants boarded here, part of the migration of six million who were seeking a new life in America. There is a trail around the town.

Bolton – the captain of the *Carpathia*, Arthur Rostron, who responded to the *Titanic*'s distress calls, was born in Bolton. There is a plaque at his birth place.

Dalbeattie – the senior officer of the *Titanic*, William McMaster Murdoch, was born here. He was on watch when the iceberg was struck and took a leading role in helping passengers into the lifeboats. There is a memorial plaque to him at the Town Hall.

Captain Smith, captain of the *Titanic*, was born in *Lichfield*, and Jack Phillips, the wireless operator, was born in *Godalming*.

(Based on Hodgman, 2012)

Other significant events such as the Gunpowder Plot, which has links in Warwickshire, London, Northumberland, York and Worcestershire, have similar local potential.

Teachers' toolkit 6.1 Identifying significant local people and events

- *Are you aware of any nationally significant people or events represented in the local area?*
- *Use web searches and local history books and material produced by the local history library or societies to supplement an awareness of local place names (see p.114).*
- *Consider 'famous' individuals and events who might well have been studied in many schools at either key stage – are there local traces?*

Characteristics

A local area can offer an insight into what it was like to live at a time in the past – historical situations. Different localities will always offer an individual flavour to this because of a variety of cultural and geographical difference (the nature of employment for instance; the amount of wealth in an area; its links with London as a generator of ideas and fashion and as the centre of power; the nature and extent of transport links). Nevertheless, there is usually enough in common for aspects of the bigger conceptual picture to be developed. Local example 6.5 shows how local enquiry can move on to making generalisations through questioning and further research.

Local example 6.5 The Wilson family

An example is provided by some mosaic plaques in a church in south east London: St Bartholomew's Church, Sydenham. The two mosaic plaques tell a fascinating family story and they provided enough information to outline family events over a thirty year period and to invite questions about the bigger story.

Sacred
To the memory of Emma
Who died 24 Nov, 1840 aged 3 days
And of Richard who died 2 Dec 1844, aged 6 days,
children of Richard and Emma Wilson
of Perry Vale

Sacred
To the memory of
Richard Wilson of
Molesworth House Brighton,
Who died 22 Sept 1869 aged 69
Also of Emma his wife who
Died at Perry Vale, Sydenham
29 Nov 1844 aged 34

These plaques would work very well with the trio of questions promoted by such primary historians as Hilary Cooper (Cooper, 2000, 2006; Turner-Bisset, 2005):

- What does this tell us for certain? What do I definitely know about this?
- What can we hypothesise from this? What reasoned guesses can I make?
- What would we like to find out? What does this source not tell me?

We have encouraged students working with these to initially draw a timeline of the events and to sketch the family tree to help understand the events and relationships. The questions generated can be both **specific**:

- Were the family rich or poor?
- Where in Perry Vale did they live?
- Was Richard the elder in Brighton when he died?
- How long had he been there? Who had the plaque placed in the church? Did they have any other children?
- Did Richard marry again?

and **general**:

- Was it typical for two babies to die in a family?
- Was it common for children to be named after their parents?

These can lead in to generalisations about life in the Victorian era, a part of the bigger picture.

In using such evidence with children, we would always argue that it is most helpful if the teacher rehearses the enquiry process during their own planning stage, identifying key questions that they think it important that the children ask, as well as some of the more obvious ones.

One of the characteristics of history is that sometimes we never do know the answers and this is perhaps one of the hardest things for young children to grasp. In the case of this evidence, the work of the children can be left as a series of questions with some facts and some hypotheses. Alternatively, with a little bit of research, additional information can help to answer some of the questions. In this case, some elementary research using the census and church records revealed the following:

Local example 6.5, continued

- the family were middle class, Richard being a merchant;
- they had married late and Emily was their first child;
- they had two other children in between Emily and Richard (meaning that in the space of four years, Emma had four children!);
- both surviving children were girls and one of them was also called Emma;
- these girls survived infancy and were living in Brighton with Richard in 1861;
- finally, the church appears to have no record as to who ordered and paid for the plaques.

The mechanics of research like this are covered in chapter 5.

In identifying links with the national picture in local examples 6.1, 6.2 and 6.5, what we have essentially been doing is building on our understanding of some of the key historical concepts: change and continuity; chronological understanding; historical situations (events, people, characteristics); cause and effect and historical evidence (see Figure 1.1 on p.18); alongside the geographical concepts such as process; interrelationships and interdependence. The links or connections are, amongst other things, about: trade; work; exploration; migration; culture; language; fashion; disease. They are about people, things and ideas. Some of these links are evidenced in the lives of the children and their families. Figure 6.1 begins to demonstrate how to identify links between the personal or local and the national.

Teaching and learning about people and events through the local

In the same way that enquiry questions form the basis of finding out about the past of a locality, so they help to form a basis for understanding about people and events. A starting point in the local is through fieldwork, the use of other primary sources or story which can help to generate such questions using activities which are highlighted throughout the book. Sites and places locally can provide useful starting points when considering individuals, events and period characteristics. Although much of this has been explored in chapter 3, we will make a few additional points here. There are places and sites across the whole of Britain which have a national or even global significance.

Change may have been part of a national trend. For instance, rural to urban migration and urbanisation which were experienced across the country.

An event may have been a *shared national experience* or a version of it, for instance the Second World War.

A local event may have had national *significance*, for instance the burning down of the Crystal Palace.

An *individual* who was born or lived in the area may have had a nationally *significant* impact, for instance Joseph Lister, who worked in Glasgow and developed the use of antiseptics in surgery.

A *feature or building* in the area may be of national *significance*, for instance the first iron bridge.

A local *feature* may be *characteristic of the period*, for instance the architectural style of local Victorian housing.

A *transport feature* – a canal or a line of Roman road – may provide evidence of trading links showing *the interrelationships* with other areas.

The economic *activities* in the local area may have national *links* through trade, for instance the movement of coal from the Tyne to the Thames.

There may be clear *causes and effects* of an event such as the growth of housing in an area following the arrival of the railway.

Figure 6.1 Personal/local: national links – helping to make the connections.

Plaques: The Blue Plaque scheme is a national one run by English Heritage. The plaques commemorate significant individuals who have lived in an area, sometimes even for a relatively short period. Some local areas have their own schemes. They are helpful indicators of an area's links with significant people.

Statues: these can commemorate events and people both of local and, more usually, national significance. Purkis (1995) claims there are more memorials to Queen Victoria than to any other person, many commemorating her jubilees. They form a useful starting point for further research and, like all traces of the past in the environment, are themselves useful evidence. The following questions could be used in exploring this evidence:

- Describe the clothes – what does this tell you about that person and their role?
- Are there any objects which provide clues about their work?
- Are there any animals and what is their significance?
- What does the inscription tell you?
    - Dates of a person's life
    - The date of an event
    - A reason the person is being commemorated

Place names: Street names and also pub names may reflect battles and national events, as well as generals, politicians, monarchs and other individuals of national significance connected with them such as Alma, Sebastopol, Balaclava (battles of the Crimean War); Coro-

nation (for instance named in 1838 or 1902); Lord Raglan; Blenheim; Nightingale; Albert; Livingstone; Gladstone and so on.

More recently settlement names have commemorated significant events and people such as Telford (the road maker); Peterlee (after the miners' leader); Waterloo (after the battle); Ironbridge (after the first iron bridge); Westward Ho! (after Charles Kingsley's book); Victoria (after Queen Victoria); Peacehaven (to commemorate the end of the First World War); Saltaire (after the industrialist Titus Salt); Bournville Port Sunlight (after Sunlight soap).

Local newspaper stories: Local and sometimes national newspapers carry local history stories which can be used. One in the *Guardian* newspaper in 2012 led to the further investigation of a story about a local school teacher who challenged the establishment by teaching Darwinism in the village school of Fishlake, East Yorkshire in 1908 (local example 6.6).

Local example 6.6

In 1908 Miss Winifred Gould taught the local children in Fishlake Endowed School about Darwin's theories of evolution. The local vicar, a trustee of the school, took exception to this and accused Miss Gould, the head of the school, of infidel teaching. In spite of a local inquiry clearing her name (on the grounds it seems that the children were too young to understand Darwinism), the vicar continued to accuse her publicly. The children were removed from the school, and had to walk to Stainforth, several miles away. Miss Gould eventually took the vicar to court and won notional damages at the Leeds Assizes.

Based on information from: http://www.guardian.co.uk/theguardian/2012/mar/14/archive-1908-teaching-darwinism-in-schools; http://www.fishlakevillage.co.uk/history.htm)

In order to start thinking about some of the ways in which personal and local might connect to the national, and to a national chronology, the questions in the following teachers' toolkit may be helpful.

Teachers' toolkit 6.2 Connecting the personal and local to the national

Based on the information gathered using the toolkits in chapters 2, 3, 4 and 5, compile a chronological list of personal/family and local history. Local examples 6.1 and 6.2 will help.

Where possible give dates.

Consider each item in relation to the following:

- *Is this person or event of national significance? Does it/he/she have an impact beyond the immediate family or local area?*

- *Are the activities of people linking with other places through trade, transport, migration etc.?*
- *Could this feature be typical of the period?*
- *Might this change be part of a bigger pattern of change?*
- *What time period does this aspect of personal/family or local history relate to? What was happening nationally at this time?*
- *Are there published books about local events and individuals?*

Narrative and story in history

Davies and Redmond (1988) have described stories as 'a cultural universal' and certainly stories are a key attribute of human culture. Bage (1999) also explores the significance of story personally and collectively as a means of organising our understanding which is fundamental to human experience. In primary education generally and history education specifically, it has long been identified as a valuable approach to teaching and learning.

Turner-Bisset (2005) discusses the way in which we organise experience, drawing on the theories of Bruner; the 'logico-scientific' and the 'narrative' modes encompass the two key approaches to history. This former approach has been extensively drawn on in the first chapters through the use of evidence as part of historical enquiry. The use of narrative can complement this and is a powerful way of engaging children and, alongside enquiry, represents key approaches in the teaching and learning of history.

In relation to history specifically, Husbands (1996) refers to the way 'narrative shapes are built into the way we think about the past'. This narrative approach to history is represented in many traditional history books for children and the narrative approach is also apparent in particular in the genre of biography. It is an approach which has the potential to explore the concept of historical interpretation and which can also contribute to the concept of chronology as well as to different aspects of historical knowledge and understanding. It can also provide a powerful stimulus to enquiry.

We tend to think of story as part of the fiction genre, and yet the term 'history' itself reminds us of the importance of narrative in the discipline. Husbands (1996) has suggested that teachers and historians have been sceptical about the role of story in history; the term narrative, even though it implies a coherent line of argument and therefore some intellectual rigour, has become linked to a form of history which conveys one version of the past to a passive audience. An interesting and classic example of history as narrative is *This Island Story* by H.E. Marshall, first published in 1905 and then republished one hundred years on. This narrative account of British history actually begins in the style of a story – 'Once upon a time there was a giant called Neptune . . .' (Marshall, 1905:1), begging the question of the fictional or otherwise nature of its contents. However, Husbands (1996) emphasises the use of story to stimulate thinking about history, a point supported by Cooper (2002) who reminds us that stories require the active imagination of children and by Turner-Bisset (2005) when she reminds us that history is a narrative based on evidence.

Both fiction and non-fiction narratives may be used in the classroom to support history learning. Non-fiction books about a significant person, a significant event, or a particular period of history would include biographies, eye-witness accounts, diaries and recounts. There have been non-fiction story books written specifically to support National Curriculum

history such as the GINN history story series for Key Stage 1 covering significant events and people. However, sometimes the most effective stories seem to be those which are not intentionally written to support history teaching, for instance those of Michael Morpurgo or Rosemary Sutcliffe and which are classed as fiction.

Such fiction books which have accurate period detail (but with fictional people) can be used. They may be written at the time being represented as in the case of Dickens's novels for instance – period fiction – or in the present period. Some crossover genres may need care in their use such as the fictionalised eye-witness accounts in the Scholastic 'My Story' series which are diaries written by fictional characters but focusing on particular events (The Crystal Palace; The Titanic; The Blitz). Picture books which are especially useful for younger children, but which should not be forgotten for older ones, feature in both the fiction and non-fiction categories.

We need to be selective in our choice of books both for ourselves and in our choice for the classroom, making a judgement about the historical accuracy just as we should be doing with reference books, including those aimed at primary children.

Reflection

- *What stories have I read, fiction or non-fiction, with an historical setting or content?*
- *As a child? An adult? A teacher?*
- *Did I consider them to be historically accurate?*
- *Did they inspire me to find out any more about an aspect of history?*

Using story in local history

For family and personal history there is a wide range of picture books focusing on children or families that can be used to help develop important concepts. In nursery and reception, these do not necessarily need to have formal history content but they might for instance chart the passage of time over a single day or explore different points of view. Stories with historical content might relate to generations (*Grandma's Bill* by Martin Waddell); to change over time or give accurate period detail (*Peepo* by the Ahlbergs).

For history of localities, the most likely relevant ingredients in a story are those of people and events. Some of these will be published as part of a series but it is always surprising how through the initiative of local authors, museums or even school-based projects books about local individuals have been written and published (see resources list). Collicott (1993) looks at stories which have a local setting and global links. She herself has researched and written these stories. They require commitment and time for research, but can provide material for significant schemes of work.

Story as a pedagogical approach

Turner-Bisset (2005) explores the use of story as a powerful approach to teaching where our need to know what happens next draws us in and engages us. This aspect is explored in further detail by other writers such as Cox and Hughes (1998), Fines and Nichol (1997),

Vass (2000) and Farmer and Cooper (1998) in their discussions of the importance of narrative to our historical thinking and of its centrality to our history teaching. Between them they explore a range of reasons for and advantages of using story:

- engages children and is memorable;
- flexible in the depth in which they can be used;
- has potential for linking with other resources;
- can introduce difficult concepts and issues;
- helps to link the past to the present through children's own experiences;
- creates an historical context within which historical vocabulary is used;
- provides a framework for developing chronological understanding through the sequencing of key events;
- provides a framework for exploring cause and effect, and human emotion and motivation;
- can generate curiosity and thence lead to enquiry questions;
- can help young children understand in particular about the distant past.

Alongside these advantages, the above writers and also Husbands (1996) emphasise that storytelling can put the narrative and therefore the control in the hands of the teacher.

A story offers an interpretation of history and not only has the author selected the information of the events to be included, but also both the way these are put together and the manner of the telling contribute to creating a particular version of history – an historical interpretation. As Vass (2000) points out, because powerful emotions can be raised by storytelling we need to be particularly careful about how those stories are used. He suggests that effective use of story in teaching to develop historical knowledge and understanding needs to involve discussion, careful consideration and analysis to help shed light on the past. He is persuasive in asserting that even young children should be encouraged to think about what parts of a story might be true.

Reflection

- *To what extent is narrative/story being used to support the teaching of history in your school?*
- *Is this true for all age groups or just for younger children?*
- *How are these chosen? Is historical accuracy an issue?*

For short stories a basic introductory sequence might start with a simple reading of the story to the class. In doing this you will rely on a number of storytelling skills – sitting so that all the children can see you and also the pictures if relevant; varying voice tone, volume and pitch; giving characters distinctive voices; reading the book and looking at the children at the same time; using pauses effectively, for instance, for dramatic effect. This might then be reinforced by doing one or two of the following: reading in sections; using a story bag of relevant artefacts or additional pictures; allowing children to listen to a taped version; reading with interaction using questions which encourage observation, comparison, association,

understanding of time, imagination and curiosity; encouraging children to retell the story to each other, for instance with their talk partners.

These techniques give opportunities to engage children's interest in the story, helping them understand the basic elements and events and helping them to remember the key points. Fundamentally, in order to build on the story to develop historical knowledge and understanding, children need to have a basic familiarity with it. Follow-up activities will depend on the nature of the story, the role the story has in the overall unit of work and the specific learning intentions. In the following suggestions, reference has been made to the story 'Peepo' to exemplify the activities:

1. To develop chronological understanding – place the events in the story in sequence using pictures or captions. Space the pictures according to the time intervals involved. Children could be asked to represent the story in a specified number of pictures, each with a title. In the example of 'Peepo', the events in the story take place across a single day.
2. To help understand why people did what they did – discuss why individuals acted in a certain way then use speech balloons linked to pictures to indicate actions. Select pictures which might represent why someone did something. Use a sorting activity to identify likely and unlikely reasons for an event. In 'Peepo', we might consider how the family has been affected by the war.
3. To develop historical understanding – look for similarities and differences with the present day (for example clothes, artefacts). Record in a simple table. Any of the rooms in the house represented in the illustrations of 'Peepo' could be compared to one in the present day.
4. To help understand different viewpoints – identify any bias in the story, for instance through the use of positive or negative adjectives for particular characters. Identify fact and opinion in the story and discuss what they think is 'true'. Discuss the story from two different points of view. Individual children can retell the story with a set number of pictures and compare their 'version' with someone else's. The events of the day in 'Peepo' could be discussed from the perspective of the child and the mother who share some experiences but also do different things.
5. To initiate historical enquiry – generate or respond to questions for further research. Hot seating could be used. Cross-check the reliability of historical information. One of the characters in 'Peepo' – father, mother, grandmother or child – could be hot seated.
6. To develop enquiry skills – children identify clues in pictures or text which help them to decide if it is set in the past (or for older children, when in the past). Use the clues in the pictures which help them to find out more about the past. 'Peepo', as well as providing lots of clues that it is set in the past, has a specific setting in the Second World War which could be identified by older children through the evidence in the picture.
7. To develop communication skills – make a display using elements from the story chosen by the children as a starting point. For 'Peepo' a display could be structured around a timeline.

The sorting activity referred to in the first and second activities above represents one version of a very helpful generic activity which can be used in history to develop understanding. It works particularly well in following on from a story, but could also follow a video or teacher exposition. In these activities children work in groups to facilitate discussion and

are given a set of cards which have to be sorted in a particular way. The strengths of such an activity are not only the discussion it facilitates but also the freedom from writing, and the ease with which a change of mind can be enacted. Sorting might involve:

- putting cards into chronological order. This can be extended to involve the positioning of a key event so that in effect cause and consequence are becoming apparent;
- categorising reasons for an action as 'likely' or 'unlikely' and 'short term' or 'long term'; 'cause' and 'consequence'. In such sorting activities, it is always useful to have a 'uncertain' category, and to have some cards for which it is easy for children of all abilities to make a decision, and others which are likely to promote discussion;
- ranking to show level of significance, for instance the importance of reasons for an event; the degree of difference;
- Sorting into fact and opinion.

This activity should always be modelled first. It is easy to differentiate, for instance by varying the number or difficulty of the cards given or by allowing children to add their own cards.

The national to local perspective

We referred above to the need to develop chronological understanding by linking the personal and local with a national framework. Of course there is not one agreed national chronology in terms of content and any produced in connection with the National Curriculum for history are bound to be controversial. It is something neither historians nor politicians are likely to agree on. However, for the beginner historian, starting with their immediate and own chronological frame of reference is useful. The development of chronological understanding at a national level is developed further.

Next steps

In the next chapter, we explore the concept of chronology which is fundamental in helping to form a framework for the bigger picture. We also look at the developing overview of history which children will need as they progress in their understanding of key concepts such as cause and consequence, historical significance, and change. It can be read as a stand-alone chapter, although it links well with both this chapter and the one which follows – also about the bigger picture.

Useful websites and resources

National level resources which can be used for research to develop local knowledge:

List for famous significant people commemorated through the blue plaque scheme: http://www.plaquesoflondon.co.uk/

And a list of the different plaque schemes across England: http://www.english-heritage.org.uk/content/imported-docs/p-t/plaques-register.pdf

For significant people elsewhere in the UK: http://www.historic-scotland.gov.uk/index/places/commemorativeplaques.htm

http://www.ulsterhistory.co.uk/plaques.htm

100 Places That Made Britain, by David Musgrove, BBC Books (2011)
Landmarks of Britain, by Clive Aslet, Hodder & Stoughton (2005) lists 500 places of significance across Britain from earliest times to the present day and geographically from Cornwall to the Orkneys. It provides such delights as the place where tea may have first been served in 1658.
Local Heroines: A Travel Guide to Women's History in Great Britain, by Jane Legget, Pandora (1994)
The Classical Music Map of Britain, by Richard Fawkes, Elliot and Thompson (2010)
Ian Dawson's ideas on his thinkinghistory website: http://www.thinkinghistory.co.uk

Local stories

A few examples of stories which have been published locally for significant people:

Some True Stories of Mary Anning, by Jo Draper, Lyme Regis Museum
Thomas Coram, The Man Who Saved Children, by Harriet Amos and Alice Mayers, The Foundling Museum, London
William Brookes and the Olympic Games; *Eglantyne Jebb Saves the Children*; and *Charles Darwin*, all by Dorothy Nicolle, Blue Hills Press, Wem, Shropshire

Chapter 7

A chronological interlude

Time and time again

Introduction

This chapter is here in recognition of the important role of chronological understanding in history, in response to the weaknesses apparent in children's understanding of time (Ofsted, 2011), and with awareness of the increasing emphasis being put on children having a chronological framework. In chapter 4 we began to explore ways of developing a child's understanding of the recent past, in particular their own life and the lives of adults around them. In this chapter we will explore further the development of historical time and extend our consideration of time into the more distant past. As well as making reference to current understanding through research on this issue, there are practical suggestions for teaching chronology.

Chapter objectives

By the end of this chapter you should:

- have developed an understanding of the importance of chronological understanding to the subject as a whole;
- have started to think about a chronological framework;
- be familiar with a range of strategies to develop children's chronological understanding.

Chronological understanding

> I know what time is, but if a man asks me what it is, I cannot tell him.
>
> (St Augustine, quoted in Low-Beer, 1991)

The importance of a chronological framework for the understanding of history is accepted by most primary historians; it is seen as being of fundamental importance to the subject and is widely recognised as one of its key concepts. 'Chronology . . . provides a mental framework or map which gives significance and coherence to the study of history' (DES, 1991:9). At one level such a framework can be a mechanistic scheme populated by dates which have little real significance for the individual. At another level a chronological

framework can support a real understanding of change and continuity; of cause and effect; of historical situations; significant events and people. Through such a framework an individual's current learning can fit into the bigger historical picture and how it relates to 'today'. Cooper (2012) identifies asking questions about change and time as being central not only to historical enquiry but also to historical understanding. She also comments on the possibility that an understanding of time and chronology can help children's developing sense of identity by helping to place them in a temporal and cultural context and by helping them to form relationships with their families and then with wider groups so we can see its significance in wider terms.

A chronological framework can develop over time with the benefit of teaching, through regular use and reference to this structured overview and through a growing awareness of the significance and value of such a device. Our personal experiences suggest that the more active the use made of a chronological framework, the more real value it has. It is also important to recognise that the longer an individual has lived, the more depth and breadth a chronological framework has; having lived at least half a century somehow makes a considerable difference to an appreciation of the passing of time at both a personal and an intellectual level! This 'length of life lived' element is of course outside our control, but does serve to highlight the nature of the challenge in helping children to develop an understanding of historical time at a comparatively young age with so few years 'under their belts'.

It is quite a challenge also, given that time is an enormous and complex concept, one which Hoodless has described as a 'many-faceted notion' rather than a single concept (1996:8). Time has a range of significances in different cultures and in different academic traditions. Some aspects of the measurement of time are linked to astronomical phenomena (the circulation of the earth around the sun); others are arbitrary (the length of an hour). The points from which time is counted (which 'bit' of time is 1 AD; which 'bit' of time is 1 January) is certainly arbitrary. Additionally, Hodkinson (2003) has argued that we have not perhaps been helped in the challenge of developing children's chronological understanding through the framework provided by the National Curriculum 2000 and the QCA schemes of work where the learning tasks, vocabulary and use of resources are 'vague and inconsistent'.

Given these issues it is perhaps not surprising that in successive Ofsted reports on history in schools including the most recent (Ofsted, 2011) chronological understanding features as a concern. Hoodless (2002) has suggested that there have been concerns over the teaching of chronological understanding since the late 1970s. Pupils are seen as having a weakness in understanding the overarching historical narrative; their chronological understanding is fragmented and there is a lack of a coherent chronological framework. Teachers seem to find it difficult to establish a clear mental map of the past for their pupils. Ofsted sees this in part, like Hodkinson, as being the result of the fragmented nature of the National Curriculum, but also being about teachers' lack of expertise. Nevertheless, a key recommendation of the report is thus that primary schools need to focus on developing chronological understanding and so there would seem to be a related issue of teachers' chronological understanding. Nor is this just an issue in schools; Lowenthal comments that,

> Even in modern book learning societies, the past for most people is largely chaotic and episodic, a hodgepodge of chronologically unknown or mistakenly connected figures and events. In this heaving and formless sea stand a few islands of stratified narrative, on which we huddle for calendric security.
>
> (1985:220)

In addition, Clare (2006) maintains we never do 'get a handle' on time. This suggests how hard establishing this framework is for the non-specialist primary teacher.

Ofsted have commented that a lack of continuity is a problem in developing historical thinking (2011) and in regard to this the locality has an advantage: the local as a context can provide continuity. It can be a familiar and recurring reference point as a chronological framework is developed.

Fortunately, perhaps, of all historical concepts chronological understanding is the one which seems to have been most researched and is one for which there is an increasing amount of practical guidance. In fact the teaching and learning of chronology could occupy a whole book in itself and we must be content to summarise much of what is known and to refer the reader to some particularly useful sources.

From research the following key points emerge about children's understanding of time:

- The concept of time develops with memory and language.
- On balance there is a view that teaching in chronological order is not necessarily important.
- We need to be careful about the use of subjective terms such as 'a long time ago' and 'old'.
- Young children distinguish more easily between the distant past (as opposed to the recent past) and the present. This does not imply of course that the recent past should not be used in the teaching of history, but that to help children to learn how to sequence, bigger intervals between the material used is most helpful.
- Children's chronological understanding develops at very different rates and is not age related. Retention of knowledge, on which chronological understanding must depend, does seem to be related amongst other things to mathematical and reading abilities.

(Barton, 2000; Hodkinson, 2002, 2003; Cooper, 2012)

Babies exist solely in the present and a sense of the past and the future emerges only slowly over the first years of life. Even at the point where a child has some understanding of past and present, this past is chaotic (Wood, 1995). Another way of thinking about this is that the schema held for the past by young children is initially undifferentiated; it has no depth and structure. By schema we refer to a mental structure of existing ideas, a framework of understanding that represents some aspect of the world. We can support the emergence of the schema through helping to develop a child's memory and the repeated use of appropriate language.

The role of timelines

In order to comprehend and manage the concept of time, we resort to the use of metaphors, and the commonly used one is that of distance. Distance is used as a means of expressing the length of time where length is usually used as a substitute for duration. We use some of the same general words for both time and distance – short and long for instance, and we refer to different scales. In a visual form, this is shown as a timeline. A line, straight or otherwise, is used to show the relationship between events in time – sequencing, intervals, duration. The past is conventionally shown on the left-hand side of a straight horizontal timeline, perhaps because of the direction in which Western cultures read and write, and at the bottom when using a vertical system, perhaps because of the link to archaeology.

Maddison (2011) stresses the importance of teachers placing as much emphasis on duration of events and the interval between them as on sequence when using timelines. These are two of the three key aspects of historical time which we need to be aware of when teaching

history; the order in which things have happened (sequencing); how long things have lasted (duration); and contemporaneity (a sense of period). To this some writers add a sense of historical perspective, i.e. a sequencing of the periods over a long length of time.

Timelines can be constructed by going back in time from the present (a retrograph) or by working forwards from a point. Retrographs are particularly useful in building up an initial understanding of a new aspect of chronology – where this part of the past is in relation to now – and is one way in which timelines can build on prior knowledge. Levstik and Barton stress the importance of relating new time-related information to existing knowledge (2011).

It is important in terms of developing an overall chronological framework that timelines are used not only to help understand the period being studied, but also to help to fit this into the broader chronological context. The use of a whole school timeline showing all the periods being studied is important for Key Stage 2 children in particular. Different versions can then be available for them to refer to in the classroom. Of necessity, where a very long period of time needs to be shown, the scale of the timeline will be very small, or there may need to be a change of scale so that the more recent two thousand years is on a larger scale than the earlier periods.

Hodkinson (2009) has stressed the need to use a variety of different multi-sensory approaches to teaching chronology and the idea of creating human timelines with children fits particularly well with this (Dawson, 2013). Dawson's ideas, although requiring quite a lot of practical preparation and needing much space, are engaging and interactive and will work on a number of time scales – for the creation of a two thousand year line, or part of the twentieth century, as in the case of local example 7.1. They can also help with the understanding of BC and AD, with the numbering of the centuries, and with the overlapping of historical periods such as the Romans with the Saxons.

Local example 7.1

The personal can be used to develop a chronology back to the start of Victorian times in five generations as recommended by Dawson (2010). It takes only five generations in my family. The information can be used to create a human timeline with children taking the part of the family members. The use of photos would bring this to life further. This also highlights some national and wider geographical links.

<table>
<tr><th>1819</th><th>1822–1903</th><th>1855–1936</th><th>1881–1962</th><th>1910–1998</th><th>1949–</th><th>2013</th><th>Years</th></tr>
<tr><td rowspan="3">Birth of Queen Victoria</td><td>Great great grandfather William</td><td>Great grandma Wise</td><td>My nana, Edith</td><td>My mother Nora</td><td>My birth</td><td rowspan="3">NOW</td><td>Person</td></tr>
<tr><td>Buckinghamshire</td><td>Italy</td><td>Bermondsey</td><td>Thornton Heath</td><td>Newcastle</td><td>Place of birth</td></tr>
<tr><td>A bigamist who began as a railway navvy and became an Inspector of railways in Australia</td><td>Brought up 5 children with little support</td><td>Did her husband's job as travelling rep. during the Great War</td><td>Met my father on a walking holiday in the Lakes and left her London roots when she married</td><td>Grew up in Newcastle but moved to London to work</td><td>Personal</td></tr>
</table>

For work in the local area we suggest that a local timeline is developed to which is added national chronological reference points.

Task

The activity is based on one undertaken by our undergraduate students to chart a timeline of their own lives, alongside which they subsequently develop a local history and a national history timeline.

- *Chart your own timeline using about ten key points. Parallel to this add in a number of national and international events working initially from memory. If you can extend the personal line back in time to involve aspects of your family history then do so, complementing this with appropriate wider events. You may be covering aspects of the last one or even two hundred years.*
- *Can you identify conventional time periods on this?*
- *Figure 7.1 on p.129 will remind you of some familiar periods if needed.*

The use of dates

Dates are simply the numbers with which we are counting the years from an agreed starting point. Fines refers to them as 'fixed points around which we may weave our understanding of motivation, cause and consequence' (2011:7). They provide a shared means of understanding when in time something took place and they can help us to understand sequence and duration. However, chronological understanding does not spontaneously come about merely because events are taught with the use of dates and in date order (Dawson, 2011).

Our structuring of time using dates is governed by our system of numbers using base ten, that is we make use of decades, centuries and millennia in order to help us understand the passing of time and the characteristics of periods, even though this is an artificial construct. Furthermore, our division of time into BC (or BCE – Before the Common Era) and AD (or CE the Common Era) is determined by the Christian tradition. The use of these conventions helps us to impose a pattern on the passage of time and what has happened in the past and thus aids our understanding, but they are constructs and not absolutes.

Learners need to know dates in order to help build up points of reference. Barton (2000) has concluded from his research that there is no reason *not* to refer to dates with young children, as they know what they are and what they sound like from daily use at school if nowhere else. However, we do need to acknowledge that the ability to completely understand the full significance of dates (as opposed to knowing dates by rote) is dependent on children having a certain level of mathematical understanding; for instance to be able to work with numbers in the hundreds and thousands – adding, subtracting, counting forward and backwards – to understand the different ways of saying these numbers; and then to be able to work with negative numbers.

Fines (2011), like Cooper, stresses the importance of questioning in order to help children develop their understanding when using dates around sequencing and duration, and also to help understand the significance of time for the people in the period.

Sense of period

Developing a sense of period is about helping children to understand what a particular period was like – what might, for instance, differentiate the Victorian era from the Georgian. According to Fines (2011), this should also include not just what this period was like, but also what came before and what came after. Whilst, as adults, we may query the suitability and fixed nature of time periods which are be defined by the reigning dynasty, we believe in practice this can be a helpful device for helping young children to structure time. Towards the top end of Key Stage 2 it may be helpful to use a wider range of terminology and to know that there are different periods which may overlap (for instance the Saxon period overlaps with both the Roman and the Viking eras and the Victorian period overlaps with the Industrial Revolution). In terms of teaching and learning activities, sorting artefacts or pictures into different time periods is a useful group activity, while using anachronisms can be a fun approach. Anachronisms are literally things which are out of period – usually a modern item erroneously placed in an historical context.

Time future

In chapter 4 we suggested that developing children's understanding of the future can help to develop their chronological understanding. Not only could older children think about this in relation to their own lives, they can also begin to think of future generations. A useful activity linking past and present is to bury a time capsule containing items from the local area, present and the past, and to include a message for future residents. The following case study provides another approach to linking past, present and future.

Case study 7.1 Past, present and future in a local park

A class of children in west London undertook a project on their local park with the support of their local urban studies centre. The project began with some extensive work on the park as it is today. This work included mental mapping the park to show what they knew of the park already and then some in-depth interviews of the workers in the park. The pupils were then set the task of identifying a location for an ecological area drawing on the environmental work they had done previously. They shared their ideas with the council's conservation officer who in turn shared with them the plans for the park. The children were able to monitor the progress of change in the park and were themselves involved in the planting of trees.

Work on the history of the park then built on the children's extensive knowledge of the geography of the park and in particular on an awareness of the fact that the park was constantly changing. They were able to produce an extensive list of the changes they already knew of and this awareness of change provided an important foundation for looking at historic change which they did by first comparing a map of 1863 with one of the present day. They followed this up by taking photos of the park to put alongside a number of historic photos obtained from the local history library. The children came up with their own questions about past events in the park which they were able to answer by examining documents at the library as well as by drawing

on prior learning, for instance from talking to the park workers and to members of the public in the earlier part of the project.

The children then worked on a number of ways of presenting this information to members of the public with an exhibition and slide show marking the park's centenary. One of the strengths of the work was the development of the children's chronological understanding; one of them commented that in fifty years' time she would be able to tell her children that she had helped to create the ecological area they were looking at.

Duration

In identifying duration, timelines can be visually helpful. In order to help provide structure for a timeline, we recommend the use of colour and different numerals (larger, bolder) to emphasise the ten- and hundred-year divisions, and the named periods. This distinctive notation can be helpful in highlighting length of time.

Helping children to link past, present and future as discussed in chapter 4 is also important and the following case study helps to highlight how well these can work together in a locally focused history and geography project.

The use of terminology

Terms relating to the passing of time need to be used in conjunction with dates and alongside the use of timelines. They should be used consistently both by an individual teacher and also across a school. Particular care is needed in using terms such as 'a long time ago'. As children get older 'a long time ago' will change in meaning, for instance, and adults will also use it to denote different lengths of time. It may be helpful to use an additional descriptor such as 'before you or your parent was born'. Time-related vocabulary relates to the duration of time and also to the labelling of periods of time, which may be in an unspecific way (such as 'the past') or in a specific way (such as 'the Victorian era'). Figure 7.1 gives a selection of useful time-related vocabulary. The terms related to period may be helpful in beginning to build a chronological framework. These have been selected because they seem to be the ones most commonly used with Key Stage 2 children and are more familiar to the non-specialist.

Enquiry and developing chronological understanding

Within all activities focusing on developing chronological understanding, the use of questions is vital. Figure 7.2 outlines a range of questions that can be used in conjunction with the three aspects of chronology we have been discussing.

Summary

The following key points summarise our advice in helping to develop children's sense of time:

When in time
Past/present/future Then/now A long time ago/recently Yesterday/today/tomorrow Last/this/next week/month/year Later than/earlier than Before/after When (I was born/you were little/Queen Victoria was on the throne) BC/AD
Duration
Day/week/month/year Decade/century/millennium Period Era Generation Lifetime
Period names (These are ones which have been commonly used in primary education)
Stone/Bronze/Iron Age Celtic Invaders and settlers = Roman/Saxon/Viking Norman Medieval Tudor Stuart Georgian Victorian Edwardian Windsor
In relation to artefacts etc.
Old/new Ancient/modern Antique/recent Aged Obsolete Old fashioned Out of date

Figure 7.1 Time-related vocabulary.

- Relate time to the children themselves – their lives and the lives of people they know; their own current knowledge; their immediate surroundings – using timelines and key vocabulary, and family structure;
- Help children to understand there are patterns of time;
- Use the tangible and visible – artefacts, site visits, museums, fieldwork;
- Make regular use of timelines through both display and interaction during lessons; These should show both the specific period being studied and the overview linking across periods. A range of different scales, styles and approaches should be used;
- Use narrative accounts and discuss the sequencing of events;
- Encourage thinking about on-going change and about the future, making use of cross-curricular links to geography;

Sequence

- When did this happen?
- Where does it fit in with other things we know about?
- How does it relate to us?
- Which came first?
- Could these two historical people have met each other?
- Could your parent have met this historic person?
- Which event is the more recent?

Duration

- How long did that event last?
- Which of these events lasted the longest?
- How many generations did that last?
- How long was that artefact in use for?
- What was the interval between these two events?
- Was that longer than your/your parents' lifetime?

Sense of period

- What were the dates of this period?
- What would you have seen? (What did people wear? What was the environment like? How did they spend their leisure time? What work did people do?)
- What technology did people have? (How did they make things? What household objects were there? How were their houses made?)
- What did they know?
- What were their beliefs, values and attitudes?
- Who lived then? What happened then?
- What happened before/after this period?
- How was this period similar to (or different from) that period?
- What was so special or distinctive about this period?

Figure 7.2 Questions to help develop children's chronological understanding.

- Encourage children to explain their decisions about chronological order, for instance when sequencing, dating;
- Help develop children's memories both generally and specifically related to history including the use of dates. Consider the use of rhymes and music to aid memory. Use quizzes;
- Use appropriate language on a systematic and regular basis starting in Key Stage 1, ensuring there is some agreement among staff to avoid vague and subjective terms such as 'long ago' being used;
- Encourage an awareness of the duration of time, for instance by relating this to children's experiences.

(Adapted from Stow and Haydn, 2000)

But finally, and perhaps most important of all, time and chronology need to be taught, retaught and reinforced on a regular basis (Hodkinson, 2011b; Dawson, 2013). The teaching of chronology should be a constant feature of the teaching of history and should be

taught in a sustained way. Cross-curricular opportunities can be taken to work on sequencing or dates in maths sessions, or to explore time-related vocabulary in literacy. Short activities can be used on an informal or 'drip feed' basis, for instance using five minutes for a quiz; discussing briefly a 'this day in history' event (for instance taking ideas from the BBC website) once a week; adding an event to the class timeline.

Next steps

In the following chapter we return to the geographical context which was explored at the national level in chapter 6. We are broadening out the local through the web of connections with the wider world which seem present even in the remotest of areas.

Further reading

Time and Timelines in the Primary School, by Pat Hoodless, London: Historical Association (1996)

Primary History, Issue 59, Autumn 2011 is devoted to chronology including an article on developing chronological understanding on a local history study. It also contains a table showing expectations of chronological understanding for older primary children by Hilary Cooper

'Planning for chronological understanding', by Alan Hodkinson, *Primary History*, Autumn 2009, pp. 17–19

Research on chronological understanding is well summarised by Stow and Haydn in 'Issues in the teaching of chronology', *Issues in History Teaching*, edited by Arthur and Phillips (2000)

Useful websites and resources

Activity ideas

Videos featuring classroom activities can be accessed at http://www.teachersmedia.co.uk/videos (KS2 History – Teaching Chronology; KS1/2 History – Time and Place; KS2 history – Chronology Workshop; KS1/2 History – What's in it for you) or via the TES resources website

Ian Dawson's website has many practical suggestions for chronology (as well as other aspects of history): http://www.thinkinghistory.co.uk/Issues/IssueChronology.html

The archived website of QCA gives many ideas on chronological understanding: http://webarchive.nationalarchives.gov.uk/20080520144420/http://www.qca.org.uk/history/innovating/improving_learning/chronological_ks12/index.htm

Developing your own national chronological framework

The BBC website is useful in developing a framework and providing definitions: http://www.bbc.co.uk/history/british/launch_tl_british.shtml or that of Woodlands School: http://www.chiddingstone.kent.sch.uk/homework/timeline.html

Chapter 8

Local–global links

And on to the wider world

Introduction

This chapter is based on a number of key assumptions. First, that most local areas have historical links not only at a national level, but also at an international one. Beginning with the local should not mean ending with the local. Second, that children's knowledge and understanding of the wider world can be deepened through having a greater awareness of themselves (Bage, 1999): primarily through their local roots and community and then by making links and connections to both the national and global dimensions. Third, that all children, in any location, have 'a history' and recognising that those histories are important in the global context will promote both inclusion in history and an inclusive history. We have included heritage in this chapter because we wish to acknowledge its importance in local and international perspectives as well as the more obvious national.

Chapter objectives

By the end of this chapter you should:

- understand the links between the local and the global in history;
- be able to relate this perspective to your own local area;
- have an understanding of how those links may be revealed by evidence in the local area.

Going beyond the local and the national

In chapter 6, we focused on the national dimension. This reflects the change in emphasis in school history in England which has become more explicitly focused on national British history and its chronology. However, we believe, for a variety of reasons, that it is not possible to consider British history in primary education as if the group of islands off the north west coast of the continent of Europe (the British Isles) existed somehow in isolation from the rest of the world. The history we teach in schools needs to have an international dimension, an awareness of global links.

The first reasons are to do with history itself. The history of Britain is linked geographically, socially and economically into the wider world and it is difficult to make sense of British

history without a sense of those links (Collicott, 1990a). These links are about ideas, cultures and commodities and have come about through exploration, trade, conquest, migration and colonisation. Britain is interconnected with the world and has been so for all its history, sometimes at the instigation of its inhabitants, sometimes at the instigation of people from elsewhere. As Collicott (1990b) has pointed out, engaging in trade and conquest has established Britain in a two-way movement of people and ideas and this is exemplified in a range of physical, social, cultural and economic ways.

Furthermore, our involvement in and with places around the globe has meant that those places have had an impact on us (Visram, 1994). The understanding of interrelationships is as important a concept in history as it is in geography and present day interrelationships can only be fully understood in the context of the interrelationships of the past. These ongoing relationships continue to impact both on British people and on people in other countries. Our outlook is to acknowledge the importance of a global perspective, even when the main focus remains the local/national.

These links have resulted, through the movement of people, in Britain having a diverse population and this diversity has its roots at least as far back as the Roman period. Indeed as Fryer has reminded us, 'There were Africans in Britain before the English came here' (1984:85). The movement of people both into and out of the country has been significant and it is as important to talk of a diverse past as much as it is of a diverse present. We believe, like Collicott (1990a) and Claire (1996), that it is important that children understand this cultural diversity as well as the global links.

From an educational perspective, we believe understanding the diversity represented by British history is relevant to all children. It has a specific role in relation to inclusion and identity in situations where a school has a diverse population, ensuring that all children see history as being relevant to themselves. Where a local school community is not apparently diverse, there may still be family links with places near (Ireland, Sweden) and far (Australia, South Africa).

The global links are important not only at a national level; local communities have rarely been completely isolated and have been involved in such links. Histories do therefore involve an awareness of both the local and the global (Tosh, 2010). We might think, for example, of how international warfare might generate the need for ships and therefore for more materials with which to build them, leading to an impact on areas supplying timber, as happened, for instance, to the Tudor dockyards at the time of the Armada. We might think about how the plague arrived at Eyam in a basket of linen from London and further afield. Some of these links have left more tangible evidence.

A number of writers explore the links of Britain in terms of local–global links. Collicott (1990a and 1993) refers to local stories in a wider context and uses examples to show a perspective that is about starting from a locality and seeing the wider connections and relationships. In her local area, Haringey, Collicott (1990a) identified a range of physical features giving an indication of the nature of the physical evidence of these connections: Dutch gables and Indian domes in local buildings; numerals linked to Arabic culture; the paisley pattern – originally an Indian motif; a range of foods from around the globe. This approach is also advocated by Levstik and Barton (2011) who see the importance of the global connections of both the local and the national. These local connections are not only important in terms of local history and Collicott (1990a) reminds us that local evidence can add information to the national story that is not apparent from other evidence.

It can be easy to be unaware of the significance of the links we have with places around the globe, and sometimes a significant change of perspective at a personal, subject or institutional level is required. Within the domain of local history there is some growing awareness of, for instance, the history of ethnic communities and migration. However, while this has been acknowledged by some local historians such as Killingray (2011), it has also not been recognised by others. At a personal level, it was not until black history began to receive a higher profile, many years after our own primary and secondary education, that we began to understand some different perspectives on British history. At an institutional level, an example of changing perspectives was provided by the Museum of London when it was curating its 'Peopling of London' exhibition in the early 1990s. It had initially seemed that there was little material in the museum's collection which was relevant. However, it was quickly realised that this was not the case and that it was a question of cutting across the existing categories into which artefacts had been placed in order to find the relevant artefacts. The resulting exhibition charted Britain's links with other areas from earliest historical times (Merriman, 1993). When Britain was connected to mainland Europe, groups of people were able to move north and west easily across what is now the continental land mass, coming from as far away as the Mediterranean and the Middle East. Even after separation from the rest of the continent occurred about 8,000 years ago migration is believed to have continued, and for the period before the arrival of the Romans, there is evidence in Britain of the influence of ideas and of trade with other areas.

So, people with diverse cultures, beliefs and ethnicities have been coming here since the beginning of recorded time and before, and perhaps we might argue as Frow (1996) has that everyone who lives in Britain today is either an immigrant or descended from one. More recently, over the last millennium people have come to this country for a whole range of reasons: as slaves or as servants; as refugees (religious, political, because of war or famine); for economic advancement; as settlers and as invaders. They have come in response to varying push and pull factors, sometimes being actively encouraged, sometimes received begrudgingly, some fleeing from physical danger or from persecution; others have come offering their labour or their skills or for marriage.

Immigration is not the only process through which links have become established. Another is exploration motivated by the search for new lands to colonise, or for commodities to trade. In British history, this has been in evidence since early Tudor times and later led to the development of the British Empire with the imprint of British rule and cultural influence around the globe which remains today. The trading links forged through settlement and commerce impacted in turn on industry, commerce and settlements in Britain.

The movement of people from the British Isles to other parts of the world has continued in different periods. After the initial periods of colonisation some emigration has occurred in 'waves'. For instance there were intensive periods of migration during the Highland Clearances of the eighteenth century and the potato famine in Ireland during the nineteenth century. In the post-war period, emigration has continued although it was not necessarily so area-specific in place of origin, encouraged for instance by the subsidised fares to Australia in the 1960s. Links with other places have also been reinforced through travel, missionary work and exploration especially in the nineteenth and twentieth centuries.

Britain's history is inextricably linked with places around the world and as Claire (1996) points out, it is indeed difficult to make sense of its history without having some understanding of what was happening elsewhere. However, learning about the history of the world only through a British lens is unlikely to contribute to global understanding. It is important therefore that at least some different perspectives from around the globe are understood.

> One of the defining features of Britain lies in its relationship to the rest of the world and in this sense to learn about Britain's past is to learn much about the world, but we need more than a British perspective if we are to develop for a world of global interdependence.
>
> (Kitson and Husbands, 2011:153)

The geography of the wider world

In considering how this wider world dimension can be included in our approach which starts with the local, we will revisit some of the approaches of the evidence-based chapters 2 to 5, and also consider other approaches. The most important point, however, is that the wider world perspective needs to be made explicit. It is not enough merely to mention places around the world in passing nor just to refer to other countries casually without further explanation. It is essential that location should be discussed and that maps should be used to show the places being spoken of and their location in relation to the British Isles and elsewhere.

- In what direction are they?
- What other places are they near?
- How many miles away?
- How might people have travelled from or to there? How long might that have taken?
- Are they across sea or land and sea?
- Were there established routes that were used?
- How easy was the journey?
- Might their climate and physical environment be very different?

At this scale, as at the local, maps are invaluable to the historian, both historical maps – what was the known world at the time – and present day maps. They can help to show for instance places involved in historical events such as the Armada; trade routes during the time of the Roman Empire; the route of Drake when he circumnavigated the world; the journeys of Mary Seacole in and around the Caribbean, from the Caribbean to Britain and on to the Crimea. Many of these links are best understood with the additional use of globes which help to ensure we understand the actual spatial relationship between places.

Heritage

The term 'heritage' used in conjunction with the pronoun 'our' provides a powerful phrase which can 'press many buttons' for us as citizens. It has so many emotive and value-laden associations that it is difficult to use it in a neutral way. Indeed the Working Group of the original National Curriculum deliberately avoided it (DES and the Welsh Office, 1990), suggesting instead the term 'inheritance'. Historians tend to use the word carefully, seeing the complexity of a term which is linked to theme parks, historic houses and sites, television programmes, reconstructions and even retailing (Bage, 2000) as well as natural heritage such as National Parks and nature reserves (Grigg and Hughes, 2013). Lowenthal (1985)

suggests that heritage is something which is appreciated about the past and we can perhaps consider that this could be at the international, national, local and even personal levels.

The plethora of possible heritages is acknowledged by Lowenthal who states that 'No wonder heritage takes forms so diverse as to seem incommensurable' (1985:37). Heritage has now generated its own industry which plays an important part in our economy and Bage (2000) suggests it is the main way in which people in industrialised nations now experience the past. If that is the case then it is likely to be one of the ways in which at least some children are also increasingly experiencing the past. That we have an emotional and sometimes irrational relationship with the past is illustrated in Lowenthal's comment that: 'relics (of the past) once abandoned may become more treasured than those which have continued in use' (Lowenthal, 1985:240); we value what we no longer use perhaps more than that which we currently use.

The ubiquitous nature of heritage has both advantages and disadvantages. It is because of this that we feel it relevant to comment on the role heritage has to play in history education.

Grigg and Hughes (2013) explore a number of advantages of heritage education including those which are environmental, social, economic and even psychological. They suggest that it can meet children's spiritual, moral, social and cultural needs and help to define their place in the world through exploring their family, local and national heritage. We think that in both the local and national aspects of this heritage we ought as educators to be aware that heritage represents a heavily interpreted face of history – one which presents it in its most attractive light, according to Tosh (2010) – and that sometimes these interpretations, even when the heritage is clearly part of a local area, tend to emphasise the national perspective at the expense of the international, and sometimes ignore the local context. (With regard to the latter, for instance, a stately home will have drawn on local families for its employees.)

English Heritage (2011) also highlight another aspect of heritage that should be of some concern to educationalists: that some groups have traditionally not visited their sites in the numbers that might be expected – black, Asian and minority ethnic communities; those on lower incomes; young people; those with disabilities. It is to be expected that other aspects of heritage – museums, reconstructions – might similarly not attract these groups. In other words, we cannot assume that all children have experienced 'heritage' and we need to remind ourselves that even local heritage may not seem relevant to all children. As we have seen in the example above of the Museum of London, however, there is an awareness in some sectors of the heritage industry that the nature of the perspective offered is important and increasingly relevant especially for diverse communities.

One aspect of Britain's history which is becoming more apparent in the perspectives and interpretations offered in recent years is that of involvement in the slave trade. Some museums such as the International Slavery Museum in Liverpool and the Museum of London, Docklands, highlight the links of the trade with their local areas as well as general aspects. Likewise English Heritage has explored which of their properties has some level of link with slavery or its abolition and has followed this up with in-depth studies of these links in the case of four of their sites (English Heritage, 2013). Hopefully, this example of good practice will be taken up by others involved in interpreting heritage. Information from their website enables some of the impact of the slave trade on local areas to be understood. For instance, local example 8.1 explores the range of goods through which there were links to different parts of England.

Local example 8.1

English Heritage discusses the slave trade and in particular the impact of the trade on industry in Britain. Not only were there many ports other than the familiar ones – Liverpool, London and Bristol – which were involved in the trade (for instance Weymouth, Falmouth and Whitehaven), the range of manufactured goods involved in the trade was extensive and this in turn had an impact on industrialisation in many areas. Not only were goods needed to exchange for the slaves in Africa – copper, cloth, glassware, metal ware, ammunition, alcohol – goods were also needed by the plantations – cuffs, leg irons, chains and manacles. In addition goods from Africa and America such as ivory, gold, raw sugar, rum, rice, coffee, tobacco and cotton and palm oil were involved. There were particular links with the metal industries of the Black Country and the cloth industry in Lancashire, but there were also important effects on ship building, rope making, furniture and tool making and the consumables used on board ship. Finally, merchants, industrialists and others benefiting financially from the trade invested in country estates across the country.

(English Heritage, 2013)

Where there is a lack of reference to international links this is an opportunity for older children to discuss the reasons for this absence and to help them understand the complex nature of historical interpretations.

Fieldwork and heritage sites

In chapter 3 we looked at various aspects of fieldwork in local streets and spaces. We consider site visits here mainly because of their association with heritage. There is an implication certainly within literature on teaching history that sites are 'separate' from the rest of the environment and part of this is that many but not all are not within public spaces. Heritage sites vary enormously both in terms of what they are physically and also in terms of the support they might offer to school groups. They include sites owned by English Heritage, the National Trust, or private owners; they might be listed buildings or even World Heritage sites (Britain has some two dozen such cultural sites); they can be stately homes; historic industrial and commercial buildings; ruined castles or Roman remains; earthworks or burial mounds.

If it is available, it is always worth arranging a visit supported by educational staff at the site. In arranging this, however, we would recommend talking in advance about any particular requirements you might have. At most sites 'off the peg' sessions are offered, but staff may be happy to accommodate requests to make sure the local context is explored – the links of the site with its immediate locality – and also the global connections. While some quite humble buildings may have these global connections, it is undoubtedly the case that many sites and buildings identified as part of national or world heritage have more extensive connections.

In terms of a stately home or large mansion, we might for example think about the source of the wealth which helped to create the house; materials used in the buildings and the furnishings; the origins of plants in its grounds; the architectural style; the dates of the house

in relation to the slave trade. If you are particularly interested in the links to the slave trade, look out for any of the following:

- furniture or floorboards made out of mahogany or other hardwoods
- people of African origin in paintings
- tea sets, punch bowls and sugar bowls/nips (see Figure 8.2 on p.143)
- pictures or porcelain with tropical scenes and fruits
- fabrics dyed in rich blues and reds
- typical Georgian architectural styles (such as columns and symmetry)
- Palladian architectural features, especially temples and follies in the grounds.

Key questions that might need to be asked would include:

- Where did this material/style originate?
- How did it end up here in a country house in this country?
- Who paid for these things? Where did they get their money from?

Such houses may well have a complicated mix of furniture and artefacts of many different ages and origins. If there is little on-site interpretation and no education staff to teach a session, this can present quite a challenge to the non-specialist teacher. One focus can be the rooms and the building themselves rather than the fixtures and fittings.

It is perhaps ruins which seem to be the hardest sites for children to interpret. How hard is it to imagine what it was like living in a building which now has no roof, and has grass floors, and short tumble down walls, let alone the reality of the time (no glass in the windows, localised sources of heat, lack of plumbing and so on)? For sites which have considerable remains underground and little above ground, Vass (2005) has suggested children need to do some preparatory work in the form of reconstructions, perhaps using plans of the site, and children might also discuss in advance what they expect to see and what they would like to find out. Children can be helped to 'imagine what this place was like', but the ease with which they can do this should not be taken for granted. For some popular sites, artists' impressions and reconstructions are available which should be used. Children are also likely to find 'imagining' unknown places easier if they are used to doing that as part of reading fiction (Cooper, 2004). If they have already focused on ongoing change in their locality that can also help: seeing a building actually being demolished or built, and then being reminded of the change through the use of photos. Once on site, Vass recommends that it can be treated like a maze with children following walkways and doorways through the network of rooms without using the information panels in order to do this, and initially getting a 'feel' for the building.

Possible general questions:

- What can I see?
- What can't I see?
- Why is this missing?
- Where did they cook and go to the toilet?
- What evidence is there that shows us this has changed?
- Why did this happen?
- What was the building for?
- How many people might have lived/worked here?

The nature of the questions may vary according to the main function of the site. Copeland (1993) suggests these might be: settlement/residential; defensive; religious/ceremonial or industrial. His guide provides useful approaches to each of these.

In general terms we acknowledge that 'heritage' (be it of local, national or international significance) within a locality is important, and accessible. However, we feel that its impact can be disproportionately powerful and this needs to be recognised and its use balanced by the more 'everyday' aspects of history that are closer to our daily experiences but which may not be labelled as 'heritage'.

Other local starting points

There are, however, traces of the past in local areas which are not formally part of nationally or even locally acknowledged 'heritage'. There will be remnants of the past in our social, economic and physical environment and much of this will provide us with a way into global connections. In the following we develop some of the clues that may present themselves through aspects of the locality we covered in chapters 3, 4 and 5.

1. People and the community

Oral history accounts are one way to access both the story of a person's arrival in this country and their initial time here, as well as something about their country of birth. Children interviewing parents or grandparents, or telling their own story, can reveal these connections.

2. The physical environment

We have already covered some of the basic information on using aspects of the physical environment in chapter 3. Here we want to provide some examples to show how links can be made with relative ease to places around the globe. Some of these links are explicit as in the examples in local example 8.2, while others, such as the presence of local coffee shops, may be harder to establish. What is apparent is that the use of the internet will often reveal some relevant and interesting information which may help to provide answers or lead to primary sources.

Trails

As part of the 2012 Cultural Olympiad, the Royal Geographical Society with IBG (the Institute of British Geographers) developed a series of trails in different places across the United Kingdom which celebrated links across the globe through diverse local features in twenty localities. These can be found on their 'Discovering Britain' and companion 'Walk the World' websites. They are useful in demonstrating the range of links that can be found in a local area both in terms of the nature of the evidence, and also in terms of the countries that are linked.

Local examples 8.2 Memorials: local plaques leading to international links, and researched using the internet

A gravestone: In St John's graveyard, Eltham is a gravestone for Yemmerrawanyea Kebbarah who was brought to England with another Australian aborigine, Bennelong, by Admiral Arthur Philip, governor of New South Wales, in 1793. Yemmerrawanyea lived for only a year in this country before dying in Eltham in the home of Edward Kent, possibly from tuberculosis. Bennelong returned to Australia. For a time there was a campaign to return the bones of Yemmerrawanyea to Australia (http://www.elthamse9.co.uk/tourismpostings.php?id=9194).

Memorial window in south east London: In All Saints church, Hatcham, there is a stained glass window to the local abolitionist Joseph Hardcastle, a member of the Clapham sect which fought for the abolition of slavery and which included Thomas Clarkson and William Wilberforce. Hardcastle lived locally and his work is commemorated in this window. This can lead children into a consideration of slavery and its abolition. Incidentally, this same church has a foundation stone which was laid by the social reformer and philanthropist, Lord Shaftesbury; another individual of national significance (http://www.ideal-homes.org.uk/lewisham/assets/galleries/new-cross/hatcham-house-3; http://allsaintscommunitycentre.co.uk/about.html).

A memorial plaque in Devon: A memorial at Ilfracombe highlights a fascinating and controversial international link. In 1796 a ship, 'The London', was wrecked during a storm and floundered at Raparree Cove near Ilfracombe with the loss of many on board. The ship, reportedly on its way from St Lucia to Bristol, was transporting enslaved black people, apparently captured during fighting in the Caribbean. Their bodies were buried on the beach and the event forgotten about until storms began to uncover the bodies in the 1990s (Barrow, 1998). There appears to be some controversy, however, surrounding the origins of the bones and as yet no final resting place has been agreed for them (Morris and Constable, 2007; http://www.guardian.co.uk/uk/2007/nov/06/archaeology.science).

Gravestones in East Yorkshire: In a rural churchyard in Brandesburton, East Yorkshire, are a number of graves of airmen who were killed locally during the Second World War (see Figure 8.1). A number of them were clearly German. Some simple internet research revealed information about the origins of the others (10 from the UK, 6 from Australia, 9 from Canada and 2 from New Zealand) and information about the incidents that had led to their deaths. A local reminder of the global nature of the Second World War (http://www.cwgc.org/find-a-cemetery/cemetery/2040183/Brandesburton%20(St.%20Mary)%20Churchyard; http://en.tracesofwar.com/article/18868/German-War-Graves-Brandesburton.htmrd).

Figure 8.1 Graves of foreign airmen killed near Brandesburton, East Yorkshire in the Second World War.

Plants

Throughout history, and certainly since the later Stone Age, plants have been used by people in a way which has affected their distribution (Agyeman, 1995). Plants have moved with people (that is, accidentally) and have been moved by people (that is, on purpose). Many plants in Britain which we consider to be 'native' have their origins in other parts of the globe and plant species are intertwined with the movements of people – invaders, settlers, scientists, traders and travellers. From the eighteenth century onwards plants were acquired or more formally collected by some individuals for horticultural use, or for scientific study.

In the gardens of historic houses as in botanic gardens, plants can be found that have been deliberately introduced and cultivated. Some of these have become common garden plants such as forsythia and wisteria. Others such as the rhododendron introduced in Victorian times have additionally become a problem in areas such as the Lake District. On waste ground, in hedgerows or growing wild we are more likely to find the plants which have been introduced accidentally. For example, in the north of England where shoddy was brought from Australia for the woollen industry, the seeds carried with this raw material have found their way into the surrounding landscape where the wool was transported and processed. Here they have grown and some have flourished (Agyeman, 1995).

The starting point for identifying these global connections through plants requires identifying some local plants and checking on their origins and the possible reasons for their location locally. Some plants will have a specific local connection (for instance through industry); others may have spread from elsewhere and reflect a national pattern (for instance, Oxford ragwort, originally a native of Sicily, was introduced into the country and planted in the Botanic Gardens of Oxford. It then spread along the railway embankments during the Victorian era.)

3. *Beyond memorials*

Local history centres and archives

It is increasingly likely that local historians and local history libraries are providing information on significant historic individuals from across their diverse communities. In Greenwich, for example, material has been published on Ignatius Sancho (born on a slave ship in about 1729) and Olaudah Equiano (born in the Kingdom of Benin in 1745), two black people who were part of the anti-slavery campaign and both of whom had links with the local area (Anim-Addo, 1996). Anim-Addo's book also provides a more general look at the black history of the local area.

Museums

Local museums are worth exploring for any explicit links they may make in their displays and exhibitions. Finding links through artefacts which are on display for yourself may be more challenging. However, much can be learnt from the approach of the British Museum to the history of the world in their joint initiative with the BBC, 'A History of the World in 100 Objects' (MacGregor, 2010). In approaching for instance a porcelain tea cup of the eighteenth century many links are identified.

> It is one of the ironies of British national identity – or perhaps it says everything about our national identity – that the drink which has become the worldwide caricature of Britishness has nothing indigenous about it, but is the result of centuries of global trade and a complex imperial history. Behind the modern British cup of tea lies the high politics of Victorian Britain, the stories of nineteenth century empire, of mass production and of mass consumption, the taming of an industrial working class, the reshaping of the agriculture of continents, the movement of millions of people, and a worldwide shipping industry.
>
> (MacGregor, 2010:201)

In a similar vein we might have an object such as a pair of sugar nips, which were used to crumble solid cones of sugar in the eighteenth and nineteenth centuries, through which we might explore the significance of sugar, the search for and trade in sugar, and its route to the locality (see Figure 8.2). Some objects which were used in the area may have been locally made but others may not. Even these items may help to provide links not only globally but also to different parts of Britain.

In south east London, there is a museum which provides evidence of global links not only through the artefacts on display, but also through its own history (local example 8.3).

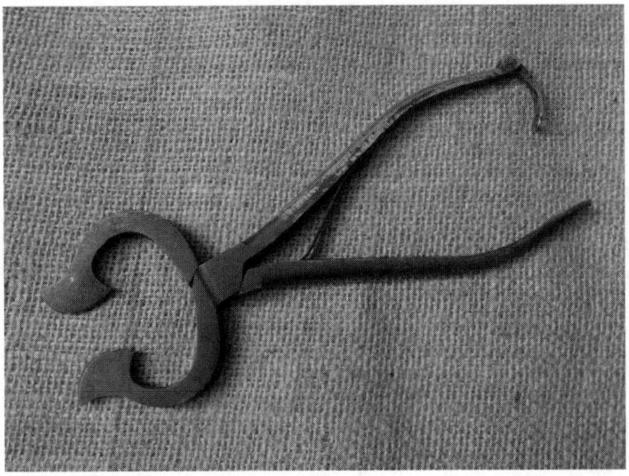

Figure 8.2 A pair of sugar nips.

Local example 8.3 Horniman Museum: where did the wealth come from?

Forest Hill in south east London during the nineteenth century attracted the middle classes to its wooded environment away from the dirt and industry of London but within easy reach of the City. Amongst the merchants in the area was a tea merchant John Horniman. He made his wealth by packaging tea rather than by selling it loose, guaranteeing its purity and its weight. The global links of his family business which was continued by his son, John were:

- the movement of tea from China, Java, Sri Lanka and India;
- the distribution of his packaged tea to an extensive export market;
- the collection of objects he and his contacts amassed;
- the travels he and his son made both as part of the tea business and in order to collect items.

The collection of objects eventually required a purpose-built building to house it and the museum and its collection was then gifted to the London County Council in 1901 (Teague, 1993). It includes such items as a bracelet from the sacking of Benin City, musical instruments from around the world and an Egyptian mummy.

In the 1980s children from a local school made a local history study of Horniman and his museum which was published in a small booklet, 'Mr Horniman and his Victorian Museum' (Christ Church Primary School, undated).

To draw together this final review of the potential of the local area to support history's bigger picture, the following toolkit encourages you to revisit earlier findings about and in the locality, and to consider their potential for unravelling the local to global links.

Teachers' toolkit 8.1 Identifying local–global links

Reflect on the information you have been gathering about the local area and identify any global links using the following:

Aspects of place: look at and for

- *Architectural style of buildings*
- *Memorials to people*
- *Evidence of*
    - *economic activity (factories making goods linked to international trade, transport, docks, warehouses, processing goods in mills and refineries such as grain, sugar, tea)*
    - *commercial activity (coffee and tea shops)*
    - *private and public wealth (country estates, grand mansions, ostentatious public buildings such as town halls)*
    - *'exotic' plants which may have been collected from abroad*
    - *institutions supporting people from abroad or travelling, such as seamen's hospitals*

Personal and family history

- *Memories and testimonies*

People

- *Do people in the area have stories to tell of their journeys from other places, or about growing up in other places?*
- *Have people emigrated?*

Events

Have there been events which have a global dimension?

- *International exhibitions such as the Great Exhibition, 1851*
- *Sporting events*

Evidence

- *Documents such as the census revealing birth places abroad; parish records referring to black servants*
- *Photos which include people of different ethnicities*
- *Artefacts*
- *Published material on the history of different communities in your local area*

Next steps

A range of links through time and between places have been explored in these three chapters. The next chapter moves on to exploring the curriculum links between history and a

range of other subjects in the primary curriculum. Many of these have arisen through the subject matter of all the chapters so far and so the links are those which we feel will serve the purpose of our 'local in history' approach.

Useful websites and other resources

http://www.english-heritage.org.uk/education/resources/slave-trade/

http://www.english-heritage.org.uk/discover/people-and-places/the-slave-trade-and-abolition/sites-of-memory/

http://www.britishmuseum.org/pdf/TheSlaveTrade_TeachersNotes.pdf

Local trails highlighting global connections can be found on a website published by the Royal Geographical Society: http://www.discoveringbritain.org/walks/walk-the-world/view-all/

Rozina Visram's book, *Asians in Britain: 400 Years of History* (2002) provides information on the Asian community in a range of places such as South Shields, Cardiff and Glasgow.

There are a number of examples of BME oral history projects such as the Black and Ethnic Minority Experience in Wolverhampton; the Chinese Oral History Project in London; the Tameside Oral History Project reflecting experiences of the Indian community; the Leicester Oral History Archive drawing on memories of arrivals from Africa and the Indian sub-continent; and Birmingham's Black Oral History Project.

For ideas and inspiration, we recommended Hilary Claire's book, *Reclaiming Our Pasts: Equality and Diversity in the Primary History Curriculum*, Trentham Books (1996) and the articles by Collicott, especially 'A way of looking at history: local–national–world links', *Teaching History*, July 1993, pp. 18–23 (see bibliography for her other articles).

All QCA material is currently archived on the National Archive website at the 'Respect for all' pages: http://webarchive.nationalarchives.gov.uk/20081105160428/qca.org.uk/qca_6753.aspx

Information on a range of black British people linked to houses in the ownership of English Heritage: http://www.english-heritage.org.uk/discover/people-and-places/the-slave-trade-and-abolition/sites-of-memory/black-lives-in-england/

For further information on these aspects go to: http://www.english-heritage.org.uk/education/resources/slave-trade/country-estates/

Very useful background information on 'British' plants and their, often global, origins can be found in *People, Plants and Places* by Julian Agyeman, Learning Through Landscapes, Hampshire (1995).

Chapter 9

Cross-curricular history

The rich tapestry

Introduction

In previous chapters we have looked at the local specifically through people and place, putting the child as the local. We have explored ideas of how to locate and use resources within these areas and have seen that the local is not isolated in its nature, but connects to the wider national and global world.

This chapter takes those ideas one stage further to look at the cross-curricular nature of history in the local. It will explore the explicit links it has with geography and citizenship and how this goes beyond the immediate or physical locality to create a deeper sense of the local: linking individuals in the community to the contribution they make in society. It will also look at specific areas that have become embedded in our history curriculum such as the recent inclusion of Black History Month and Refugee Week. It will discuss areas that may be viewed as controversial history teaching such as war and conflict.

The final section will briefly look at the more generic cross-curricular elements of literacy and the use of writing and non-fiction books in teaching and learning, and the use of ICT and the internet.

Chapter objectives

By the end of this chapter you should:

- understand the nature of cross-curricular aspects of the local in history and how it links 'the personal' to identity and to diversity in local, national and global issues, through geography and citizenship;
- have considered the links between history and other curriculum areas such as literacy and ICT and how these might be effectively incorporated into teaching in the local;
- have considered what is meant by black history and thinking of it in terms of hidden history;
- be able to discuss controversial issues and evaluate their relevance to history in the local.

The local in history and its links to . . .

Geography

As we have previously explored in chapter 2 history and geography are explicitly linked through their study of people and place. We cannot look at or understand the physical or the human environment without questioning how or why it is like that (Catling, 2006). Lambert (2009) tells us how geographical thought in the early twentieth century was dominated by 'environmental determinism', the idea being that people were conditioned or limited by their physical environment. Today this view has changed and geography is seen more as a discipline which teaches, rather than a way of thinking, which focuses on how people influence the environment through the way in which they work with each other, and with the physical world (Lambert, 2009).

This change in view is a pertinent one, as it very much brings geographical thought in line with that of Marwick when he states:

> We cannot, as I put it, escape from the past . . . The human past has [influenced] much of the built environment . . . The functional argument then is that to understand contemporary problems, to take part in contemporary debate, we need history.
>
> (Marwick 1989:17)

Whilst Marwick makes original reference to the human past as 'determining' the built environment, we have substituted the term 'influenced' for Marwick's 'determined' to more closely reflect current geographical thinking. For us it better describes the interrelationship between the two – people and place – and allows for further reflection when considering the future.

Catling takes this point further when he explains that that the connection between the two subjects runs deeper than merely identifying contemporary physical features or knowing something about the age of old features. He says it is more to do with:

> the personal and identity; with a sense of place; with understanding and valuing how any of us came to be here; about continuity and discontinuity. They (history and geography) are also to do with how the past impacts on the present and the future in a locality . . . it concerns the lives of people . . . and the marks they have made.
>
> (Catling, 2006:14)

We are now seeing a further shift in geographical thinking, moving away from just having an understanding of the 'here and now' but towards a notion of: how can we make this place, be it local or global, better (Grigg and Hughes, 2013)? We have what is now commonly known as Education for Sustainable Development (ESD). This is essentially an educational approach which considers how we might better look after the planet and the people in it.

Sustainability is an issue which all curriculum areas are concerned with, but clearly its roots lie in that of geography. However if we delve further into the concept we can see how history is essential in the process of understanding the notion of ESD. ESD has three interdependent strands: economic, social and environmental which relate to some of the 'big' questions that geography, and arguably history, seeks to answer about place, people, change, actions

and connections (Owens, 2013). If we are to consider an education for sustainability, i.e. building a better future for our quality of life, then we have to consider it in relation to the past.

Owens also points out that issues concerning ESD are value laden and emotive and these: 'are intrinsic and inescapable facets of sustainability, [and that] being properly equipped to respond to these issues also demands some degree of understanding about how and why human, biological and the physical worlds interact and affect each other' (Owens, 2013:155).

Our approach – learning in and through the local – gives both adults and children an active opportunity to learn; seeing in practice how humans and the physical world interact and being a part of the issues which concern those of sustainability. With a grasp of such issues which may be illustrated or experienced through the local, children are able to transfer their knowledge and understanding and extend it beyond to the national and global. The local provides a geographical 'here and now' and a window to the future. Learning 'how and why' the local has reached the 'here and now' through history provides an understanding and a more informed view from the window to a sustainable future.

At the heart of geography and history is the process of enquiry. Enquiry in both history and geography provides a scaffold for children to make sense of the world in which they live. Enquiry is essentially about asking questions and coming to reasoned conclusions. Questioning (as explored in chapter 10), observing, selecting and interpreting information are central to both disciplines in understanding the past and the present. And, if children are to understand the future, then they must have a developing understanding of the present and past. Geography is about the relationship between people, place and the environment and learning about the 'today'. Learning about today provides that link between the past and the future.

Pickford et al. (2013) stress the importance of enquiry, especially that of geographical enquiry, in preparing for the future, stating: 'it is one way of preparing our children for their lives in the future; lives which will be characterised by rapid technological progress and expansion, globalisation, social and cultural change' (p.84).

When we are considering the use of enquiry to explore questions or test hypotheses, particularly when trying to prepare for the future, we have to decide on what evidence we have or may want, and how we might use it. Pickford et al. (2013) make a distinction between geographical enquiry and that of history. They state that within history, because there are a limited number of like experiences to draw firm conclusions from, we have to make logical generalisations based on any evidence that we might have; for example about a particular time period or the cause or consequences of a series of events. It is from these generalisations that we can then formulate questions or set hypotheses. We then look back at these general premises to reach some kind of logical conclusions to the posed questions. This is logical deduction.

It could be argued that logical deduction is perhaps the only means of reaching conclusions in history, especially when we are faced with many interpretations of the past and we cannot set out to *test* these interpretations. However, we also have to consider how time and the duration of events and experiences may impact on the use of logical deduction; the more distant something is the less reliable a general premise may be. Therefore when using these general premises to come to any form of conclusion, they may not be as reliable as we would hope. We then may not be able to rely solely on the evidence of the past and would need to look for further evidence, particularly if we want to make assumptions about the present and the future.

Geography, however, allows us to use 'reasoned induction' – conclusions from the systematic study of behaviour, patterns and processes, as we are dealing largely with the present. The present provides far more opportunities for systematic study of observations and experiences. We are thus able to use the data and evidence from these studies to answer questions or test hypotheses that we may have about the present, enabling us to go some way in reaching firmer conclusions.

Therefore the relationship between history and geography is a pertinent one. The interconnectedness of both history and geography allows a process of enquiry in which we can draw from one form of reasoning to support the other, arguably strengthening our assumptions and conclusions about the present and the future.

The local provides a scaffold for bridging the gap between logical deduction and reasoned induction. It provides the resources, people and rich experiences which allow us to engage in a process of practical enquiry that is a blend of the two. It provides the means for first-hand systematic study: looking at what we have, observing the patterns and behaviour of people and having access to, and interpreting historical evidence within the environment. From this, we are able to combine the knowledge and understanding from both methods of enquiry to draw informed conclusions.

Local, national and global citizenship

If we are saying that history and geography are essentially about people and place and how they interact with each other, then we cannot exclude the notion of citizenship. History and geography involve trying to understand attitudes and values of people in the past and contemporary societies, in the hope that we learn to respect and tolerate other cultures and societies today (Davies, 2000; Cooper, 2006). Citizenship and education for citizenship is not a new idea and dates back to the first democratic society of the ancient Greek city-state or *polis* (root of the word politics) (Grigg and Hughes, 2013). It is essentially about becoming informed, active citizens, 'enabling people to make their own decisions and to take responsibility for their own lives and their communities' (http://www.citizenshipfoundation.org.uk/main/page.php?286).

Reflection

- *What does citizenship mean to you?*
- *What do you think are the underpinning values and principles of citizenship?*
- *What issues are citizenship concerned with?*
- *Consider what you think makes a good citizen and how they might contribute to the local, national and global community.*
- *Can you think of individuals in history whom you consider to be examples of good or bad citizens?*
- *What has influenced your choice of individuals and why?*

The concepts, values and principles of citizenship underpin the dimension of local, national or global citizenship which, as Vass points out, 'has the potential to promote

understanding that transcends time as well as space, whilst providing an immediacy and relevance to the subject of study' (Vass, 2007a:8).

Whilst citizenship may start with the individual, it by no means finishes there. We have seen throughout history how the achievements and contributions of collective communities have contributed to the wider history of the national and global world. For instance the story of the Tolpuddle Martyrs tells how a village community in 1834 rose together to fight against injustice and oppression, forming what we now know as a trade union. The contributions and achievement of different communities in the Second World War can be recognised at a local, national and global level and continue to inform our values and principles on world peace.

Education for citizenship is no doubt challenging and as Davies (2000) points out there is a chasm between the thinking of the theorists and the practice of classroom teachers. However, he advises that the challenges are not as overwhelming as perhaps first considered. History offers a vehicle through which the teaching and learning of citizenship can take place, although we should not consider history solely for this purpose, but instead must recognise the important links between the two. At a practical level, understanding the links between history and citizenship will go some way in raising the status of both history and the inherent values of citizenship. The content of history provides excellent examples through which to pursue the concepts of citizenship. The story of William Wilberforce, for example, can help older children pursue the topic of moral and social responsibility. We might use the story of 'Peepo' as discussed in chapter 6 to explore the impact of war on families. Accounts of child labour in Victorian times can open up discussions on contemporary global poverty today.

Davies, along with others such as Cooper (2012), Bage (2000) and Alexander (2010), directs us to the importance of the local in citizenship. They highlight that not only is it about the individual, but how the ethos of a school, its involvement within the local community and with the physical environment itself, all add to the preparation and education for citizenship, leading to both individual and collective senses of shared identity. Below is a case study of how one school incorporated history and citizenship through a cross-curricular approach to promote respect, understanding and local community cohesion.

Case study 9.1

During a History Theme Week, it was decided that the involvement of the local community in the activities and events would make a considerable contribution to the learning of history for the children. It would also go some way in bridging the gap between the eldest and youngest members of our community and the way in which they viewed each other, thereby strengthening community cohesion. In order to do this a tea dance was organised in the school hall. Through an historical study of music, the children had been introduced to 'tea dances' and had watched footage of the dances and music involved. They were given a budget for the purchase of tea and cakes and were responsible for ordering, organising and preparing refreshments suitable for the elderly community they were entertaining. They wrote letters inviting residents of local sheltered housing to join them for the tea dance with the possibility of learning some of the dances that they might have engaged in when younger.

Before the arrival of the visitors, the children discussed what they might want to find out about and what questions they might want to ask them about their lives and experiences. The children decided that they would not only try to learn dances of the time, but would show the residents some of the contemporary dances of today. The afternoon proved to be a great success. The immediate connection between the children and the residents was astounding, with many stories of war, evacuation, dances and experiences being passed from the adults to the children who listened with interest and awe. The children were also eager to learn the dances, and variations of waltzes and jive were taught! Through this sharing of history, the children were able to explore values, learn respect and develop a deep level of understanding of a group of people in the community whom they might not have otherwise met.

This set a precedent for the involvement of the community within the school and for the residents of the sheltered home. They continue to play an active part in the life of the school, through attending assemblies, telling their oral histories in classrooms and working alongside the children.

Citizenship and the teaching of controversial history

The aim of this section is not to impart views or make judgement on historical issues or complex themes, but rather to give the reader food for thought when faced with what might be emotive issues within the history curriculum. Within the local, there will always be issues in history in the more distant past and most certainly in the recent past that we can consider. These issues will be topical and in some circumstances very difficult from both a teaching and learning point of view. The question is: do we avoid such issues and if not, what relevance do they have in our teaching?

Before we try to consider what history we teach and to whom that history might belong, we need to think about what we mean by the term 'controversial issues'. The term 'controversial' is in itself controversial, meaning it will have different levels of application for different people. What may be considered controversial in one sense or to one person may not be the case for another. We have purposefully chosen not to define the term ourselves as we think it is one that is complex and multi-faceted in meaning. We challenge the reader to draw their own conclusion using the following reflection.

Reflection

- *Examine your own view of what 'controversial' means.*
- *When does something become controversial?*
- *Write a list of topics/areas in general that you would consider to be controversial issues.*
- *Would there be any area from your list that you would not engage children in?*
- *Ask a colleague/friend to do the same. Do you agree?*

We have become aware of how difficult it can be for trainee teachers to contemplate tackling controversial issues in the classroom, and we wonder to what extent this is also true for early career teachers. This seems to be the case not only in relation to complex present day issues, but also for historic issues that have become remote in time. The following case study helps to highlight the reactions of a group of students when talking about the recent bombings in America and in London, and then about Guy Fawkes.

Case study 9.2

During a history seminar, a discussion surrounding the events of 9/11 was brought up by initial teacher trainees and the question was asked whether it should be used within the primary classroom as an example of cause and consequence. We related the event to the recent local example of the London bombings and explored the consequences of this and its impact on the local communities, many of which the students were from or had involvement in. They were able to discuss and describe events surrounding the experience with some authority as well as clarity.

We discussed whether such events had any place in the primary curriculum and whether it was an appropriate vehicle to talk about the issue of terrorism. Students found the notion of using these particular experiences with young children quite alarming, expressing their opinions strongly that it was both distasteful and the idea of terrorism being far beyond a young child's understanding. When they were questioned about the motive of Guy Fawkes and whether he might have been considered a terrorist of his time this interpretation surprised them. The students seemed unable to see this perspective and would not consider introducing it in their teaching of Guy Fawkes. In both cases therefore the students were reluctant to refer to terrorism explicitly in the classroom but for very different reasons.

In the case of the recent bombings, students were clearly concerned about the complexity of terrorism as a concept and about the terrifying and horrific nature of the consequences. In the case of the Guy Fawkes attempted bombing, the story seems to have lost its controversial edge with familiarity and with the factor of much time passing.

What can we learn from this? Not, we believe, that controversial issues should not be addressed in the classroom, but that there needs to be a careful balance in the choice of issue, the depth of discussion, an awareness of progression in how we approach issues and a need to challenge ourselves in how we perceive the controversy. We need to feel comfortable with our own responses before managing the potential responses of children.

Claire reminds us that the remoteness of time, the absence of real people and dealing with difficult concepts often lead 'to poor historical understanding, oversimplifications, misconceptions and a-historicity, all of which are hard to shift later' (1996:6). This was certainly true of Guy Fawkes and our teacher trainees. However, history through the local and its

connections with real people and places, along with the inherent values of citizenship, allow children the opportunity to experience learning which might otherwise have been remote and hazy.

Children are more likely to be able to discuss, assimilate and apply the learning of something which is distant if they are able to link it to something which is accessible and relevant to them; for example the death of Stephen Lawrence, a young black man who was murdered in Eltham as he waited for a bus. This made national headlines and has had a lasting impact on race relations policy and practice. It has continued to feature in both national and local news. Not only are children able to explore the social and moral issues surrounding this event, but they are able to relate the learning to similar events in the past and to draw some possible correlations surrounding cause and consequence which Pickford et al. (2013) say is at the heart of logical deduction, as explored earlier in the chapter.

If we consider issues that may be controversial, such as execution (the beheading of Henry VIII's wives for instance), war or slavery, does the passing of time make them more or less controversial? It could be said, as Claire suggests, that 400 years or so has made the story of Guy Fawkes oversimplified and therefore less controversial. A more contemporary question might be: is something made more controversial perhaps when it is sensationalised by the media? And how does the use of media in history impact on the learning of young children?

In our experience even very young children have a level of understanding that is surprising. We may be failing to acknowledge the extent to which children are exposed to controversial issues through the television and media. Every day, children are increasingly confronted with images of war, murder, death, terrorism, amongst others. They listen to and no doubt engage in discussion with family and friends about such issues. Pluckrose, writing in 1991, argues that it is young children who are victims of this social phenomenon of media exposure and need particular help from school. If true then, how much more so today!

Research by Cooper in 1995 in war torn areas of Europe illustrates that young children are very able to and want to explore the controversial issues they see, hear and often experience. Our own personal experience of young children in the classroom has also highlighted an eagerness to engage in such discussions. They have been aroused by past historical issues such as the Holocaust, and contemporary history they hear or see via the media or similar; the primary classroom can provide a safe environment in which to do so. Skilful questioning and making connections between the present and the controversial issues of the past can help children begin to explore their own values and ethical and ideological standpoint. This is not, as Claire emphasised, a matter of indoctrination but one of education, with teachers enabling children to weigh up serious ethical questions and decide where they stand on them (Claire, 2007:29).

In order to begin the early process of understanding concepts such as cause and consequence that are integral to many controversial issues, activities such as a game of snakes and ladders can help young children to begin to explore the notion of why some things happens and what happens as a result.

Likewise story, particularly fictional stories, as explored in chapter 6, can also be a neutral and less threatening way to introduce children to difficult concepts and issues such as war, oppression and death. This is more so when the story is within a context that children can identify with, i.e. the family or local. The story 'Tusk, Tusk' by David McKee, for example, offers a balanced and very thought-provoking way into the issue of race, culture and conflict and does so without using those actual terms. This story has been used and continues to

Teacher/child activity

Set up a familiar game using dice and chance as a means of winning. As the children play, stop at strategic points and ask questions such as:

- *What would have happened if I had thrown a 6?*
- *Would the game have been fair if the number of throws were uneven?*
- *What would happen if only children wearing red/blue/green jumpers were allowed to climb the ladders?*

Such activities help children begin to explore and make connections in their learning, and in turn develop their conceptual understanding of potentially difficult concepts and issues in a safe and non-threatening way.

be used very successfully with very young children in exploring their understanding of such concepts. Other books such as 'One day we had to run' by Sybella Wilkes (a book where refugee children tell their stories in words and paintings) are an invaluable source to have in the classroom. This particular book introduces children to the concept of displacement, which many of them may have experienced. Certainly in many local communities refugee children and families have had to move to an area because of the threat of war, poverty or oppression in their own countries.

Again, we can see here the relevance of the local and in particular the child as the local. By exploring such issues in a sensitive and supportive way, children, whether victims themselves or whether learning about the children and families in their local communities, can develop an informed understanding of the history that surrounds them, fostering respect and tolerance and dispelling stereotypical images that they may be exposed to.

Black history or hidden history?

The content of the history curriculum is in itself a cause of controversy. The question of 'whose history?' continues to be debated, and at the time of writing is one of the most pressing topics in the field of history academia and within the wider political arena. The original message from the present government was clearly one of 'British-ness', to strengthen our national identity and to promote the 'great' in Great Britain; the draft National Curriculum document stated the need to recognise 'how the British people shaped this nation and how Britain influenced the world' (DfE, 2013b). However, this has since been modified and refers to a more two-way relationship in a global context. Whilst we can continue to debate the 'who', one fact remains: Britain is, and has always been, multicultural. Multiculturalism is not only about our influence on the rest of the world, but also about the influence of the rest of the world on us.

Despite our society having been multi-ethnic for hundreds of years, history and the writings of history have largely ignored the presence of black and multi-ethnic people in Great Britain. This has been partially addressed by the introduction of black history and more specifically Black History Month as a recent development in our British non-statutory history curriculum.

In this country, the Black History Month event had its origins in the 1980s. However, the idea originated in the United States when the historian Carter G. Woodson launched Negro History Week in an attempt to bring to the forefront the history of Americans of black, African descent. It was launched here following a campaign led by Ghanaian Akyaaba Addai Sebbo who worked for the Greater London Council (GLC), which helped him stage the first event. The main impetus for the British version had its roots in the supplementary schools movement set up in the 1960s and 1970s, following the arrival of people from the Caribbean during the 1950s and 1960s (see chapter 1). The locally fought campaign to teach black history was in response to the demands of black parents that their children should be taught about their history and culture and not the Eurocentric history that children were being exposed to at the time (http://www.black-history-month.co.uk).

Black History Month continues to feature in many of our primary schools nationally, albeit at different extents. In our visits to London and suburban primary schools, the teaching of black history has been varied, with some schools focusing on the month and others embedding it fully into their history curriculum throughout the year. Clearly we can speculate on the reason for that variation but in terms of culture, identity and citizenship we would suggest that such history should be embedded in all teaching and learning. Wilson sums this up effectively when she states: 'The benefits to be gained from devising a history curriculum designed to cater for the needs of a multicultural society are numerous both for ethnic minority children and white children. This enables the serious challenging of stereotyping and misconceptions' (Wilson, 1997). Wilson's point about stereotyping is a serious one. Whilst the achievements of black individuals in history is now rightly celebrated both locally and globally, as explored in chapter 1, the histories of other groups are rarely, if at all, recognised in our schools.

Such histories may include those of the travelling and refugee communities, and perhaps more recently that of communities coming from the Eastern European countries. As they may not be of black descent, clearly their histories are not recognised as part of 'black history' and therefore not included in Black History Month. In local areas where these families have settled we may have children and families whose culture and heritage is not being recognised as part of the local community. This may result in there being children who are failing to access their history and history in the wider context. If they are not in their country of origin and not learning about this history, nor are they learning about it in their 'now' local, what message is that giving to a child in terms of their identity, confidence and self-esteem? The exclusion of these histories is likely to bring about the stereotyping and misconceptions that Wilson talks about. If we are considering the child as the local, then we must take into account the diversity of families which we are increasingly seeing.

Here it is worth noting the distinction we make between 'inclusive history' and 'inclusion' in history; the two are often used interchangeably. We take Claire's definition of inclusive history as being: history which embraces all histories, regardless of race, ethnicity, gender or class. An inclusive history curriculum will include and recognise the struggles as well as the achievement of the young and old. Claire adds that children from all backgrounds can particularly benefit from an inclusive history curriculum.

She states:

> This history will interest and engage children, allow them to build towards the unknown from what they know and meet needs relating to self-esteem and valuing others. It

follows that a non-inclusive history curriculum must fail or disadvantage some children, those we are most concerned to encourage.

(Claire, 1996:9)

Inclusion, however, means that children (and adults) are given opportunities to access history according to the ways which benefit them, i.e. they have been *included* in the history learning. For example: a child might access historical learning through a differentiated approach (see chapter 10) or merely having a curriculum that is relevant to them, thereby facilitating effective learning. This could be through an inclusive curriculum.

If we consider the notion of an inclusive history, we need to widen the concept of 'black history' and refer rather to that of 'hidden history'. This being: significant events, individuals or communities whose history may not have been fully recognised or uncovered (and which therefore are hidden), but making considerable contribution to our local, national and global history. We are then able to give ourselves permission to include groups of people, children and events who are important to our local environment and community regardless of race, culture, gender or class, thus creating a 'history for all'.

Literacy

Writing non-fiction texts

The cross-curricular links between history and literacy, particularly writing, is very apparent. History continues to be an effective stimulus for writing because of its rich nature of narrative and story and its ability to develop and enrich children's imagination, skills and creativity. It is an excellent way in which to motivate and excite reluctant writers, particularly boys.

Writing is often the end product of historical enquiry studies (Eales, 2012). However, this should not be its sole purpose. Writing in history serves many different functions and should be utilised to its fullest potential.

Before we consider any writing task we might expect children to engage in, or the opportunities the local might have, we must consider the preparation needed before children begin to write. The following provides useful guidance when setting an historical writing task.

Guidance: Writing for history

- *Objectives must be clear, with the focus being on the historical concept that you want the child to concentrate on.*
- *'Talk for Writing' – children will need planned opportunities to discuss, debate and question the learning they are doing. Being able to articulate their thoughts, clarify meanings and orally practise their writing, they will become clearer about what they want to put on paper.*
- *Children will need to be exposed to any particular genre of writing several times before they are expected to write in the same way. In this case the genre includes historical diaries, posters, information texts and reports which they have been able to read, discuss and evaluate in terms of their purpose and style.*

- *The teacher needs to clearly model the writing to the children and set expectations.*
- *Differentiation, such as writing frames, vocabulary lists and support from peers or other adults, should be considered in order to personalise the learning.*
- *Ensure children have access to appropriate historical vocabulary and are clear as to the meanings of words – some words may have had a different historical meaning from how we might use them today.*
- *Marking and feedback should be clear, concise, focused on the history learning objective and giving constructive feedback to extend the learning.*
- *Allow the children time to reflect on their writing in terms of historical content, structure and quality.*

Writing does not have to take the form of a narrative in order for it to be of value. Children can and should engage in many different types of writing during their study. This might include making or taking notes; jottings; labels; poems or songs. Some of the more obvious forms will include: letters, stories, recounts, newspaper reports.

The history in the local acts as an excellent stimulus and provides lots of opportunities for children to engage in purposeful writing. A selection of activities, though not exhaustive, is provided in Table 9.1. These are not age-specific and offer the reader only a brief number of examples which can be adapted and added to.

Table 9.1 Writing opportunities

Time period/area of study	*Activity in the local*	*Concept*
Victorian	Write a letter to your local councillor complaining about the railway line due to run through your village	Consequence, historical situation, persuasion
Roman	Write a newspaper article from the viewpoint of the Romans reporting on a battle involving Boudicca and her tribe in your village	Cause, consequence, perspective, interpretation, historical situation
Second World War	Write a diary of the night you spent in the air raid shelter in your back garden	Historical situation, chronological order
Edwardian	Label a picture of the building with all its recognisable features that tell you it is from the Edwardian period	Description, period, interpretation
Significant local person	Write a news bulletin describing the achievements of a local person in your community	Perspective, interpretation, historical situation, communication
Local archaeological dig	Write a report on what you found in your local area	Evidence, chronological understanding, interpretation, communication
1940s	Construct a menu using the rations you have for a family dinner or tea	Interpretation, historical situations
Local street	Write a 'Rap' on what it was like to live in the house/street/building	Interpretation, empathy, chronological understanding, enquiry

Reading non-fiction texts

When we are dealing with more remote periods of history we may only have access to secondary information in the form of text books. There are many quality non-fiction texts available and these can be accessed in some local resource centres discussed in chapter 5, though schools will no doubt have their own collection. Children should be introduced to these as another form of evidence which they can use to research, access and gather information or to fill gaps in their knowledge which other forms of evidence might not do, or indeed they might not be available to use.

Non-fiction texts may be found in other formats such as on the internet, but as with primary sources children will still need to apply the skills of effective enquiry. Good quality non-fiction books provide children with clear and accessible information often incorporating a range of sources which may provide both primary and secondary evidence. However, we would suggest that where possible non-fiction books/texts should not be used in isolation but alongside other sources, so children can see how they can supplement and complement other forms of evidence in the process of enquiry. Using a non-fiction book to confirm an idea or check the reliability of another sources is good historical practice and one that should be encouraged.

Cremin (2009) and others warn of the danger of children using non-fiction text to extract or copy large amounts of information from, without considering what it is they are looking for or whether it is relevant. First, teachers will need to use their professional knowledge to consider whether the text is relevant, reliable and offers a reasonably accurate historical view or account of the period being studied. As children become more expert in asking historical questions about the use of evidence, they themselves will begin to select non-fiction books according to whether they think they are appropriate to their line of enquiry.

Teachers will also need to ensure non-fiction books and the texts are appropriate for the age and stage of learning for the children. Some texts may need to be simplified or read to the child, whilst others may not include enough information, often typical in early years non-fiction books. However, photographs can provide content which is accessible to young learners at a range of levels.

In order for children not to copy chunks of information verbatim, which is often problematic, teachers can set a different task rather than asking for a narrative piece of writing. Children can be asked to highlight, make notes, produce mind maps or make visual representations of what they read. Whatever form of information gathering takes place, children will need to have clear questions to begin with and be encouraged to identify key words and phrases within the text.

This process of gathering notes in historical research is the same for all written sources whether primary or secondary evidence, but children will need explicit teaching in the skill. Older children will need to be taught that secondary sources may also be written from one perspective or contain stereotyping and must begin to use this knowledge when considering the information they may be presented with. They need to evaluate whether the information within a book is reliable. Teachers will also need to model and ensure children are aware of how to use features such as contents, indexes etc. in non-fiction works. Children require ample teaching and learning opportunities to develop skills such as scanning and skimming of text in order to extract the information needed efficiently.

The idea of non-fiction books being used as sources of evidence can be copied by the children, whereby they produce their own non-fiction information book for an historical

Teacher/child activity

- *Provide a selection of historical non-fiction and fictional story books*
- *Allow the children to investigate the books available and ask them to categorise them (this should be done initially without guidance)*
- *Discuss with the children how they have sorted their books, and why?*
- *Now pose questions such as:*
    - *Find a book which tell us about . . .*
    - *Which books have other features which are useful for giving us information (pictures, labels)?*
    - *Which books do you think are true, and why?*
    - *Which books might contain opinions, and why?*

Questions can be differentiated according to the needs of the children. They can be adapted to suit the particular history or theme you are studying.

study. This not only illustrates their learning, but particularly develops their ability to communicate what they know. If children are able to do this for their local community they are not only sharing knowledge but also providing a valuable service to their community. There are many excellent examples of local projects where children have engaged in just that. This not only illustrates their skills as historians, but it communicates the history of their local, thereby promoting fundamental citizenship principles and concepts. One such local example involved children from the Hammersmith area who contributed to a guide for the Thames Path in their borough.

Information Communication Technology (ICT)

Ell states that local history is on 'the cusp of a revolution' (in Ell, 2011:266).

He attributes this to the rapid expansion of ICT and the wider access to participation it promotes. As explored in the earlier chapters we have indeed seen an explosion of family history, historical television programmes and local history research, and this is extremely positive. ICT gives us immediate access to a range of evidence, skills and programmes which are invaluable to our historical learning. We literally have the world at our fingertips!

The reader is no doubt more aware than we are of the range of ICT available and its possible uses, but the toolkit on the following page lists some ICT resources and how we might use them, particularly when engaging in the local.

The possibilities of being creative with ICT and history are endless. However, we have to be mindful of the potential pitfalls, particularly when using the Internet while engaging in historical enquiry.

As described in chapter 5, it is easy to become reliant on the ease of accessibility when using the internet as a research tool but we still need to evaluate, disregard some sources, assess for reliability and use alongside other evidence we may have. With this in mind, we are preparing children to make their own informed interpretation based on the evidence they

Teachers' toolkit 9.1 Using ICT resources

ICT	The use in the local
Digital cameras	*Essential for fieldwork, the camera can become your eyes and memory, the beauty being you can snap away and review later instantly.*
Recording equipment such as Digi blues, sound mats and microphones	*These are easily transportable and can be taken into the community when engaging in oral history.* *For some children it is useful to record their thoughts/notes and observations in the local rather than make written notes. It is also often easier under difficult weather conditions.*
Tablet computers	*The uses are vast – but video conferencing between children and/ or local community is a possibility. If the children cannot get to the local bring the local to them!*
Webcams	*Webcams connect 'locals' around the globe. Many schools are now participating in joint ventures where links are made via webcams. This holds many exciting possibilities for excellent teaching and learning opportunities and one which should be exploited.*
Internet search engines	*Can be used to search for census materials, online archive material, online newspapers, journals and articles relating to the local.*
ICT software programmes	*Various multi-media presentation packages are available such as Prezzi and Powerpoint which children can use a means to present their findings.*
Bebots and robots	*Can be used to explore large scale maps. Many can be programmed to take different routes and store information.*
Social media sites such as Facebook and Twitter	*Can for be useful for sharing information, engaging in historical discussions with different groups or forums and finding out about your local area and community.*

have. Clearly the skill of enquiry extends far beyond that of history learning; it is a lifelong and transferable skill.

The last caution we give concerns the use of social networking sites and open forums with children. Children must be taught internet safety and made aware of the possible dangers when engaging in any forms of social media. Schools will have policies regarding internet safety and it is essential that they are adhered to.

And so, to the last chapter

This chapter brings an end to the elements we feel are fundamental in our approach: namely people and place. The chapter itself has provided the reader with a wider per-

spective of the cross-curricular elements of the local in history and has offered some challenges and insight into areas such as 'hidden history' and 'controversial issues': themes perhaps not otherwise thought about!

The next chapter brings the approach together and will help the reader plan and teach effective historical learning in the local.

Further reading

A Teacher's Guide: Citizenship: Using the Evidence of the Historic Environment, London, English Heritage (2004)

Global Communities: Learning about Refugee Issues, by Miriam Halahmy, Primary School Teaching Resource, Department for International Development (2005)

The Life of Stephen Lawrence, by Verna Allette Wilkins, Tamarind (2012)

New Faces, New Places: Learning about People on the Move – a resource for 4–7 year olds, Save the Children Fund. An old but excellent resource with published real life stories of children who have been displaced by war. The pack offers games and activities to introduce and develop concepts.

Tusk, Tusk, by David McKee, Red Fox Picture Books

One Day We Had to Run! by S. Wilkes, London, Evans Brothers Ltd (1997)

Useful websites and resources

Many local authorities will produce and provide resources relating to Refugee Week and Black History Month. It is worth calling your local education department and asking them to put you in touch with their Ethnic Minority Achievement Services (or current equivalent). Services and department will vary from area to area.

The reader will no doubt be very familiar with the range of web resources that are available to support areas discussed in this chapter. Here we have given a flavour of those you might use or begin with.

http://www.blackhistorymonth.org.uk
http://www.movinghere.org.uk/galleries/histories/intro/intro.htm
https://secure.savethechildren.org.uk
http://www.redcross.org.uk
http://www.worldvision.org.uk

Chapter 10

Planning

Completing the jigsaw

Introduction

We have given both an understanding of why history is an important curriculum area for children and a rationale as to why the teaching and learning should be done in and through the local. We have considered in earlier chapters the resources available in the local and how to use them to make learning meaningful and relevant. This chapter brings together that understanding and our approach, and offers the reader a way to plan and implement the resulting practice with children.

It considers planning in the broadest sense. It covers long-, medium- and short-term planning and how assessment and progression make up an integral part of this process. Different planning outlines are offered for teachers to use, adapt and apply in different ways to suit their circumstances. We show how planned study units can be linked to the local and how this can be adapted to cover the primary age range. Planning in the Early Years Foundation Stage is covered separately as we feel that there is much to be learned from excellent early years practice; when planned well, it provides children with the bedrock of good history learning.

Chapter objectives

By the end of this chapter you should:

- be familiar with long-, medium- and short-term planning for the local in history across both primary and the Early Years Foundation Stage;
- be able to use questioning effectively to promote historical learning;
- have an understanding of the progression in historical concepts, skills and understanding/thinking skills and be able to differentiate accordingly;
- be able to consider the most suitable planning format to meet the needs of your class and be able to adapt as necessary.

Planning in general

It is reasonable to say that over the past few years planning has become less formulaic and more flexible, particularly in the move towards greater creativity and cross-curricular teach-

ing; however, as Phillips (2008) points out 'planning for any lesson is (always) a complex task' (p.54). Whilst some schools are still reliant on QCA units of study for history, teachers are beginning to appreciate the breadth that history has to offer in terms of topics and themes. During our time visiting schools as link tutors it is has been refreshing to see the history curriculum incorporating a wider range of people, events and approaches. However, Florence Nightingale, the Great Fire of London and the wives of Henry VIII are still very prominent in our schools and children are clearly very excited by them, where they have been taught well. Such topics are excellent to pursue and should continue to form part of the national and international history available to our children, but they can be adapted to make for a more relevant and meaningful experience for the child.

Stand-alone local history projects have also been visible in our schools, though arguably less so than the above topics, but this is not surprising given that local history is one of the statutory study areas in the National Curriculum (DfEE, 1998).

However, here we have a difficulty. The way in which these topics, including local history study, are sometimes planned and presented to the children makes them appear as unrelated areas of history. Few links are made connecting the local to the bigger picture of national and international and equally we do not always refer to the local when we engage in wider areas of history such as those mentioned above. This isolates the local from the national and global. Chapters 6 and 8 offer valid starting points and gives examples of how the local, national and international interconnect.

With planning in mind and linking to the local, we echo the viewpoint of Cooper (2006) and Turner-Bisset (2005), who offer a very compelling argument for using published ready-made history schemes with caution. Their advice suggests that the non-specialist teacher may wish to use schemes to help structure planning, especially for a new context, but advocate using both local and human resources as much as possible to ensure learning is meaningful to the children. We suggest that teaching through the local, and using people and place, should be a key part, if not the starting point, in any history planning you do. This may not always be evident in published schemes and so they will need to be adapted to suit.

Cooper (2012), Claire (1996) and Turner-Bisset (2005) offer excellent examples of how to be creative with the more familiar units of the current history curriculum and many of these ideas could be adapted to suit the National Curriculum (2014) history content, particularly at Key Stage 1. Our approach to teaching and learning through the local does not focus on particular units or areas of study (though some have been used as examples). What it offers is a more holistic approach for any area of historical study, and it is therefore compatible with any national curriculum orders.

When planning for history learning, it is important that we bear in mind at all times the statutory requirements of the current National Curriculum history orders and ensure that statutory content is covered. At the time of writing the National Curriculum 2014 has just been released and whilst this again gives some of the content, it must be remembered this is the minimum coverage and not the entire range of history that *can* or should be taught. Neither does it specify a particular approach, e.g. stand-alone units, cross-curricular, so teachers still have the flexibility to enrich children's history learning further with themes and approaches that are of interest and relevance to the child. The other point to note is that there has not been any statutory guidance as to the depth or length of time spent on each history focus and therefore teachers are still able to use their professional judgement when planning, i.e. they should take into account the interests, needs and starting points of the children in their class.

Types of planning

Long-term

Long-term planning is merely the overview that a school will adopt to ensure that history study requirements are balanced across Key Stages 1 and 2 and that statutory requirements are covered. Plans will usually focus on the individual terms for each year group and will offer a theme or topic, but this has become far more flexible than it was historically. The purpose of a long-term structure is to safeguard against areas being duplicated or not covered at all. Themes will often be loose and there is flexibility within them. Table 10.1 is an example of long-term history planning and what it might look like. We have attempted here to give examples of where and how you might start with or incorporate the local when initially faced with such a plan.

Planning for curriculum change

Clearly changes will need to be made to long-term plans according to the agreed content of the national curriculum in place at any one time. When faced with a changing curriculum, curriculum leaders should read the wording carefully with regards to the content, taking note of the words and terminology used. For example, terms such as '*such as*' and '*or*' give examples of subjects that *could* be used, not necessarily *must* be used.

For the new curriculum 2014, we suspect that themes outlined in Key Stage 2 particularly will be taken directly from the chronological framework given and this is a perfectly acceptable way of organising your long-term plan, if appropriate. However, at the time of writing there is no guidance as to depth of study into these areas, except that the framework 'will serve as an essential frame of reference for *more* in-depth study' (DfE, 2013b; emphasis added). Therefore children need to be exposed to it and to the chronological framework in which it is presented; they need be able to refer to it and make connections and comparisons to and from any other historical content that they might otherwise be studying. As discussed in chapter 7, there is no evidence that children effectively learn the concepts of chronology, which go far beyond knowing the sequence dates and events, by learning content sequentially. However, this is clearly one of the statutory requirements so children must have any specific content delivered sequentially across the year groups, which may need to be outlined in your long-term planning.

Local history content remains prominent in both Key Stage 1 and 2 of the current National Curriculum 2014, which of course, we celebrate. We would add that whatever format your long-term plan may take, 'the local' is woven throughout regardless.

We encourage teachers and curriculum leaders to continue to be creative in their approach to formulating their long-term plan, allowing as much flexibility as possible so teachers can use their professional judgement when planning for the needs of their children. Above all, we must not teach content to the exclusivity of understanding concepts and skills.

Case study 10.1 is a short overview of how one local primary school incorporated their local into their long-term planning.

Table 10.1 Curriculum planning

An example of a possible 'Seven Year Plan'. The theme areas are a mix of familiar titles and some more general. We have shown some links with the National Curriculum 2014 which schools can add to or adapt. The italics underneath these topics/themes are examples of how the local can be incorporated and used as a starting point to plan flexibility against these themes. These ideas might be something that you would develop in your medium-term planning with reference to a timeline overview.

	Autumn	Spring 1	Summer 1
Reception Understanding the World – EYFS (2012)	**All about me and my family** (This theme lends itself very well to the local) *What were you like when you were babies?* *How have you changed?* *Where do you live? What is your school like? What are your homes like? What is special about your families?* *Similarities and differences between cultures/religions/communities.*	**Toys** *What toys/games did your families play with when they were little?* *Why might this be different to your toys?* *Visit a toy shop in the area.*	**Transport** *Look at transport now in our area. What are the differences/similarities between an old train and one you might travel on now from your local area?* *Look at the bus stops in the area; have they changed?*
Year 1	**How is it made?** **(NC 2014 – the lives of significant individuals in the past who have contributed to national and international achievements . . .)** *Look at different artefacts and compare them.* *Brunel – what did he make and how? Are there any similar things in your local?* *Do you have any local engineers or any in your families?* *Look at any bridge/railway/footpath in the local area.*	**Homes** **(NC 2014 – changes within living memory . . .)** *Compare and contrast different homes in the local area. What do our homes look like?* *Visit a famous/significant house in your local area; what does it look like? Who might have lived there? You might visit a new building or housing estate and compare this to old pictures of the past.*	**Travel** **(NC 2014 – changes within living memory . . .)** *Where did our families come from?* *What is their local environment like?* *Let's send a letter – what are post boxes like now in our area; what were they like?* *What holidays have your families been on?* *Have they changed?*
Year 2	**Remembrance Day** **(NC 2014 – significant historical events, people and places in their own locality)** *Remembering a local war hero – your local archivist will be able to give information on this.* *Visit a local sheltered housing or home, for oral reminiscences.*	**Significant people and events – (NC 2014 – events beyond living memory . . . and the lives of significant people . . .)** *Local significant figure/event – See local case study 10.1.* *Have there been any fires in your local area?* *Are there any children who may have a mum/dad/nan/granddad as a nurse – compare to Florence Nightingale/Mary Seacole? Does your local area have links with either Florence or Mary?*	**Pride and achievements** **(NC 2014 – events beyond living memory . . . and the lives of significant people . . .)** *Talk to people in your community about their achievements and successes.* *What is your local area noted for – goods/trade/sport . . .*

	Autumn	Spring 1	Summer 1
Year 3	**Hidden histories (Black History Month) (NC 2014 – a non-European society . . .)** *Look at hidden histories in your area.* *Contact your history centres for significant black figures in your local.*	**Rome wasn't built in a day! (NC 2014 – the Roman Empire . . .)** *Are there any Roman roads, evidence of Romans in the local?* *Daily life in a Roman family. Compare to the time now.* *Did any of the key Roman figures/events live/ happen in your local area?*	**The Anglo-Saxons and Scots (NC 2014 – Britain's settlement . . .)** ***Archaeology*** *Contact your local archaeological group for local excavations in your area.* *Create one in your classroom.* *Look at migration into your area. Who has settled here?* *Look at Anglo-Saxon pastimes. Compare to the way we pass our time.* *Look at local area maps for settlements.*
Year 4	**Greensleeves (NC 2014 – a study of an aspect or theme in British history . . .)** *Look at Tudor houses in your area.* *Who might have lived there? Compare life today to that of Henry VIII.* *Look at events in your area before the Tudor monarchy.*	**Operation (NC 2014 – a study of an aspect or theme in British history . . .)** *Look at a local hospital; how has it changed?* *Look at medicine and how it has changed.* *What was the death rate in the local area e.g. 200 years ago? Why has it changed?*	**How did life change in our locality in Victorian times? (NC 2014 – a study of an aspect or theme . . .)** *This has endless possibilities – significant Victorian people, schools, trade, entertainment, examples of which have been highlighted throughout the book.*
Year 5	**Invaders and settlers (NC 2014 – the Vikings and Anglo-Saxons . . . the achievements of the earliest civilizations . . .)** *Local invasions/settlements and their impact on the local area over time.*	**Britain since the 1930s – WWII (NC 2014 – a study of an aspect or theme in British history . . . Local history study)** *In our experience WWII offers a wealth of local starting points and most children have connections either through family and community.* *How has the local area changed since WWII?* *(See chapter 9 for other activities/ideas)*	**A street in time (NC 2014 – a local history study . . .)** *Choose a local street and track the changes on a timeline – houses, shops, people, jobs* *Look at the census for that street to see what can be discovered.* *Compare pictures.* *Comparing our local with a contrasting local over time (history and geography).* *Visit a local heritage site/park/house.*
Year 6	**All change . . . (NC 2014 – changes in Britain from Stone Age . . .)** *Look at early settlements in the local area.* *Compare tools/trade of the time.* *Are there any heritage sites in your local?*	**Tomb raiders (NC 2014 – the achievements of the earliest civilizations . . . Ancient Greece)** *Look for evidence of Greek/Egyptian style architecture and tombs.* *Explore local burial grounds now.* *Are there local explorers?*	**A self-chosen theme such as 'Crime and Punishment Across the Ages' (NC 2014 – a study of an aspect . . .)** *Look at local crime and punishment records.* *Visit a police station/gaol or a building that might have been use for punishment.* *Look at local events/papers across time.*

Case study 10.1 Integrating Crayford history projects into the curriculum of St Paulinus

At St Paulinus I have been delighted to incorporate local history projects into our school curriculum either as discrete sessions or as part of our termly curriculum planning. Children from all years have benefited from these projects, which have enabled teaching staff to ensure the delivery of a creative curriculum that has, over time, included elements from every curriculum area.

It was some years ago that Peter Daniels from Westminster Archives approached the school to enquire about providing projects relating to local history. It was at this time, the school decided to review the whole school history curriculum. To this end World War II and local history was allocated to Year 6. Thus an exciting challenge was set, to teach not only required elements but couple them with meaningful facts relating to Crayford and to many of the children's family history.

The first thing I did was to merge the planning from the projects with QCA planning – this was a very simple task to do. The topic books provide a wealth of information, are beautifully illustrated and easy for the children to understand. To enhance these projects the children have been involved in animation, art, drama, literacy, RE and musical productions. The animations have proved to be a fantastic teaching tool in subsequent years.

Teaching the curriculum in this manner has enabled me to ensure all children have been given the opportunity to consider how Crayford has changed due to historical events, the actions of famous people and the industrialisation of the area. For the children who have family in the area, learning in this manner adds the additional stimulus of not only being able to discuss events with parents, aunts, uncles and grandparents but also opens the opportunity for them to ask questions about their ancestry, which supports the development of self motivation towards their own learning.

Autumn Term Year 6	
World War I and II	William White: Remembrance (Crayford in WW1) Bartram, The Blitz and Beyond (Crayford in WW2)
Autumn Term Year 5	
Victorians	Fabric of Our Town: Swaisland Project (Crayford Victorians)
Spring Term Year 6	
Art/Design and Technology, Music	Fabric of Our Town: Swaisland Project (Crayford Victorians)
PSHE	Cholera Project (Cholera in Bexley, Crossness sewage works)
Summer Term Year 6	
History of the local area	A Magnificent Town and its Flying Machines Hiram Maxim/Alcock and Brown aviation project.

(Sylvia Smith – Year 6 teacher)

Planning: from medium to the short term

Medium-term planning looks at a series of lessons that might be taught from a given theme/topic usually taken from the long-term plan. It will outline content, skills and knowledge which need to be taught and will often have a cross-curricular element; though we issue a word of caution here. Despite history having many rich cross-curricular links, specific learning objectives should be history-focused and must include an element of enquiry. If history is being taught in a cross-curricular way, and this is becoming increasingly more common, one or two subsidiary objectives can be noted and used to inform other curriculum areas but should not be the main teaching within the lesson. For example, if children are making a 3D model of a Victorian house but may not be using the correct joining techniques, this might be something to note for your design technology planning focus but would not be something you would spend time on during the history part of the lesson; rather you would focus on the Victorian features they might include.

When planning we promote creativity, flexibility and the need to be prepared to change to allow for child-led and child-initiated learning. Medium-term plans should incorporate the broad knowledge, skills and understanding within the aims outlined in the programme of study. It is important that medium- and short-term planning is reviewed and adjusted according to ongoing assessments made. No plan should be followed verbatim without continually reviewing what the children have learned and where they need to go next. Sometimes a concept or a skill may have to be taught several times in a number of ways before learning can be considered embedded. If children cannot apply learning then learning has not been learnt!

As with all planning, there is no set or agreed format and schools are becoming far more flexible in their required levels and depth of medium- and short-term planning. It is no longer a requirement to produce a lesson plan either for Ofsted or for senior management during observations; however there is a statutory duty to plan and there is a statutory duty for you to demonstrate that you are planning. A slight contradiction in terms! In other words something will have be recorded either electronically or on paper to show what you are doing with the children.

Many schools have now combined medium- and short-term plans which provide a route through teaching and learning, incorporating progression and providing coherence.

All planning, particularly medium- and short-term plans, serve three main purposes:

1 it organises your thoughts into a coherent structure which you are then able to adapt where necessary, identifying and subsequently filling any gaps in teaching and learning;
2 it allows others, who may need to take over from you at any point either in the long or short term, to see where your class is in their learning, therefore ensuring continuity and progression;
3 it acts as a point of reference for noting down evaluations, assessments and significant outcomes for children, which is easily accessible to other members of staff, senior managers and external agencies. For yourself, it is an aide memoire, which is vital for the vast amount of information that we as teachers need to know and carry around.

In addition, for yourself when considering the content of a medium-term plan and having the local as a stimulus in mind, teachers need to consider the following questions:

- What do I know specifically about my class, groups of children and individuals?
- What are their interests? This does not have to be history or local specific at this stage but will serve as a starting point.
- Where do the children live/come from?
- Do they have specific connections with the local, i.e. are their family from the local originally, or do they work within it?
- Are there connections with other possible 'locals'?
- What is the prior learning of the children? This information is not always accessible so plan an 'assess and review lesson' to find out.

Figure 10.1 is a simple format showing an exercise that can be done in groups/pairs/individually for any theme, area of history learning, such as enquiry.

- What do children need to be moved on to next in terms of knowledge, skills and understanding? (See steps in progression.)
- What do I know about the local which can be linked to the required learning? Your audit will tell you this.
- What might I want the children to learn specifically about local people and places?
- What resources do I have in the environment and what do I have or can I bring into the classroom – physical, human and documentary?

Plans may be in various formats and if your school permits flexibility it is important to find one that suits your style of teaching and learning.

Medium/short-term planning may take the form of:

- topic web planners
- mind maps
- tabular
- day books with bullet points in
- a combination of all the above.

Summary of planning

Schools will have their own long and/or medium-terms plans which will outline specific learning areas and for some there will be an obligation to follow this planning; but again any planning that is presented can and should be adapted to suit the needs of each child.

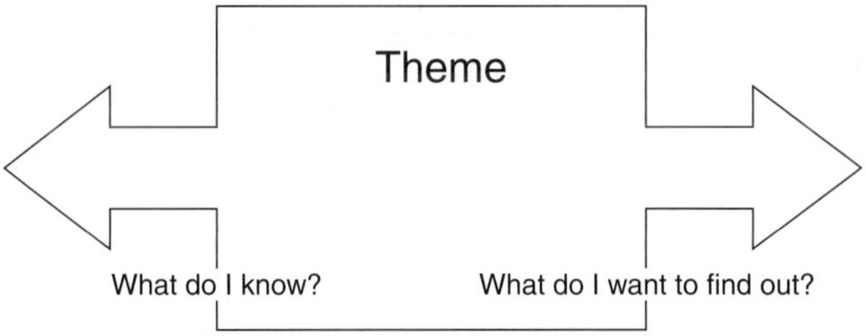

Figure 10.1 Assessing prior learning.

- A given theme or topic can be taught through another topic – we would urge that as many history topics as possible start with the local, but should at least have a local element in them, e.g. what Roman activity was present in your town/village? Or how has Roman life influenced what you see around you?
- A given theme or topic can have different starting points, e.g. a particular episode or person may dictate the particular starting point, for example in 'Britain since the 1930s'. Many schools will cover the obvious topics such as the Second World War, but you may want to focus on a particular change in the local which had a significant impact on your town/village at a different time. This may include the relatively recent past such as the technology explosion in the 1980s.
- Emphasis can be put on areas where there is relevance and interest – what aspect of the Victorians will excite the children you teach?
- Less engaging areas (which might be less engaging as a result of limited resources or teacher/child interest) can be used for an explicit skills lesson, such as scanning or skimming historical text or recognising fact from opinion. This will free up more time for in-depth study where concepts, skills and understanding can be embedded fully.

Always speak to the history coordinator and/or the overall curriculum leader in your school to discuss any changes that you feel would be beneficial to the children.

Teacher's audit and preliminary planning

Before we embark on any history planning, particularly when we want to use the local as a starting point or to consider its potential, it is essential that teachers review what they know, what resources or sources of information they may already have and what they may still need to find out about. A short amount of preparation can save several wasted hours and will ensure you are fully prepared to help children with their historical learning. As busy teachers, we realise time is at a premium and the 'walk or visit' that you may have done, using the teachers' toolkits in chapters 2, 3, 4 and 5, will serve you for most of your initial planning and is a good opportunity to take that all important lunch time walk! Having undertaken many preliminary investigative walks during our years as primary practitioners, we can assure teachers that such activities can be done in a very short time. Walks in the local can be done either during a lunch time or during an allocated planning, preparation and assessment time (PPA), which is a justified and valid use of time.

Teacher audit: What local history do we have?

- *Using the toolkit ideas offered in chapters 2, 3 and 4 and following your preliminary investigations into the local environment, look at the evidence you have gathered.*
- *Organise what you have into the different types of evidence:*
  - *pictures/photographs of the physical/built environment*
  - *notes taken from observations*
  - *sketches*
  - *notes from conversations*
  - *documentary evidence*

- *What things are rich in evidence?*
  - *a particular period?*
  - *any significant people linked to the area?*
  - *any significant events?*
- *Can you make any immediate links between the evidence? What is the evidence telling us? For instance what does the census tell us about a particular building or house?*
- *Make a list of questions you might ask about the sources.*
- *Begin to think about where the best place might be to find possible insights to some of these questions.*

The evidence gathered during the walk can be linked to the long-term planning in your school and begin to form the basis of your medium-term planning. Children can also be involved in this process; either they can use the evidence that you have provided and pose their own questions to formulate a collaborative class medium-term plan or, as we shall explore later in the chapter, they can undertake the preliminary walk themselves and design their own individual lines of enquiry (see p.173).

Historical enquiry

Historical enquiry is at the heart of all history and therefore must be at the forefront when we begin to plan. At its simplest it involves purposeful talk, asking and answering questions, selecting and interpreting evidence and using the information gleaned from that evidence, and developing lines of enquiry (Bage, 2000; Grigg and Hughes, 2013).

O'Hara and O'Hara (2001) point out that children are naturally curious, and good history planning provides an opportunity to capitalise on that curiosity through historical enquiry. Historical enquiry draws heavily on children's investigative skills. Children need to learn how to find, select and structure historical information. They need to develop their ability to question through lots of opportunities to engage in listening, describing, explaining and debating (purposeful talk) as well as being able to present and communicate their understanding (historical interpretation).

Often planning focuses on the child producing a piece of work which is used as evidence of their learning, and of course this is important. This may take the form of piece of writing, a project or a presentation. It is understandable, with demands on teachers having to 'deliver' in a system that is constantly under pressure, for teachers to focus on concrete outcomes to illustrate the learning. This may, however, result in less emphasis on enquiry, because of its complex nature, and more on factual learning. Nevertheless we have to ensure that we do not fall into the trap of simply providing children with information, like a list of dates or events, without the opportunity to engage in the historical process of enquiry. If this happens and enquiry is not at the heart of planning, we are not allowing them the opportunity to develop the skills and concepts for learning to take place (Pluckrose, 1991).

Asking questions

> Who questions much, shall learn much, and retain much.
>
> (Francis Bacon, 1561–1626, British statesman and philosopher)

Questioning is at the heart of historical enquiry. Asking questions in history and, more importantly, getting children themselves to ask questions, is vital if we are to enable them to take their learning forward beyond the classroom. Bage states: 'Questions fuel history . . . Teachers' questions are important, but only insofar as they act as models and prompts for those in which children have a genuine stake and over which they have control' (Bage 2000:19). If questions are not encouraged or used we are in danger of going back to a type of history learning where children are the passive recipients of information, accepting all information as representing the truth. Fines and Nichol (1997) not only stress the importance of children asking questions individually but also how working with each other and with the teacher to ask and answer questions places the learning in a context which is socially constructed: again fundamental for effective teaching and learning.

For children to be able to ask questions in any context and become skilled in doing so this approach has to begin at an early age. At face value this may seem obvious to most readers; however, in our experience of working in schools with children and with teacher trainees, this has not always been the case. Teacher talk and the need to get through units and vast amounts of information and targets have tended to dominate our classrooms and this may (have) inadvertently stifle(d) the art of good questioning and discussion. If children are not explicitly taught to ask questions or given the opportunity to do so they will find it increasingly difficult as they move through their schooling.

Reflection

- *Consider an article, a documentary or a story that you have engaged with recently. Did you question it at all or did you accept it at face value?*
- *Would you question a professional opinion on something in order to find out more information?*
- *Do you feel confident in asking questions?*
- *What was your experience of asking questions when you were at school?*

Children not only need the opportunity to ask questions, but also quality time must be devoted to it. They will also need encouragement and praise for doing so – no question is a 'silly' question. We would advocate that speaking and listening opportunities which include posing and answering questions are planned into every history lesson.

When we are considering enquiry and more specifically the notion of asking and answering questions, we have to accept that there are many uncertainties in history and that finding answers to questions has two aspects:

1 We may not have enough evidence (or any at all) to even begin to form an answer.
2 Our answers are only interpretations – others may disagree.

Sometimes we can only synthesise the information we have and make an informed interpretation of the evidence. We would also argue that children need to be aware of this and accept that history is an interpretation and often there may not be answers.

In our experience of trainee teachers, adults can often get frustrated at not knowing 'the answer'. During almost all historical enquiry seminars where trainee student teachers

were asked to investigate artefacts using their questioning and hypothesis skills, there was always a question of 'what is it?' or 'can you just tell us?' When the answer was 'no', students were clearly troubled at not being given the information and this caused a further, though valid, discussion. This is something that in our opinion is attributable to an education system where testing and getting it right is at the forefront. This culture of instant answers has perhaps been further perpetuated by the rapid expansion of the internet with answers at our fingertips through smart-phones, tablets and computers – the recent inclusion of 'google' as a verb in our dictionaries is testimony to that. This is not necessarily a negative; quite the contrary – the internet provides us with a valuable resource and should be used for history teaching and learning and with children (see chapter 9). However whilst we still have a culture where 'getting it right' remains prominent, we need to educate our children that in some circumstances and in particular in history we may not get to any answer, let alone right answers. It is important that teachers model this, sometimes planning explicit examples.

Historical enquiry, questioning and the local

The local provides the ideal context in which we can engage in historical enquiry and begin to ask enquiry questions. The process is one in which children can and should be involved. A teacher will have to assess the area initially, having used the toolkit, but can involve children in the evidence building and research questions. The audit can be used to plan a walk with the children with a possible starting point being 'What history is in our local area?' You may want to introduce this as a TASC activity, the process of which is explained at the end of this chapter. The 'walk' may be limited to a couple of streets and you may want to assign evidence gathering to different children. For example, one group of children can look specifically at houses or a building, another may look at street furniture, some may sketch or others conduct interviews. For those children who for some reason or other may not be able to go on a walk, an alternative approach might be that they begin to look at documentary evidence back in the classroom.

When the evidence and information have been gathered teachers will need to guide children, through skilled questioning, to sieve through the information and help them to eliminate sources that are not relevant. Children will then need to begin to raise questions in order to follow a line of enquiry.

Even children in the early years can engage in this process and in our experience, when given the opportunity, they will ask very pertinent questions. For young children, for example, your walk may involve the immediate area of the school, or to the edge of the playground if you have view of a street. You will need to point out specific features, such as windows, plaques or signs, but young children will love taking pictures when given a camera and produce drawings and have conversations about features they see. Back in the classroom the early years teacher can elicit enquiry questions from children through skilful pedagogy and modelling.

There are many activities that can be used from an early age that will help develop the art of questioning, some of which are listed at the end of this chapter. Not all will necessarily need to have an historical focus – for example the potato activity in chapter 4 – but will act as a fun way to begin to pose questions. However Nichol offers a simple format of trigger question words for children: how, what, why, when, where, who and why, which are described by him as 'question heads' to use when generating the questions (question tails) to begin to solve 'history mysteries' (Nichol in Cooper, 2012).

For example, focusing on a person highlighted on a census return as an example, these generic interrogatives can generate question tails such as:

- *How* did he travel to work?
- *What* was his house like?
- *When* was he born?
- *Where* was he born?
- *Who* is in his family?
- *Why* did he move here?

Bloom's Taxonomy also provides a framework in which questioning and higher-order thinking skills can be developed, and gives links to progression, outlined below. Bloom, writing in 1956 (see for instance Harnett and Whitehouse, 2013), proposed a theoretical ranking of six levels of thinking that learners go through. He suggests that thinking moves from a basic, concrete level of knowing something to being able to synthesise and evaluate. This framework extends beyond the first level as indicated by Nichol's format and is useful, particularly when considering differentiation within your planning.

Figure 10.2 gives an overview of the types of possible questions which could be asked at each level of thinking. A local perspective has been used.

Progression in historical skill, concepts and understanding

Progression is about how pupils' learning advances: the gradual gains in knowledge, skills and understanding that children make through different approaches, styles and techniques. Chambers and Donert (1996) define progression as 'the careful and deliberate sequencing of learning so that children can build their current learning on previous experience and also prepare for future learning' (Chambers and Donert in O'Hara and O'Hara, 2001).

Progression has to be planned for and assessed. It is not sequential nor is it time- or age-bound. Some children may progress quickly in one concept or skill, but may go back and forth within another before the learning is embedded. When thinking about progression we have to consider how thinking itself develops and how we might progress this. Bloom's Taxonomy (and Figure 10.2) provides an overview of this.

A general progression of historical skills and concepts can be viewed in Table 10.2. In summary children will move from simply describing to beginning to offer explanations and justifying. Likewise, they will move from asking and answering simple why and how questions, to asking what if . . .?, then to questioning motives, ideas and happenings.

Differentiation

Differentiation and assessment go hand in hand with planning with one informing the other. The main ways to differentiate within lessons are:

1. The use of resources
2. The support given
3. How you might group or pair learners
4. The complexity of the activity
5. The use of questions
6. Time given

A street in time . . .

Evaluation – discriminating between ideas and making judgements based on reasoned argument

Useful verbs	Example questions in the local
Judge *Select* *Choose* *Decide* *Debate*	How do you think . . .

Synthesis – involves combing ideas/evidence to make some new

Useful verbs	Example questions in the local
Create *Invent* *Imagine* *Propose* *Predict* *Devise* *Justify*	Imagine you are a worker on the land. What might your day look like? Predict what you think happened 50 years later in the area, when the factory arrived?

Analysis – to break down evidence into its components so it can be understood

Useful verbs	Example questions in the local
Compare *Contrast* *Examine* *Explain* *Categorise* *Separate*	Compare the different trades in the area. What does this tell you about the change in society? Explain why so many children died in the area at this time?

Application – applying knowledge or understanding in different contexts

Useful verbs	Example questions in the local
Solve *Use* *Show* *Examine* *Complete*	Use the house details to discover more about the house in the street. Show how the cooking would have been done.

Comprehension – understanding information or making sense of ideas

Useful verbs	Example questions in the local
Explain *Interpret* *Discuss* *Compare* *Distinguish*	Explain how you know the road was once in the middle of farm land? Discuss why you think Mr A had to work such long hours?

Knowledge – involves recalling previously learned information

Useful verbs	Example questions in the local
Tell *List* *Describe* *Relate* *Locate* *Find* *State* *Name*	Tell me what you can see now in the street. Locate the old bakery in the picture. Name the family on the census.

▲ Higher order thinking skills

Lower/middle

Lower order thinking skills ▼

Figure 10.2 Questioning to promote thinking in the local, using Bloom's Taxonomy and the theme 'A street in time'.

Table 10.2 Broad outline of progression

	From early years →					to Year 6
ENQUIRY	• Investigate places, objects, materials and living things by using all of their senses. • Identify and talk about some features, expressing likes and dislikes • Identify old and new objects • Describe and handle objects from the past	• Ask questions about artefacts from familiar contexts from the past • Handle and draw objects • Find answers to simple questions from a small range of sources • Use oral sources/ displays/pictures to find information	• Ask appropriate questions • Observe/handle sources to answer simple questions • Use a wider range of sources • Begin to make deductions from pictures • Recognise there are several ways they can find out about the past • Know there is a range of evidence	• Ask and answer questions using at least one source • Use sources beyond simple observation to answer questions • Use a range of sources to construct the bigger picture • Recognise that different evidence tells us different things • Compare sources of information and their different interpretations	• Begin to make inferences and deductions from sources • Begin to select and combine information from different sources • Use a range of sources to reconstruct aspects of life in another period	• Select/combine information from a range of sources to undertake enquiry and reach supported conclusions • Evaluate sources of information • Identify sources useful for a particular task • Use sources critically • Select and organise information to produce structured work using appropriate dates and terms.
CHRONOLOGY	• Begin to use everyday terms associated with the passing of time such as before, yesterday, today • Can discuss simple events in their own lives	• Use simple features to sequence a small number of objects • Begin to offer reasons why something is old/older	• Show knowledge and understanding of aspects of the past beyond living memory • Compare own life with past and recognise similarities and differences	• Describe and compare some characteristic features of a period • Compare and contrast aspects of then and now • Realise that the past can be divided into different periods	• Describe characteristic features of past societies and periods • Sequence main events and changes within a period • Identify changes within and across a period	• Describe and explain differences within periods • Describe features and make links between past societies and periods • Use knowledge of a particular society/period to make connects with another

	• Consider differences between themselves as babies and as they are now • Can sort pictures or objects related to babies, children and adults		• Know some main events and people • Place events on a timeline • Sequence main events and objects	• Recognise some similarities and differences between periods and use appropriate terminology	• Show knowledge and understanding of aspects of British history and the wider world within a chronological framework	• Describe the legacy of one period to another
CAUSES and EFFECTS	• Suggest a possible outcome for an action	• Recognise reasons for people in the past acting as they did • Describe how people in the past lived differently • Give one or two reasons for an action • Give simple results of an action • Use the vocabulary of simple cause and effect	• Begin to offer reasons for and results of main events and changes • Understand the impact of an event on people's lives	• Begin to understand why people make the decisions they make	• Understand the impact of an event on people's lives • Know that a particular period has influenced life today • Identify the main cause of an action/event	• Describe and make links between changes and causes of change • Begin to understand that causes can be grouped generically

Table 10.2 Continued

	From early years →					to Year 6
INTERPRETATION	• Begin to know about their own culture and beliefs and those of other people		• Begin to identify some ways the past is represented • Recognise that people may have different interpretations of events	• Identify the ways the past is represented • Understand strengths and weaknesses of eye-witness accounts • Understand why people make different interpretations • Know an event can be interpreted in different ways by different people • Form an opinion about an individual's contribution to history	• Understand that aspects of the past have been represented and interpreted in different ways • Begin to suggest reasons for different interpretations • Understand why some interpretations might be negative • Show an awareness of the range of possible interpretations • Understand different interpretations of individual's contribution to history	• Know some events, people and changes have been interpreted in different ways and suggest possible reasons • Interpret an event from one perspective then compare with others • Assess the importance of individuals in history from differing perspectives • Recognise that new evidence may change an interpretation

There are many excellent texts from which the reader can build on their general understanding of the importance of differentiation and for a generic overview of the theory behind differentiation and assessment. Here we provide a broad overview of how using the local can facilitate differentiation quite easily.

The scope of the local environment provides immediate differentiation in itself. Children do not need enhanced literacy skills in order to observe and discuss what they can see in the locality. Chapters 2, 3 and 4 give excellent examples of activities in which children can participate at their own level, particularly when following a trail, or walking in the local. Artefacts, visual and oral sources again enable all children to access learning, but use of such resources is particularly suited to those who may struggle with literacy. Being able to access learning will not only progress their understanding but will also raise their self-esteem and confidence levels; it puts all children on an equal footing. Written sources can be read or simplified in order that children do not have to decode complicated pieces of text – paired/group work is very good for this. See chapter 5 for an example of a transcript.

Several different types of resources can be looked at in one activity, one per table or group, for instance, and differentiated according to the needs of the children. Each group can then feed back to the rest of the class so learning is shared and modelled. Discussion in and about the local and the use of questions will enable children to verbalise their thoughts and communicate their understanding.

Assessment

There is no statutory duty to assess in history, although ongoing formative assessment and assessment for learning (AfL) must be carried out so that progression can be planned for; a report on these aspects must be provided to parents and carers at the end of the year. However, children should very much be a part of the assessments made and discussion of the next steps of learning should be formulated together with the teacher.

In our experience, historical understanding and learning is sometimes judged upon the child's literacy ability, i.e. on the assumption that not being able to 'write it down' equates to a lack of understanding. We would recommend that when you are considering ways children may communicate their findings and historical understanding, you incorporate various different ways and opportunities for them to do this. We have experienced children who, though being supported for low literacy and numeracy skills within school, were in fact excellent historians. An investigation was launched in our school after a number of children tracked on the SEND register with specific literacy or maths needs did not seem to make progress in history. It appeared that most history assessment was based on written evidence which was not always appropriate for some individual children. Training was delivered to help teachers identify children's alternative strengths and to consider other forms of assessment. Many of the children identified were, for example, able to reason orally and observe accurately so these were encouraged to communicate their understanding in other ways such as drawing and role play, rather than through written methods. As a result many children showed significant progress in their learning, moving them from needing intervention to age expected levels. This raised attainment, self-esteem and promoted self-motivation in learning.

Planning in the early years

History in the early years is part of the 'Understanding the World' area of learning within the Early Years Foundation Stage Curriculum (Early Education, 2012). This curriculum is set out in ages and stages of development and suggests that by the end of the early years phase children are expected to have achieved the following concepts and skills in history:

- talking about past and present events in their own lives and in the lives of family members;
- knowing about similarities and differences between themselves and others, and among families, communities and traditions;
- knowing about similarities and differences in relation to places, objects, materials and living things;
- talking about the features of their own immediate environment.

Relatively little has been written about young children's learning in history; however, research by Cooper (2002) has shown that young children are more than capable of learning and understanding historical concepts, engaging in historical discussions and thinking in historical ways than previously realised. Most writers would agree that Piagetian theories of early conceptual development led to deficit views of young children's ability to think beyond that of the concrete and themselves (Wood and Holden, 1995). For some schools and practitioners however, we fear it may still very much be the view held; in our experience there has been an observable lack of historical challenge within early years settings. Personal small scale unpublished research of the author has shown similar findings to that of Cooper (2002) and others such as Pluckrose (1991) and Claire (1996) and the conclusions concur; that we often underestimate the abilities of young children to understand and interact with what might be considered difficult historical concepts (Hales, 2000). The message here is quite simple: begin planning for early years as soon as possible and allow young children the same opportunities as older children. Ensure they have the experience of being able to handle, observe and play with artefacts; that questions are modelled and encouraged on a daily basis and that historical language, particularly around the passing of time, is embedded into everyday activities. Young children can and should engage in history through the local wherever possible. The use of story in this process is particularly useful.

Outlined in Figure 10.3 are some generic activities and suggestion that can be easily adapted and used in any early years nursery or reception class and should be a minimum in any setting. We have included the most obvious concepts and skills that are being covered as it is often difficult for a non-specialist to recognise the history that is going on, particularly in early years.

TASC: an approach in which to drive planning in the local

During our time as practitioners one of the most effective ways we have seen and used to plan and engage children in historical enquiry and learning is through an approach pioneered by Belle Wallace (2003) known as TASC.

TASC, an acronym for Teaching Actively in a Social Context, provides the framework for effective historical enquiry. It centres around the TASC wheel (Figure 10.4) and encompasses the elements of historical enquiry in a way that both teachers and children can navigate in a systematic and logical way. The onus of learning is placed on the child, with them engaging in enquiry-based learning (Bage, 2000), posing questions, looking at evidence,

Activities/suggestions	*Concepts and skills*
Artefacts, old and modern, can be put in the role play areas for children to play with. Observe the children using the objects, noting down what they say about them and how they describe them, and use the notes for discussion in either focus groups or a short whole class carpet session. Again, in our experience, even very young children will handle and use artefacts with care if they are trusted.	*historical enquiry, empathy, using artefacts, questioning*
Invite an adult in to talk about an aspect of their life. This could be about work, food or toys. Encourage children to think of questions to ask them.	*questioning, historical enquiry*
Use a box, suitcase or bag to reveal items that tell them something about you.	*historical enquiry, using evidence*
Sort photographs into old and new (see chapter 5 for further ideas).	*chronological understanding, using sources*
Display and use terms such as now, today, yesterday, tomorrow, then, after.	*chronological understanding, sequencing*
Sequence events and activities of the school day, the child's day, on a simple timeline.	*chronological understanding, sequencing*
Discuss past events which are special such as Christmas, birthdays, weddings, Divali.	*chronology, interpreting*
Look at similarities and differences of a range of things – objects, photos, people.	*observing, interpreting*
Use story/nursery rhymes and poems to introduce ideas.	*interpretation, communication,*
Talk about what has happened in the news (in our experience, children are very knowing about local, national and world events and want to talk about them).	*describing, questioning, reasoning, interpreting*
Play: what questions can we ask . . .	*questioning, discussing, interpreting*
Describe . . . to your friend.	*observation, interpreting*
What can we see beyond the school gate?	*observation, interpreting, describing*
Get an adult to dress up as an historical character for the children to question.	*questioning, discussion, cause and effect motive*
Ask what shapes you can see in the houses/school/ buildings.	*observation, interpreting, describing*

Figure 10.3 Early years activities.

generating ideas, testing hypotheses and evaluating outcomes. Because of its correlation with historical enquiry it provides an effective way for children to develop their problem-solving skills and enhance thinking. It provides a creative learning community within the class which encompasses all the cross-curricular areas outlined in chapter 9 and therefore is a holistic approach to teaching and learning.

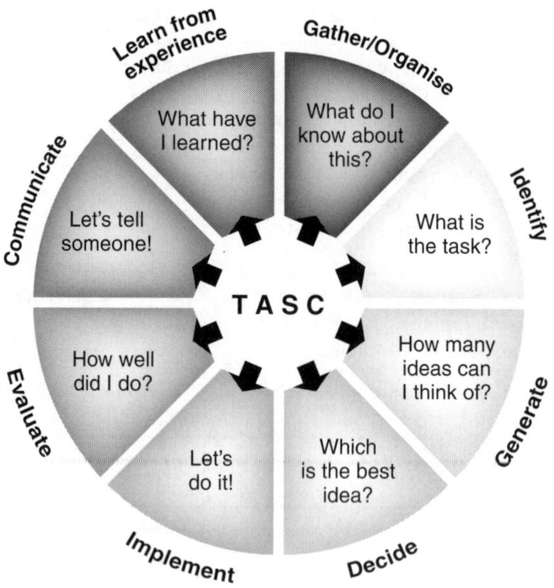

Figure 10.4 TASC wheel (with permission from Belle Wallace).

It allows children to:

- think and behave imaginatively – 'what if . . .?', 'I wonder why . . .';
- plan purposefully – raising questions, objective-led, and striving to make connections;
- generate new thinking and ideas, looking at things differently;
- value quality outcomes, reflecting critically and inviting constructive feedback.

Originally conceived with the gifted and talented children in mind, it was soon recognised that the concept behind TASC benefited children at all stages of learning. In our experience its structure particularly suited children who may have additional educational needs. The TASC wheel can also be adapted for young children using pictures. It is flexible in its nature; children and teachers may choose to focus on one part of the wheel or use it as a medium-term plan, with a series of activities linked to each section. Belle Wallace provides many excellent examples of using TASC in historical learning; further reading can be found below.

And so the journey continues . . .

We cannot presume that this is the end of the 'learning to teach primary history' story for the individual reader; indeed we propose that this is just the beginning! We hope that readers will continue to develop their understanding and enthusiasm of history through doing 'history in the local'.

Further reading

Nuffield Primary History Project: Teaching Primary History, by J. Fines and J. Nichol, London: Heinemann (1997)

Creative Teaching: History in the Primary Classroom, by R. Turner-Bisset, London: David Fulton (2005)

Teaching Thinking Skills Across the Early Years, by B. Wallace, London: Taylor and Francis, Routledge (2002)

Using History to Develop Thinking Skills at Key Stage 2, by B. Wallace, London: Taylor and Francis, Routledge (2003)

Thinking Skills and Problem-Solving: An Inclusive Approach, by B. Wallace, J. Maker, D. Cave and S. Chandler, London: Taylor and Francis, Routledge (2004)

Teaching Problem-Solving and Thinking Skills through Science, by B. Wallace, D. Cave and A. Berry, London: Taylor and Francis, Routledge (2008)

TASC International: Thinking Actively in a Social Context: Theory and Practice, by J. Maker and R. Zimmerman (2009)

Useful websites and resources

tasc@dobcroft-inf.sheffield.sch.uk

http://www.youtube.com/watch?v=bWedTbuAtR4 – a fun five-minute YouTube clip of the British Empire

Final reflections

To a certain extent local history in its wealth of resources and detail can be almost as overwhelming as national or global history. Sometimes the fascination it can have for the enthusiast means that research and exploration become rambling and unfocused. In our endeavours to show the rich potential of the local, we have cast our net sometimes broadly and sometimes in depth to find examples and possibilities. In practice, it is easy to become over-immersed in one aspect and to follow a link which takes you somewhere that is quite remote (geographically or conceptually) from the starting point. At other times threads can lead to dead ends. However, this is the excitement of history and, more specifically, of history through the local.

As primary practitioners, however, we constantly remind ourselves that 'less can be more' when working with children; small quantities of well-chosen material can result in excellent learning. We hope that some of our examples – the Wilson family or Mary Bax for instance – show how much can be learnt from apparently insignificant beginnings.

In writing about the evidence of a range of local areas, we have tried to demonstrate that everywhere does have 'history', and that this history provides a way in to understanding the wider context both within and beyond Britain. There is no excuse to say, 'But we don't have any local history. Nothing happened here.' Everywhere has an interesting past: '*even the dullest suburb of a dreary town or the most woebegone hamlet in a dismal county*' (Lewis, 1989:9).

Bibliography

Agyeman, J. (1995) *People, Plants and Places*, Hampshire: Learning Through Landscapes.

Ajegbo, K. (2007a) 'In my view: history and identity', *Primary History* 46: 6.

Ajegbo, K. (2007b) *Diversity and Citizenship: Curriculum Review*, Nottingham: DfES.

Alexander, R.J. (ed.) (2010) *Children, Their World, Their Education: Final Report and Recommendations of the Cambridge Primary Review*, London: Routledge.

Anderson, C. and Moore, A. (1994) 'Making history happen outside the classroom', in Bourdillon, H. (ed.) *Teaching History*, pp. 196–208, London: Routledge.

Andretti, K. (1993) *Teaching History from Primary Evidence*, London: David Fulton.

Anim-Addo, J. (1996) *Sugar, Spices and Human Cargo: An Early Black History of Greenwich*, Greenwich, London: Greenwich Leisure Services.

Appleby, J., Hunt, L. and Jacob, M. (1994) *Telling the Truth about History*, New York: W.W. Norton.

Arthur, J. and Phillips, R. (eds) *Issues in History Teaching*, London: Routledge.

Asari, E., Halikiopoulou, D. and Mock, S. (2008) 'British national identity and the dilemmas of multiculturalism', *Nationalism and Ethnic Politics* 14(1): 1–28.

Bage, G. (1999) *Narrative Matters: Teaching and Learning History through Story*, London: Falmer Press.

Bage, G. (2000) *Thinking History 4–14: Teaching, Learning, Curricula and Communities*, London: RoutledgeFalmer.

Baker, A.R.H. (2003) *Geography and History: Bridging the Divide*, Cambridge: Cambridge University Press.

Bakhtin, M. (1981) in Carruthers, E. and Worthington, M. (2006) *Children's Mathematics: Making Marks, Making Meaning, Birth to Eight Years*, London: Sage.

Ball, R. and Stobart, J. (1996) 'Community identity and the local government review', *Local Government Studies* 22(1): 113–126.

Barrow, P. (1998) *Slaves of Raparree*, Bideford, Devon: Edward Gaskell.

Barton, K. (2000) 'Enriching young children's understanding of time', *Primary History* 59: 16–18.

Benjamin, F. (1995) *Coming to England*, London: Pavilion.

Blyth, A., Cooper, K., Derricott, R., Sumner, H. and Waplington, A. (1976) *Place, Time and Society 8–13: Curriculum Planning in History, Geography and Social Science*, Bristol: Collins.

Blyth, J. (1982) *History in Primary Schools*, Milton Keynes: Open University Press.

Blyth, J. (1988) *History 5–9*, London: Hodder & Stoughton.

Blyth, J. (1994) *History 5 to 11*, London: Hodder & Stoughton.

Blyth, J. and Hughes, P. (1997) *Using Written Sources in Primary History*, London: Hodder & Stoughton.

Boulton, G. (1991) 'Relict geography: maps as records', *Teaching Geography* 16(4): 173–174.

Brand, J., Casey, M. and Mahon, S. (eds) (1980) *History in the Primary School*, London: Inner London Education Authority Learning Materials Service.

Bryson, B. (1996) *Notes from a Small Island*, London: Transworld.

Byrom, J. and Riley, M. (2011) 'Making the most of particular people and places in history', *Historical Association Annual Conference* Manchester, 5 June. Available at: http://www.history.org.uk/resources/secondary_resource_4469_58.html (Accessed 3 June 2012).

CABE (Commission for Architecture and the Built Environment) (2010) *Unforgettable Lessons: An Introduction to Engaging Places*, London: CABE.

Cannadine, D., Keating, J. and Sheldon, N. (2011) *The Right Kind of History: Teaching the Past in Twentieth-Century England*, Hampshire: Palgrave Macmillan.

Card, J. (2010) 'Printed pictures with text: using cartoons as historical evidence', *Primary History* 56: 10–11.

Carr, E.H. (2001) *What Is History? The George Macaulay Trevelyan Lectures*, Hampshire: Palgrave Macmillan.

Catling, S. (1998) 'Children as map makers', in Scoffham, S. (ed.) *Primary Sources: Research Findings in Primary Geography*, pp. 10–11, Sheffield: Geographical Association.

Catling, S. (2003) 'Curriculum contested: primary geography and social justice', *Geography* 88(3): 164–210.

Catling, S. (2006) 'Geography and history: exploring the local connections', *Primary History* 42: 14–16.

Claire, H. (1996) *Reclaiming Our Pasts: Equality and Diversity in the Primary History Curriculum*, Stoke-on-Trent: Trentham Books.

Claire, H. (2004) 'Oral history: a powerful tool or a double edged sword?', *Primary History* 38: 20–23.

Claire, H. (2006) 'Reflections on writing "The Song Remembers When"', *Primary History* 44: 12–13.

Claire, H. (2007) 'History, citizenship and controversy', *Primary History* 47: 28–30.

Clare, J.D. (2006) 'Teaching chronology', Greenfield History Site. Available at: http//www.johndclare.net/Teaching/Chronology.htm (Accessed 25 October 2012).

Clifford, S. (2013) 'Parish maps: places, people and parish maps'. Available at: www.commonground.org.uk/parishmaps/m-pp0.html (Accessed 4 September 2010).

Clifford, S. and King, A. (1993) 'Losing your place', in Clifford, S. and King, A. (eds) *Local Distinctiveness: Place, Particularity and Identity*, London: Common Ground.

Coard, B. (2004) 'How the West Indian child is made educationally subnormal in the British school system: the scandal of the black child in schools in Britain', in Richardson, B. (ed.) *Tell It Like It Is: How Our Schools Fail Black Children* (2nd edn), pp. 27–59, Bedford: Bookmark.

Collicott, S.L. (1986) *Connections: Haringey Local–National–World Links*, London: Haringey Community Information Services in association with Multi-cultural Curriculum Support Group.

Collicott, S.L. (1990a) 'What history should we teach in primary schools?', *History Workshop Journal* 29(1): 107–110.

Collicott, S.L. (1990b) 'Who is the National Curriculum for?', *Teaching History* 61: 8–12.

Collicott, S.L. (1992) 'Who is forgotten in HSU Britain since the 1930s?', in *Primary Teaching Studies* (6)3: 252–268.

Collicott, S.L. (1993) 'A way of looking at history: local–national–world links', *Teaching History* 72: 18–23.

Cooper, H. (1995) *History in the Early Years*, London: Routledge.

Cooper, H. (2000) *The Teaching of History in Primary Schools Implementing the Revised National Curriculum* (3rd edn), London: David Fulton.

Cooper, H. (2002) *History in the Early Years* (2nd edn), London: Routledge.

Cooper, H. (ed.) (2004) *Exploring Time and Place Through Play*, London: David Fulton.

Cooper, H. (2006) *History 3–11: A Guide for Teachers*, Abingdon: David Fulton.

Cooper, H. (2010) 'International perspectives on history education', *Education 3–13*, 38(3): 219–223.

Cooper, H. (2012) *History 5–11: A Guide for Teachers* (2nd edn), Abingdon: Routledge.

Copeland, T. (1993) *A Teacher's Guide to Geography and the Historic Environment*, London: English Heritage.

Corbishley, M., Fordham, J., Gay, S., Hollinshead, L., Spicer, S. and Walmsley, D. (1999) *Primary History: Using the Evidence of the Historic Environment*, London: English Heritage.

Corrigan, E.M. (1995) 'Battling on: family history in the primary classroom', *Teaching History* 81: 14–18.

Cox, K. and Hughes, P. (1998) 'History and children's fiction', in Hoodless, P. (ed.) *History and English in the Primary School*, pp. 87–102, London: Routledge.

Cremin, T. (2009) *Teaching English Creatively*, London: Routledge.

Cresswell, T. (2004) *Place: A Short Introduction*, Oxford: Blackwell.

Crosby, A. (2005) 'Maps and the local historian: three handbooks', *The Local Historian* 3: 201–205.

Davies, I. (2000) Citizenship and the teaching and learning of history, in Arthur, J. and Phillips, R. (eds) *Issues in History Teaching*, pp. 137–147, London: Routledge.

Davies, J. and Redmond, J. (1988) *Coordinating History across the Primary School*, London: Falmer Press.

Dawson, I. (2010) 'Using personal and family histories in the classroom'. Available at: http://www.thinkinghistory.co.uk/Issues/FamilyHistories/FamilyIndexhtml (Accessed 11 October 2011).

Dawson, I. (2011) 'Seeing the bigger picture, developing chronological understanding', Thinking History Conference, London: London History Forum.

Dawson, I. (2013) 'Chronological understanding'. Available at: http://www.thinkinghistory.co.uk/Issues/IssueChronology.html (Accessed 15 October 2012).

DCSF (2007) *Guidance on the Duty to Promote Community Cohesion*, London: DCSF.

Dean, J. (2010) 'Urban spaces near you', *Primary History* 55: 28.

DES (1991) *History in the National Curriculum*, London: HMSO.

DES and the Welsh Office (1990) *National Curriculum History Working Group: Final Report*, London: DES.

DfE (1995) *History in the National Curriculum*, London: HMSO.

DfE (2011) The Education and Inspections Act 2006. Available at: http://www.education.gov.uk/aboutdfe/foi/disclosuresaboutchildrenyoungpeoplefamilies/a0077108/community-cohesion (Accessed 12 December 2012).

DfE (2012a) *Statutory Framework for the Early Years Foundation Stage: Setting the Standards for Learning, Development and Care for Children from Birth to Five*. Available at: https://www.education.gov.uk/publications/standard/AllPublications/Page1/DFE-00023-2012 (Accessed 5 January 2013).

DfE (2012b) *Teachers' Standards*. Available at: http://webarchive.nationalarchives.gov.uk/20130401151715/https://www.education.gov.uk/publications/eOrderingDownload/teachers%20standards.pdf (Accessed 5 January 2013).

DfE (2013a) *Departmental Advice on Health and Safety for Schools: Role of the Educational Visits Coordinator (EVC)*. Available at: http://www.education.gov.uk/aboutdfe/advice/f00191759/departmental-advice-on-health-and-safety-for-schools/educational-visits-coordinator (Accessed 4 March 2013).

DfE (2013b) *The National Curriculum in England: Framework Document for Consultation*, February, London: DfE.

DfEE/QCA (1998) *A Scheme of Work for Key Stages 1 and 2: History*, London: QCA.

DfEE/QCA (1999) *The National Curriculum. Handbook for Primary Teachers in England. Key Stages 1 and 2*, London: DfEE/QCA.

DfEE/QCA (2000) *A Scheme of Work for Key Stages 1 and 2: History*, London: QCA.

DfES (2006) *Learning Outside the Classroom Manifesto*, London: DfES.

Dillon, J., Morris, M., O'Donnell, L., Reid, A., Rickinson, M. and Scott, W. (2005) *Engaging and Learning with the Outdoors – The Final Report of the Outdoor Classroom in a Rural Context Action Research Project: Final Report*. NFER. Available at: http://www.nfer.ac.uk/nfer/publications/OCR01/OCR01.pdf (Accessed 12 December 2012).

Disney, A. and Hammond, P. (2002) 'Using historical maps in the primary classroom', *Primary History* 32: 22–24.

Driver, F. and Samuel, R. (1995) 'Rethinking the idea of place', *History Workshop Journal* 39(1): v–vii.

Dyer, C., Hopper, A., Lord, E. and Tringham, N. (eds) (2011) *New Directions in Local History since Hoskins*, Hertfordshire: University of Hertfordshire Press.

Dymond, D. (2009) *Researching and Writing History: A Guide for Local Historians* (3rd edn), Lancaster: Carnegie.

Dymond, D. (2011) 'Does local history have a split personality?' in Dyer, C., Hopper, A., Lord, E. and Tringham, N. (eds) *New Directions in Local History Since Hoskins*, pp. 13–28, Hertfordshire: University of Hertfordshire Press.

Eales, J. (2012) 'Writing history', *Primary History* 60: 5.

Early Education (2012) *Development Matters, Early Years Foundation Stage*, London: Early Education.

Ell, P. S. (2011) 'Local history in the twenty-first century: information communication technology, e-resources, grid computing, Web 2.0 and a new paradigm', in Dyer, C., Hopper, A., Lord, E. and Tringham, N. (eds) *New Directions in Local History Since Hoskins*, pp. 247–266, Hertfordshire: University of Hertfordshire Press.

Ellis, B. (2005) 'My favourite geography book', *Geographical Association Magazine*, 1.

English Heritage (2010) *Heritage Learning*, 43, London: English Heritage.

English Heritage (2011) 'Outreach'. Available at: http://www.heritage.org.uk/publications/outreach/ (Accessed 15 February 2013).

English Heritage (2013) 'Researching slavery connections'. Available at: http://www.english-heritage.org.uk/discover/people-and-places/the-slave-trade-and-abolition/slavery-and-the-british-country-house/ (Accessed 3 March 2013).

Eurydice at NFER (2010) 'Unit for England, Wales and Northern Ireland'. Available at: http://www.nfer.ac.uk/nfer/index.cfm?73DA0842-C29E-AD4D-09B9-F45A781F13BD (Accessed 11 December 2012).

Farmer, A. and Cooper, C. (1998) 'Storytelling in history', in Hoodless, P. (ed.) *History and English in the Primary School*, pp. 35–51, London: Routledge.

Fines, J. (2010a) 'Doing local history', *Primary History* 55: 6–7.

Fines, J. (2010b) 'Doing local history through maps and drama', *Primary History*, 55: 35–51.

Fines, J. (2011) 'Teaching time', *Primary History*, 59: 7–8.

Fines, J. and Nichol, J. (1997) *Teaching Primary History*, Oxford: Heinemann.

Fisher, T. (1998) *Developing as a Teacher of Geography*, Cambridge: Chris Kington.

Fogleman, K. (1991) *Citizenship in Schools*, London: David Fulton.

Frow, M. (1996) *Roots of the Future: Ethnic Diversity in the Making of Britain*, London: Commission for Racial Equality.

Fryer, P. (1984) *Staying Power: The History of Black People in Britain*, London: Pluto Press.

Fyson, T. and Ward, C. (1973) *Streetwork: The Exploding School*, London: Routledge and Kegan Paul.

Garner, I. (2000) 'Problems and inconsistencies with Kolb's learning styles', *Educational Psychology: An International Journal of Experimental Educational Psychology* 20(3): 341–348.

Gove, M. (2012) 'Heritage schools: part of the government's vision for cultural education'. Available at: http://www.english-heritage.org.uk (Accessed 15 February 2013).

Grigg, R. and Hughes, S. (2013) *Teaching Primary Humanities*, Harlow: Pearson.

Hales, A. (2000) 'Too young to understand: the teaching of cause and consequence at KS1 using children who have been displaced by war', unpublished manuscript, London: South Bank University.

Hales, A. (2011) 'Alternative placements in initial teacher training', unpublished manuscript, London: University of Greenwich.

Halewood, J. (2000) 'A treasure trove of local history: how to use your local record office', *Primary History* 24: 10–11.

Harnett, P. (2007) 'Foundation Stage and Key Stage 1 history [early years]: history and citizenship education – teaching sensitive issues, Part 1', *Primary History* 46: 26–27.

Hartnett, P. and Whitehouse, S. (2013) 'Investigating activities using sources', in Cooper, H. (ed.) *Teaching History Creatively*, pp. 29–50, London: Routledge.

Hawkey, K. and Prior, J. (2011) 'History, memory cultures and meaning in the classroom', *Journal of Curriculum Studies* 43(2): 231–247.

Hazareesingh, S. (1994) *Speaking about the Past: Oral History for 5–7 Year Olds*, Stoke-on-Trent: Trentham, in association with Save the Children.

Hewitt, M. and Harris, A. (1992) *Talking Time! A Guide to Oral History for Schools*, Tower Hamlets: Learning by Design.

Hicks, D. (2001) *Citizenship for the Future: A Practical Classroom Guide*, Godalming: Worldwide Fund for Nature, UK.

Historical Association (2011) 'Urban spaces'. Available at: http://www.history.or.uk/resources/primary/_resource_3878_139.html (Accessed 5 April 2012).

Hodgman, C. (2012) 'The Titanic disaster', in *BBC History* magazine 13: 4.

Hodkinson, A. (2002) '"History Howlers", amusing anecdotes or symptoms of the difficulties in the retention and ordering of historical knowledge?', *Primary History* 32: 28–31.

Hodkinson, A. (2003) 'The usage of subjective temporal phrases with the national curriculum for history and its schemes of work', *Education 3–13: International Journal of Primary, Elementary and Early Years Education* 31(3): 28–34.

Hodkinson, A. (2009) 'Planning for chronological understanding: areas of learning and the development of effective practice', *Primary History* 53: 17–18.

Hodkinson, A. (2011a) 'Enhancing temporal cognition, practical activities for the primary classroom', *Primary History* 59: 19–20.

Hodkinson, A. (2011b) 'Primary history in the twenty first century: back to the past?', *Primary History* 59: 6–7.

Holloway, L. and Hubbard, P. (2001) *People and Place: The Extraordinary Geographies of Everyday Life*, Edinburgh: Pearson Educational.

Hoodless, P. (1996) *Time and Timelines in the Primary School*, London: Historical Association.

Hoodless, P. (2002) 'An investigation into children's developing awareness of time and chronology in story', *Journal of Curriculum Studies* 34(2): 173.

Hoodless, P. (2008a) *Teaching History in Primary Schools*, Exeter: Learning Matters.

Hoodless, P. (2008b) 'Every Child Matters: addressing the needs of the children in learning about the past', *Primary History* 50: 14–17.

Hoskins, W.G. (1955) *The Making of the English Landscape* (1st edn), London: Hodder & Stoughton.

Hoskins, W.G. (1984) *Local History in England* (3rd edn), London: Longman.

Howson, J. (2007) 'Is it the Tuarts and then the Studors or the other way round? The importance of developing a usable big picture of the past', *Teaching History* 127: 40–47.

Hughes, P. (2000) *Primary History Curriculum Guide*, London: David Fulton.

Hume, B. and Sevier, A. (1991) *Starting with Me: Topic Ideas for the Teaching of History, Geography and Religious Education to Children from Five to Seven*, Twickenham: Belair.

Husbands, C. (1996) *What Is History Teaching? Language, Ideas and Meaning in Learning about the Past*, Buckingham: Open University Press.

Jackson, A.J. (2006) 'Process and synthesis in the rethinking of local history: perspectives contained in essays for a county history society, 1970–2005', *International Journal of Regional and Local Studies* 2(1): 5.

Jackson, A. (2008) 'Local and regional history as heritage: the heritage process and conceptualising the purpose and practice of local historians', *International Journal of Heritage Studies* 14(4): 362–379.

Jenkins, K. (1991) *Re-thinking History*, London: Routledge.

Killingray, D. (2011) 'Immigrant communities and British local history', *The Local Historian* 41(1): 4–11.

Kimber, D. and Smith, M. (1999) 'Field work, visits and work outside the classroom', in Ashley, M. (ed.) *Improving Teaching and Learning in the Humanities*, pp. 101–118, London: Falmer Press.

Kitson, A. and Husbands, C., with Steward, S. (2011) *Teaching and Learning History 11–18: Understanding the Past*, Maidenhead, Berkshire: Open University Press.

Lambert, D. (2009) 'Education for geographical understanding', *Primary History* 53: 26.

Levstik, L.S. and Barton, K.C. (2011) *Doing History: Investigating with Children in Elementary and Middle Schools*, London: Routledge.

Lewis, C. (1989) *Particular Places*, London: British Library.

Lewis, M., Wray, D. and Mitchell, C. (1995) *Extending Interactions with Texts: Theory into Practice*, Cambridge: Blackwell.

Lively, P. (2011) 'My hero: WG Hoskins', *Guardian*, 26 November, p. 6.

Lomas, T. (2002) 'How do we ensure really good local history in primary schools?' *Primary History* 30: 4–6.

Lomas, T. (2009) 'History coordinators' dilemmas: archaeology', *Primary History* 51: 29–30.

Lomas, T. (2011) 'What makes good primary history'. Available at: http://www.history.org.uk/resources/primary_resources_4128.html (Accessed 12 December 2012).

Low-Beer, A. (1991) 'From "Once upon a time" to historical time', in *Primary History Today Occasional Paper 2*, pp. 29–32, London: Historical Association.

Lowenthal, D. (1985) *The Past is a Foreign Country*, Cambridge: Cambridge University Press.

Lydden Valley Research Group (2006–13) History of the Lydden Valley, Available at: http://www.lyddenvalley.org.uk/crime.php (Accessed 4 October 2011).

MacGregor, N. (2010) *A History of the World in 100 Objects*, London: Penguin.

Mackintosh, M. (2004) 'Past, present and future', *Primary Geographer* 53: 14–15.

Maddison, M. (2011) 'Developing children's chronological understanding: the view from Ofsted', *Primary History* 59: 8–9.

Malone, K. (2008) *Every Experience Matters: An Evidence Based Research Report on the Role of Learning Outside the Classroom for Children's Whole Development from Birth to Eighteen Years*. Available at: http://theacornproject.net/2013/01/17/every-experience-matters-research-summary/ (Accessed 5 March 2013).

Manning, M. and Granström, B. (2001) *What's My Family Tree?* London: Franklin Watts.

Marcus, S. and Barker, R. (1997) *Using Historic Parks and Gardens*, London: English Heritage.

Marshall, H.E. (1905) *Our Island Story: A History of Britain for Boys and Girls from Romans to Queen Victoria* (centenary edn), Cranbrook: Galore Park; London: Civitas, 2005.

Martin, F. (2006) *Teaching Geography in Primary Schools: Learning to Live in the World*, Cambridge: Chris Kington.

Marwick, A. (1989) *The Nature of History* (3rd edn), London: Macmillan Press.

Mason, C. (1993) 'The Original Homeschooling Series', Home Education, Vol. 1 of the Charlotte Mason Series, p. 280. Available at: http://www.amblesideonline.org/CM/vol1complete.html#1_5e (Accessed 5 January 2013).

Massey, D. (1995) 'The conceptualisation of place', in Massey, D. and Jess, P. (eds) *A Place in the World? Places, Cultures and Globalization*, pp. 45–86, Oxford: Open University Press.

Masters, C. (2009) *Essential Maps for Family Historians*, Newbury, Berkshire: Countryside Books.

May, S., Banks, V. and Richardson, P. (1993) *Fieldwork in Action: Planning Fieldwork*, Sheffield: Geographical Association.

Merriman, N. (1993) 'The invisible settlers: from prehistoric times to the Huguenots', in Merriman, N. (ed.) *The Peopling of London*, pp. 28–46, London: Museum of London.

Milner, A., Jewson, T. and Scoffham, S. (2004) 'Using the school locality', in Scoffham, S. (ed.) *Primary Geography Handbook*, Sheffield: Geographical Association.

Moore, H. (1988) 'Ancient history: things to do and questions to ask', in Cooper, H. (ed.) *Exploring Time and Place Through Play*, pp. 65–76, London: David Fulton.

Morgan, A. (2011) 'What is place based education?' Available at: http://lssf.co.uk/placebased.aspx (Accessed 5 March 2011).
Morris, S. and Constable, N. (2007) 'Prisoners or slaves? New row over wreck's bones', *Guardian*, 6 November, p. 16.
Nichol, J. (2010) 'In my view: difficult and challenging reading: genre text and multi-modal sources – textbreaker', *Primary History* 56: 8–9.
Nieftagodien, N. (2010) 'The place of "the local" in History Workshop's local history', *Journal of African Studies* 69(1): 41–61.
Ofsted (2008) *Learning Outside the Classroom: How Far Should You Go?* London: Ofsted.
Ofsted (2011) *History for All: History in English Schools 2007/10*, London: Ofsted.
O'Hara, L. and O'Hara, M. (2001) *Teaching History 3–11*, London: Continuum.
Ould-Okojie, J. (2007) 'Exploring our roots, oral history in the local community', *Primary History* 46: 18–19.
Owens, P. (2013) 'Geography and sustainability', in Scoffham, S. (ed.) *Teaching Geography Creatively*, pp. 154–167, London: Routledge.
Oxfam (2006) *Teaching Controversial Issues*, Oxford: Oxfam Development Education.
Parsons, M.L. (1996) 'Let's grab a granny off the street', *Teaching History* 84: 30–33.
Phillips, I. (2008) *Teaching History: Developing as a Reflective Secondary Teacher*, London: Sage.
Phillips, R. (1998) 'Contesting the past, constructing the future: history, identity and politics in schools', *British Journal of Educational Studies* 46(1): 40–53.
Pickford, T., Garner, W. and Jackson, E. (2013) *Primary Humanities: Learning through Enquiry*, London: Sage.
Place Based Learning UK (2013) Available at: http://www.placebasedlearning.co.uk/philosophy.asp (Accessed 4 March 2013).
Pluckrose, H. (1989) *Seen Locally*, London: Routledge.
Pluckrose, H. (1991) *Children Learning History*, Herts: Simon & Schuster Education.
Pryor, F. (2011) *The Making of the British Landscape: How We Have Transformed the Land from Prehistory to Today*, London: Penguin.
Purkis, S. (1989) 'Primary history and the National Curriculum', in Campbell, J. and Little, V. (eds) *Humanities in the Primary School*, pp. 71–84, London: Falmer Press.
Purkis, S. (1991) 'Thanks for the memory: oral history', *Primary History Today, Occasional Paper* 2, London: The Historical Association.
Purkis, S. (1993) *A Teacher's Guide to Using School Buildings*, London: English Heritage.
Purkis, S. (1995) *A Teacher's Guide to Using Memorials*, London: English Heritage.
Purkis, S. (2003) '"Mrs Rainbow told us what things were like when she went to school": history in the early years', in Whitbread, D. (ed.) *Teaching and Learning in the Early Years*, pp. 321–340, London: RoutledgeFalmer.
Quinlan, M. (2005) *British War Memorials*, Authors Online.
Redfern, A. (1996) *Talking in Class: Oral History and the National Curriculum*, Essex: Oral History Society.
Reeves, M. (1980) *Why History?* London: Longmans.
Richardson, B. (ed.) (2004) *Tell It Like It Is: How Our Schools Fail Black Children* (2nd edn), Bedford: Bookmark.
Rickinson, M., Dillon, J., Teamey, K., Morris, M., Choi, M.Y., Sanders, D. and Benefield, P. (2004) A Review of Research on Outdoor Learning – NFER. Available at: http://www.field-studies-council.org/documents/general/NFER/A_review_of_research_on_outdoor_learning.pdf (Accessed 4 July 2011).
Riden, P. (1998) *Local History: A Handbook for Beginners* (2nd edn), Merton: Priory Press.
Riley, M. (1997) 'Big stories and big pictures: making outlines and overviews interesting', *Teaching History* 88: 20–22.
Robinson, V. and Hale, S. (1989) *The Geography of Vietnamese Secondary Migration in the UK* (No. 10), Centre for Research in Ethnic Relations.

Rogers, A. (1972) *This Was Their World: Approaches to Local History*, London: British Broadcasting Corporation.

Rosenberg, D. (2007) 'Teaching about racism, fairness and justice through key people', *Primary History* 46: 11–13.

Rougvie, D. (2007) '"I could change the world if I put my mind to it": teaching controversial issues and citizenship through a project on heroes and heroines', *Primary History* 46: 14–15.

Rowbotham, S. (1977) *Hidden from History*, London: Pluto Press.

Royal Society for the Encouragement of Arts, Manufactures and Commerce (RSA) (2010) *The RSA Area Based Curriculum – Executive Summary*. Available at: http://www.thersa.org/action-research-centre/learning,-cognition-and-creativity/education/practical-projects/area-based-curriculum (Accessed 4 July 2012).

Scoffham, S. (ed.) (2013) *Teaching Geography Creatively*, Abingdon: Routledge.

Sheeran, G. and Sheeran, Y. (2009) 'Opinion: "No longer the 1948 show": local history in the 21st century', *Local Historian* 39(1): 314–323.

Simchowitz, C. (1995) 'The development of temporal concepts in children and its significance', *Teaching History* 79: 15–17.

Simmons, R. (1990) *Eltham in the Making, Vol. 1: from Roman Times until 1939*, London: The Eltham Society.

Snell, K. (2010) 'Parish pond to Lake Nyasa: parish magazines and senses of community', *Family and Community History* 13(1).

Spence, M. (2007) *The Making of a London Suburb: Capital Comes to Penge*, Monmouth: Merlin Press.

Spencer, C. and Blades, M. (1993) 'Children's understanding of places: the world at hand', *Geography* 78(4): 367–373.

Spurgeon, D. (1992) *Discover Eltham and its Environs; A Comprehensive Guide to Eltham, Eltham Palace, New Eltham, Mottingham, Kidbrooke and Shooters Hill*, London: Greenwich Guide-Books.

Steele, J. (ed.) (1997) *The Streets of London: The Booth Notebooks; South East*, London: Deptford Forum Publishing.

Stow, W. and Haydn, T. (2000) 'Issues in the teaching of chronology', in Arthur, J. and Phillips, R. (eds), *Issues in History Teaching*, pp. 83–97, London: Routledge.

Swift, D. (2005) 'Why valuing places is no fairy tale', *Teaching Geography* 30: 8–11.

Syson, D. (2009) 'Is Britain becoming a one-child nation?', *Observer*, 15 March. Available at: http://www.guardian.co.uk/lifeandstyle/2009/mar/15/single-child-families (Accessed 12 July 2011).

Tanner, J. (2010) 'Geography and the emotions', in Scoffham, S. (ed.) *Primary Geography Handbook* (revised edn), pp. 35–47, Sheffield: Geographical Association.

Taylor, C. (2005) 'W.G. Hoskins and "The Making of the English Landscape"', *Local Historian* 41(4): 74–81.

Taylor, L. (2005) 'Place: an exploration', *Teaching Geography* 30: 14–17.

Teague, K. (1993) *Mr Horniman and the Tea Trade*, Horniman, Forest Hill, London: Public Museum and Public Park Trust.

Temple, S. (2010) 'What is the future for primary school history in England?', *Education 3–13* 38(3): 233–241.

Temple, S. (2013) 'Using archives creatively', in Cooper, H. (ed.) *Teaching History Creatively*, London: Routledge.

Thompson, P. and Cort, B. (2008) 'Whose community? The shaping of collective memory in a volunteer', *Oral History* 36(2) 'Connections': 89–98.

Tormey, R. (2006) 'The construction of national identity through primary school history: the Irish case', *British Journal of Sociology of Education* 27(3): 311–324.

Tosh, J. (2008) *Why History Matters*, London: Palgrave Macmillan.

Tosh, J. (2010) *The Pursuit of History: Aims, Methods and New Directions in the Study of Modern History* (5th edn), London: Pearson.

Turner-Bisset, R. (2005) *Creative Teaching: History in the Primary Classroom*, London: David Fulton.

Twells, A. (2008) 'Community history', in Making History, the Changing Face of the Profession in Britain. Available at: http://www.history.ac.uk/makinghistory/resources/articles/community_history.html (Accessed 4 October 2012).

University of Cambridge Faculty of History (2013) 'What are historical sources?' Available at: http://www.hist.cam.ac.uk/prospective-undergrads/virtual-classroom/historical-sources-what (Accessed 1 February 2013).

Vass, P. (1993) 'Have I got a witness? A consideration of the use of historical witnesses in the primary classroom', *Teaching History* 73: 19–24.

Vass, P. (2000) 'Telling the truth? Using story to teach history to young children', in Clipson-Boyles, S. (ed.) *Putting Research into Practice in Primary Teaching and Learning*, pp. 115–126, London: David Fulton.

Vass, P. (2005) 'Piecing together the puzzle: some thoughts on historical sites', *Primary History* 39: 34–36.

Vass, P. (2006) 'What do we think we are?', *Primary History* 43: 17.

Vass, P. (2007a) 'Citizenship: a subject for our times?', *Primary History* 46: 8.

Vass, P. (2007b) 'Dealing with the dead: identity and community – monuments, memorials and local history', *Primary History* 46: 20–21.

Vaughan, C. (2009) 'How to read a prison roll', *Who Do You Think You Are?* May: 49–61.

Visram, R. (1994) '"British history: whose history?": black perspectives on British history', in Bourdillon, H. (ed.) *Teaching History*, pp. 53–61, London: Routledge / The Open University.

Vygotsky, L. (1962) *Thought and Language*. Available at: http://books.google.co.uk/books?hl=en&lr=&id=B9HClB0P6d4C&oi=fnd&pg=PR4&dq=vygotsky+s. (Accessed 20 October 2012).

Wall, R., Woollard, M. and Moring, B. (2004) *Census Schedules and Listings, 1801–1831: An Introduction and Guide*, Colchester: University of Essex.

Wallace, B. (ed.) (2003) *Using History to Develop Thinking Skills at Key Stage 2*, London: David Fulton.

Waller, M. (2002) 'Museums: entries to learning', *Primary History* 61: 6.

Walters, R. (2012) 'An introduction to history', in Driscoll, P. Lambirth, A. and Roden, J. (ed.) *The Primary Curriculum*, pp. 78–98, London: Sage.

West, J. (1981) 'Primary school children's perspective of authenticity and time in historical narrative pictures', *Teaching History* 29: 8–10.

Wiegand, P. (1992) *Places in the Primary School*, London: Falmer Press.

Wilkinson, A. (2011) 'What might we expect pupils to "know and can do" at the end of Key Stage 2?', *Primary History* 59: 15.

Wilson, G. (1997) 'Our history or your history? (Part 2)', *Teaching History* 86: 6–7.

Wood, L. and Holden, C. (1995) *Teaching Early Years History*, Cambridge: Chris Kington.

Wood, M. (2010) *The Story of England*, London: Penguin.

Wood, M. (2012a) The Great British Story: A People's History, Episode 1, Britannia, BBC Worldwide [DVD].

Wood, M. (2012b) The Great British Story: A People's History, BBC TV Blog, 25 May. Available at: http://www.bbc.co.uk/blogs/tv/2012/05/great-british-story-michael-wood.shtml (Accessed 29 August 2012).

Wood, S. (1995) 'Developing an understanding of time: sequencing issues', *Teaching History* 79: 11–14.

Wrenn, A. (2007) T.E.A.C.H.: Teaching Emotive and Controversial Issues at KS3. Available at: http://www.history.org.uk/resources/secondary_resource_1140,1151_11.html (Accessed 4 March 2013).

Index